Windbreak

also by
Linda Hasselstrom
ROAD KILL *(poetry — Fall 1987)*
GOING OVER EAST
CAUGHT BY ONE WING *(poetry)*
JOURNAL OF A MOUNTAIN MAN: James Clyman *(editor)*
WHEN HOT SPRINGS WAS A PUP *(editor)*
THE BOOK BOOK: A Publishing Handbook
BIRD BEGINS TO SING: Northwest Poetry and Prose *(editor)*
NEXT-YEAR COUNTRY: One Woman's View *(editor)*

Windbreak

A Woman Rancher on the Northern Plains

by Linda Hasselstrom

Barn Owl Books
Berkeley, California, 1987

The poem "When My Father Waters His Trees"
previously appeared in an anthology, *Woman Poet: The Midwest*, Women-in-Lit-
erature, Inc., 1985. "This Is" previously appeared in the *Great Plains Poetry Anthology*, Point Riders Press, 1983. "Hands" appeared in *From Seedbed to Harvest: The
American Farmer*, Seven Buffaloes Press, 1985.

"Bone," and many of the others, appeared in *Caught By One Wing*, Julie Holcomb
Press, San Francisco, 1985.

Some of the other poems appeared in the following publications: *Green Bowl,
Poet's Portfolio, Juxtapose, Midwest Quarterly, South Dakota Review, Country
Woman, Northwoods Journal, Free Passage, Jump River Review, Passages North*.

Published by Barn Owl Books
Box 7727, Berkeley, California 94707

Designed by Elizabeth Doris
Calligraphy by Sandy Diamond
Photographs by Ken Norgard
Map by Ellen Pofcher
Printed in the United States of America
10 9 8 7 6 5 4 3 2 1

Library of Congress Cataloging-in-Publication Data
Hasselstrom, Linda M.
    Windbreak : a woman rancher on the northern plains.
    1. Hasselstrom, Linda M.—Diaries.   2. Authors,
American—20th century—Diaries.   3. Ranchers—
South Dakota—Diaries.   4. Ranch life—South Dakota.
5. Ranch life—Poetry.   I. Title.
PS3558.A7257Z477   1987   818'5403   [B]   87-11428
ISBN 0-9609626-3-8

*P*rairie winds, which blow almost constantly,
may vary from gentle breezes to eighty-mile-an-hour, roaring,
twisting terrors, accompanied by lightning, hail, and pounding rain —
all in the course of one spring day. In winter, wind piles snowdrifts
behind every building, every clump of grass, every pebble. We often say
that a wind came all the way from the North Pole and there was nothing
in the way to slow it down.

A little hill that breaks the wind can save a herd of cattle in a blizzard. A
row of carefully nurtured trees protecting a house can allow a man or
woman to breathe in a blizzard and warm up a little, and then go on
with the business of trying to save the cows.

A windbreak is a precious thing. It is a promise in fall,
a lifesaver and a place of warmth in winter, a sign of hope in spring, and
a place of loveliness in the dry heat of summer.

We all need a windbreak.

Thanks to my parents, who have allowed
me to combine my writing work with the work of
operating the ranch, and been patient when I neglected
the latter for the former.
Thanks to the many friends who have encouraged me to
write about my ranching experiences, especially those
who read and critiqued *Windbreak* in manuscript.
Thanks to George, for cooking, cleaning, and doing
chores when I was writing.
And thanks to Gina, who made it work.

CONTENTS

PREFACE

Windbreak represents one year of life on a ranch, beginning in fall as we prepare for our most severe test of the year. At that time we are fixing fences, moving hay, cutting firewood and stocking up on winter feed for the cattle and ourselves. In winter, while my parents vacation in Texas, my husband George and I move the cattle closer to home, and our main daily job is providing them with feed. In spring we calve the cows out, often during the worst of the spring blizzards. During summer we maintain the cow-calf herd, fix fences, and put up hay for winter.

I was born in Texas and moved to South Dakota with my divorced mother, Mildred Bovard, when I was five years old. We lived in Rapid City while she supported us by working as a secretary. Until I was in school, my maternal grandmother spent part of her time away from her own ranch home to help take care of me.

When I was nine my mother married John Hasselstrom, and we moved to the ranch where I now live. That year I began writing my first novel. With $80 saved from my allowance I bought a horse, something I'd dreamed of since I'd opened *Black Beauty* under the Christmas tree. Both horses and writing have been part of my life since.

I attended grade school in Hermosa, where the school was divided into two rooms, with two teachers, for eight grades. I graduated from high school in Rapid City in 1961. During a couple of summers I worked as an intern on the *Rapid City Daily Journal.*

My mother was determined I should not marry a rancher; my stepfather was silent on the subject, but thought I should go to college. I attended the University of South Dakota in Vermillion, four hundred miles away in the muggy southeastern corner of the state. I studied writing, edited the school newspaper, won a few journalism awards, and published my first chapbook of poems on a handfed press in an instructor's basement. I graduated with a major in English and did a year of postgraduate work at the same campus while working as a reporter on the nightside staff of the *Sioux City Journal.*

In 1966 I married a divorced man with three children and moved with him to Columbia, Missouri, where we enrolled in graduate school at the University of Missouri-Columbia. While working on an M.A. in American literature, I taught at women-only Christian College (now Columbia College) and was a grader for classes at the university.

Our marriage shaky, my husband and I returned to the ranch in 1971. I established a literary magazine, *Sunday Clothes: A Magazine of the Arts,* and Lame Johnny Press (named for a horse thief hanged not far from the ranch). I also did some writing of my own. When my husband decided ranch work wasn't for him, we moved to Spearfish, South Dakota, where I taught for a year at Black Hills State College, in the northern Black Hills.

The marriage ended in 1973, and again I returned to the ranch. I continued to operate the press and publish the magazine. I also resumed my own writing, neglected during my teaching. I've been away from the ranch for only brief periods since then, usually for editing jobs or workshops.

In 1979 I married George Snell. His parents had also divorced when he was five years old, and he was raised by his grandparents, who own a cherry orchard in Michigan. While serving in the Air Force, he was diagnosed as having Hodgkin's disease and told he might live for a few months or as long as five years. Nevertheless he married and fathered a son, and began attending Black Hills State College for a teaching degree. After his divorce he was one of my students in an English literature class. He still complains about his grade.

George and I have no children of our own. I keep in touch with my three stepchildren, and George's son, Michael, spends part of each summer and a week at Christmas with us.

I operated Lame Johnny Press from 1971 to 1985, when I closed it to devote more time to writing both poetry and prose, and to environmental activism. I earn extra money by giving workshops in writing and publishing. I'd like to combine my separate existences as rancher and environmentalist, but both sides sometimes view me with suspicion, and I come into conflict with each on occasion.

Although some of my background sets me apart from other ranch women, I think our differences are much outweighed by our similarities. Millions of women have loved or hated ranches or farms; in some way I feel I am writing their stories as well as my own.

The Hermosa community is largely composed of one-family ranches, many of them established in the late 1800s. My grandfather Hasselstrom left Sweden in 1883 and came West as a single man with a wagon train of other homesteading Scandinavians in 1886. After establishing a homestead he married a widow who had also homesteaded. Her place is now owned by my uncle Harold, my stepfather's oldest brother.

Ours is not one of the huge ranches of the fictional West, but an extended family operation that accommodates my parents and my husband and me. We usually run from 125 to 150 cows of Hereford or Angus ancestry along with six to eight bulls. We sell the best of the year's calves in the fall as our major crop, along with cows culled from the herd because of age, infirmity, or other reasons.

Ranch work, like most jobs, has its routine, its repetition. Our drama comes with the cycles of nature; with the endless absorption with birth and death; with the lives of our neighbors and friends; with the weather, which is a character in the story of our lives.

Only the details vary. In an open winter, for example, we might bring the cattle home from summer pasture as late as Christmas day. In 1985, one of the worst winters in memory, we brought them home in a blizzard on November 8. They stood, struggling to survive, in the icy corral until January 4, because the snow was too deep for them or our vehicles to move. Most of them lived.

My parents own and operate the ranch where I live, with our assistance. Obviously, their lives are closely involved with ours. But my father values his privacy intensely, and out of respect for his wishes I have minimized mention of my parents in the journal. In referring to my father, I mean the man who is technically my stepfather, the only real father I've known. My biological father is dead.

A glossary has been added for those who are not familiar with some of the terms and operations of a ranch.

Linda Hasselstrom
Hermosa, South Dakota, 1987

INTRODUCTION

The ranch where *Windbreak* takes place is located on the plains in southwestern South Dakota. The Black Hills lie about a mile to the west, and the Badlands begin about fifteen miles to the east. The Black Hills feature tree-covered hills, granite outcrops, man-made lakes and meadows filled with buffalo and deer. Mount Rushmore, Gutzon Borglum's carving of four presidents, is perhaps the most famous spot in the Hills, also famous for the towns of Deadwood, where Wild Bill Hickock was killed, and Lead, home of the world's largest gold mine. The hills also shelter several wildlife parks and considerable amounts of wilderness area.

The Badlands, on the other side of the ranch, are deeply eroded, almost treeless ridges with very little water and a staggering quantity of fossils.

We're twenty-five miles south of the state's second largest town, Rapid City, and slightly over five miles from the small pioneer town of Hermosa.

South Dakota is divided in half vertically by the Missouri River; "west river" is supported primarily by cattle ranching and tourism; in "east river" the land is flatter and receives more rainfall, supporting farming and the state's largest city, Sioux Falls, as well as most of the educational institutions and most of the population.

We go to the Black Hills or the Badlands as to foreign countries, to show visitors the beauty; the prairie is our world.

Driving down our bumpy graveled entrance road you'd see a collection of ranch buildings similar to many others in the region. We have a slightly faded red barn; a set of corrals in need of repair; a chicken house left over from a commercial poultry operation, now used for feed storage, as is an old granary; a large garage for my parents' car and the ranch trucks and tractors; and my parents' house. The ranch buildings are sheltered by a few native cottonwood trees, along with rows of cedar and pine trees planted by us or the former residents.

A quarter-mile closer to the highway, on top of a windy hill, my husband and I (and a lot of our friends) recently built a home, its shoulders hunched against the north winds. From our windows we can see long distances; no trees interrupt the view.

The prairie is smoothly rolling, with bulges and crevices like the skin of a plump old woman. Occasionally chunks of limestone outcrop, making miniature canyons covered with lime-green lichen. After a heavy rain pools of water appear, lying on limestone close to the surface, furnishing brief watering places for frogs, antelope, cattle.

Though some trees occur naturally on the prairie, they thrive mostly in the bottoms of gullies or dry creeks where they get occasional runoff, or where underground water is close to the surface. The prairie is rich with grasses that provide excellent forage. From a distance, green or gold buffalo grass and sideoats grama mingle with the big and little bluestem and blue grama to make a colorful, shifting tapestry. We have no creeks or other natural flowing water on the ranch — only wells, dams, and dugouts. Most of our moisture comes in the form of spring snowstorms and rain.

Many of our neighbors' ranches are similar to ours, though some are dairies, or other types of cattle ranches. But family-owned ranches are in trouble here, as elsewhere in the nation. Many sons and daughters have chosen other professions, so we are surrounded by ranches where no child will inherit the land. One nearby ranch was sold to a camping syndicate. We're apprehensive about changes which might threaten our livelihood by changing the agricultural nature of the community.

A ranch may operate in several ways. Some ranchers buy yearling cattle, fatten them in summer, sell them in fall, and go south for the winter. We run a cow-calf operation, raising cows to breed and selling their calves; such an operation demands almost constant attention. Our 365-day-a-year-job is raising those calves to become beef.

What we're really selling is grass packaged inside a cow. Ranchers have a close relationship with grass, learning which kinds provide the best grazing, how to recognize overgrazed land, and what to do about it. The old ranchers in the area would hesitate to call themselves environmentalists — or even take offense at the idea — but they take good care of the land so it will continue to support their cattle.

Living on a ranch has made me intensely grateful for joys that might seem small to someone else. I love not only the easy beauty, but the hard loveliness of the clean patterns of birth, life, and death. It's easy to appreciate a fawn, harder to appreciate a cow. It's easy to be joyous at the idea of birth, harder if that birth involves two hours' struggle in the slime and stench of a barn at midnight.

In saying this I'm not suggesting that ranchers are tougher or more noble than the rest of the world because of what we endure. That wouldn't be in character; the natives tend to be restrained. One of our neighbors, now dead, fell off a sixty-foot silo a few years ago. He was horribly injured, with numerous broken bones, internal injuries, and a concussion. When he could have visitors, he said, "You know, if I'd known how bad I was hurt, I'd have died."

Mingled with the threads of my story are the skeins of others: a neighbor's accident, a horse's survival, my husband's health. Real life, as Meridel

LeSueur says, is not a straight line, or a matter of who wins, but a series of interlocking events. Sometimes the only common element is a single observer.

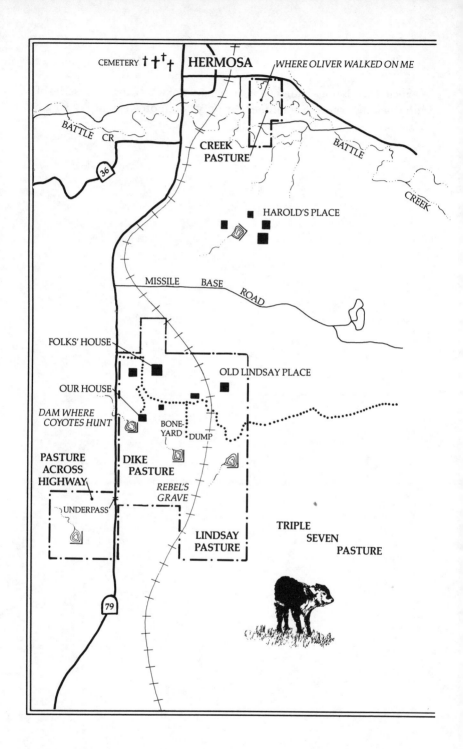

CEMETERY † † † † **HERMOSA** *WHERE OLIVER WALKED ON ME*

BATTLE CR

36

CREEK PASTURE

BATTLE CREEK

HAROLD'S PLACE

MISSILE BASE ROAD

FOLKS' HOUSE

OLD LINDSAY PLACE

OUR HOUSE

DAM WHERE COYOTES HUNT

BONE-YARD

DUMP

PASTURE ACROSS HIGHWAY

DIKE PASTURE

REBEL'S GRAVE

UNDERPASS

TRIPLE SEVEN PASTURE

LINDSAY PASTURE

79

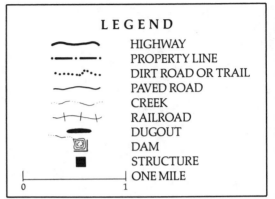

LEGEND

～	HIGHWAY
—··—··—	PROPERTY LINE
·····•····	DIRT ROAD OR TRAIL
～	PAVED ROAD
～	CREEK
+—+—+	RAILROAD
▬	DUGOUT
▣	DAM
■	STRUCTURE

0 |————————| 1   ONE MILE

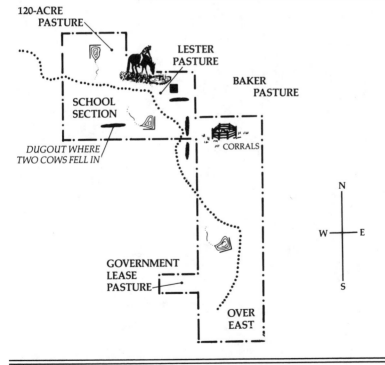

120-ACRE
PASTURE

LESTER
PASTURE

BAKER
PASTURE

SCHOOL
SECTION

*DUGOUT WHERE
TWO COWS FELL IN*

CORRALS

N
W——E
S

GOVERNMENT
LEASE
PASTURE

OVER
EAST

Fall

Rankin Ridge: Only An Ancient Moon

—for Lawrence

The sun drops below the high tree.
Elk cows the color of grass move
out of the pines,
up the meadows toward a pond.
Dark among the trees the bulls pace,
snort, begin to bugle.
That sound flows across meadows like water,
opening like a piccolo, rising to a keen,
a cry, a wail, a ululation for our night.

The moon lifts, huge, gold, flattened,
pushing to higher air,
becoming small, silver, distant.

The cows graze silent in the glowing grass.
The bulls wait at the edge of the trees,
bugling.
The moonlight flickers
at sounds too high for human ears.

September

September 1   Low 54, high 85.

Something woke me at 3 a.m. yesterday, and I got up and began to wander through the house, looking out the windows. To the east, the horizon was a flickering red and gold. For a minute I just stared, before realizing it was fire, a towering wall of flames.

I called the fire number while tearing off my nightgown, and by the time I was dressed George had the pickup ready, with a tank full of water and a bundle of feed sacks. We honked as we went through my folks' yard, and I saw the bedroom light go on. We took our regular trail over east, only we threw all the gates back out of the way; behind us in the darkness we could see the lights of the neighbors' pickups and the fire trucks. When we got to my uncle Harold's pasture, we saw a lone figure silhouetted against the fire, bending as he beat at the ground — my uncle's hired man.

Our area is served by volunteer fire departments, and who is manning the trucks depends on who's available when the fire siren blows. Getting the men and trucks together takes time, so we're all volunteer fire fighters. Our standard method is to wet a gunny sack and use it to beat out the flames. When the sparks have been beaten down in one spot, you move ahead and repeat the operation. Every foot of fire is sometimes beaten out in this way if the trucks are busy somewhere else. Any flaming cow chips within five feet of the edge of the fire must be kicked well back into the burned-over zone. They hold sparks for hours, and are light enough to be blown out into the unburned grass.

The wind was blowing hard, and twice it blew flames up into my face, jumping over the spot I'd been wetting down. The roar of the wind, the crackling fire and my own hoarse breathing were all I could hear when I stopped to rest. I deliberately slowed my pace, afraid I'd pass out.

The next time I looked up, I seemed to be alone in the dark. A long tongue of flame had shot down a gully, and I could see pickup lights ahead of it, searching for a way to get to it. Figures appeared and disappeared as the flames flickered. I stayed in the same area, working back and forth along the side of the fire. Once I saw a cow chip spinning over the dry grass, throwing sparks like a pinwheel. By the time I'd caught and soaked it, I had a new trail of fire to put out.

About sunrise, I saw men gathering around a pickup about a half mile north of me. Aunt Jo, Harold's wife, was passing out cups of coffee. I joined them, and listened to fire stories for a few minutes. Several of the men came in coughing like their lungs were on fire, and then lit cigarettes. I kept following the coughs, looking for George, since his breathing is so precarious, but couldn't find him or my father. Finally Jo spotted me. "Come on. We're going to town for stuff for sandwiches."

I was too tired to argue with her. When I piled my first armload of sandwich meat on the counter at the store, the clerk peered at me and said, "For gosh sakes, I didn't recognize you. You burned your face off, honey." She slapped a package of ointment on the counter and said, "Put some of this on it. And Josephine, put that checkbook away. We'll donate this stuff. And come back if you need more."

By the time we got back several new areas of fire had spread east and south, and a slurry bomber was working back and forth over the Badlands. We picked a spot close to where the fire chiefs were parked, talking on their radios, and started making sandwiches. Soon several other women had driven up, with pots of coffee or boxes of food, and the fire fighters began to drift in as if they could smell the coffee.

One of our neighbors still had his pajama top on, stuffed into his jeans. Another man held up the wreckage of his hat; he'd come without a sack, and had beaten on the flames with the hat. My uncle Harold came in for coffee, much to Jo's relief; he'd been helping to drive his and the neighbors' cows out of the fire's path.

I stayed with the lunch crew until late in the afternoon, since I couldn't find either of our pickups, or my husband or father. I saw our nearest neighbors, as well as people I hadn't seen since I was in high school. Close friends and enemies drank coffee, stuffed sandwiches in their faces, and went back to the fire. Every now and then the wind would change, and we'd throw everything in the pickup and get it out of the way, then fight fire for awhile until the wind switched again.

At dark, the front of the fire — fifteen miles away — was under control.

By that time, the reporters had been out, and the Highway Patrol had blocked a couple of ranch roads to keep spectators out. One child was missing, and officials were afraid he'd been burned. George finally appeared, black smudges on his face, and a definite wheeze in his throat. After he'd eaten we came on home, and found my father already here and my mother worried about us. George and Father had both gone ahead of the fire, to the east side, and fought over there most of the day. They were happy to report the fire didn't get to our pastures over east.

September 2   Low 58, high 92.
I'm still thinking about the fire, with the burned out areas lying on the horizon like a dark cloud. The fire chiefs found the fire's starting point beside the railroad tracks. Trains start many of our fires because of the tall dry grass along the tracks and the frequent sparks from the smokestacks or wheels. It burned fifteen thousand acres, and was more than fifteen miles long. Some of the ranchers in the Badlands saw it coming and were able to plow fire-guards to stop it. Ranchers who lost grass, haystacks, or cattle are talking of suing the railroad.

None of this, except the size of the fire, is especially unusual. I've fought many fires like this, and I'm a "newcomer" — only been here thirty years. Every year the railroads start dozens of fires, and every year we fight them, but the situation never seems to change.

George and I took my horse, Oliver, and went over east to our summer pasture at 7 a.m. The air stayed cool until noon, but it was windy and very dusty. We talked a little in the truck of what fall meant to us as children. For me, the first hint of cool air and yellowing leaves meant tragedy: I had to turn my horse out in the pasture and go back to school. Until the next spring, I wouldn't be able to ride out alone over the prairie, going to my favorite places, day-dreaming and making up stories while the horse grazed. George, who was always big for his age, said, "When the other kids played King of the Mountain, I was the mountain."

I know he's worried about his weight, but he has been losing; he's down to 240 pounds, which on his six-foot-plus stack of big bones isn't bad at all.

After three dry years, the big dam in the government lease pasture has only a small pool of water in the center of acres of deep black mud. Since the cattle risked getting bogged down in the mud to get a drink, we moved them out. George led with the truck and the horse and I followed, moving forty-seven pairs — cows and calves — into the school section where a dugout provides abundant water. We sorted eight dry cows back to the leased pasture and left the neighbor's bull with them. We've tried to get him out on several occasions, but he's snorty, so we left him for the Triple Seven riders to find. The trip over east to our summer pasture is always a major undertaking: six miles through pastures owned by neighbors to the nearest point of our land, opening ten wire gates and closing each carefully so the neighbors' cattle don't get out. We always take fencing tools, posts and wire, a little food and water, and make sure the first aid and snakebite kits are in the pickup, along with shovels for fighting fire or digging post holes, ropes, halters, saddles and bridles in case we have to ride. I've walked home when the truck became stuck in snow or broke down, and my father once arrived home with a shoe full of blood after cutting himself while fencing.

The drive is necessarily slow, sometimes an hour each way, since we follow pasture trails. I entertain myself as we drive remembering other trips, on long hot days, when my father talked about the history of this land as he has known it or heard it from others.

We're never bored; seeing the same scenery over and over only seems to make us notice more, so that we spot any change in the landscape, and any interesting animal behavior. Today we saw, high in the sky, a huge spiraling flock of birds, apparently riding the thermals. When we got closer and used the monocular, we discovered they weren't cranes, as we expected, but hawks. I've never seen so many together — thirty to fifty — and they simply stayed in formation, spiraling around and around for at least a half-hour while we sat beneath them and watched. I've always assumed hawks migrated alone. Perhaps their being together was sheer chance, and they were only playing with the winds.

The Lester pasture is our way of remembering Silas Lester, who homesteaded there, and Maude, the wife he got through a newspaper advertisement. He — or perhaps she — planted seven cottonwoods, the only ones on our land in this whole stretch of country; we eat lunch gratefully in their shade in July and August. The alfalfa Silas sowed in the bottom still fattens our cows in early summer. Their frame house was torn down years ago; cattle have rubbed the limestone walls until they have begun to disappear into the earth. Pieces of an old Model-A lie nearby. When they could no longer make a living, they sold their land to the Hasselstroms and disappeared from this area, perhaps to begin fresh somewhere else.

We still use their piped spring for cattle, and the water is clear, fresh and cold on a blistering day. The tank is filled with moss and frogs, but we keep a dipper hanging on a post and catch water from the pipe to drink. It tastes of earth and the roots of buffalo grass. On summer days I take my shirt off, dip it in the water, wring it out and put it back on, shivering. Then we rest under a big cottonwood, backed between the tree's thighs, leaning back against the rough bark. With no water visible, we seem to feel it drumming under the tree's bark, like the earth's heartbeat.

I've prowled through the remnants of the Lesters' lives over the years, and found a brass label from a cream can, marked "Silas Lester"; it's on a shelf in my study. In their dump, I found a single glass saltshaker wrapped in thin beaten silver with a carved pattern, a delicate thing someone might give a new bride leaving her home for a strange country; it's on my kitchen shelf.

September 3   Low 50, high 72; windy, cool, smelling like fall.

This morning I canned a bushel of tomatoes from the garden, dug and potted lavender and lilies of the valley, and with George's help dug sixty pounds of potatoes. He doesn't really enjoy the garden work as much as I do, but he's so big and so strong that he can make jobs like digging much easier. He had to stop frequently to rest because of the difficulty he has in breathing. The asthma medication doesn't seem to do any good; the doctor is wondering if he actually has asthma.

About 11 a.m. we went over east and found the cows and calves all mixed up because the neighbor's buffalo yearlings had torn the fence down. We fixed fence and tried to straighten out the pairs. The cows that don't yet have their calves will be standing at the fence bawling tomorrow, and we can finish pairing them up.

When I started to haze the buffalo back to their own pasture, a new problem developed: Oliver had never seen buffalo before. When I'd start to drive them, they'd scatter, then run up behind him and snort. He'd shiver in terror and whirl to face them. I don't blame him; those sharp horns can cut through anything, and buffalo can run faster than horses. They acted like yearling bovines: nervous, flighty, but not on the fight.

Oliver shied at rocks, trees, and the buffalo, whirling and snorting every few steps, bucking a little. The unwritten rule of horsemanship is never to hold onto the saddle horn in front of witnesses, but I don't count George as a witness any more. George insists my saddle horn has teethmarks in it where I tried to get an extra grip when holding on with both hands wasn't working, but of course he exaggerates.

After the horse calmed down, we got them out without much trouble. As we were driving home, we saw a golden eagle perched on a post. Through the monocular we could see a snake writhing in the eagle's talons while he bent his huge head and pecked at it. As I was studying him, he suddenly raised his head and his eye seemed to focus directly on mine. I had the sensation we were only inches apart, and that he was studying me as carefully as I was staring at him. We made a wide circle around him so as not to drive him off. Golden eagles are now rare here; several have been shot along the highway.

When we got home, I made dill and refrigerator pickles, finishing around 10:30. George slept in his chair after the TV news, with Phred, his cat, curled on his shoulder and our Westy, Cuchulain, sprawled in the other easy chair.

September 4   Low 65, high 86. A few high, dry clouds this morning, with no promise of rain.

George worked at fixing fence near the house while I canned another half bushel of tomatoes and hauled squash and potatoes to the basement. Mother was out in her yard, raking leaves, and we stopped to rest and visit a few times while we worked. I told her again how glad I am we don't have trees around our house to shed leaves, nor a lawn to rake; the buffalo grass and wildflowers suit me.

In the afternoon, George and I went over east again and paired up the rest of the cows and calves. The calves were hungry; some of them have been away from their mothers for two days. We let a few cows into the corral at a time and, as soon as a calf began to suck its mother, hazed the pair out again. They waited outside until the calves had sucked, then all headed for water.

My uncle Harold, whose ranch is about five miles northeast of us, called last night. Somehow we started talking about heights; he said his father (my grandfather Hasselstrom) shingled a church in Sweden with a steeple two hundred feet high. I knew he'd been a cobbler in Sweden, but this was the first I've heard of the carpentry. I wish I knew more about him, and what he thought about when he came to these wide plains. He refused to teach his children Swedish because "we're Americans now, and we're going to talk English." He chose his brand, the Bar Ninety-Nine (–99) from 1899, the year he started the ranch, and my father still uses it.

Whatever kind of man he was, he raised a good family. All of his living children are in this area so I see more of them than I do my mother's three brothers. Harold is the oldest, eighty-two, and still a big man despite the cancer that required removal of his left leg. He gets around with crutches and a wheelchair, and drives his pickup and tractor. When he was young, he did a great deal of the work on the family ranch, as well as helping the neighbors. When most men put fenceposts in, they dig a hole three or four feet deep, drop the post in, and tamp the earth carefully around it. Harold stood on the back of a wagon and drove sharpened posts straight into the ground with a sledge hammer.

My stepfather, John, was the youngest child. He suffered from rheumatic fever, which left him very slender and with a weakened heart. He went to college and then worked as an accountant for years before coming back to South Dakota and joining Harold on the ranch. The third brother, Carl, was killed in World War II.

When John married my mother, Mildred, the ranch was divided between the two remaining brothers. Harold kept the home place, and my parents built a new house near some old barns and sheds on another part of the ranch. When we married, George and I built a new house on a hill overlooking the home place.

Harold has no children, and my husband is sterile from radiation given to counteract Hodgkin's disease, so no children are growing up on the two ranches to inherit the land. I kept my own name when I married for the second time, to keep the name alive a bit longer. George doesn't seem to mind, and professes not to know me when my name appears in the paper for various environmental causes.

September 5   Low 54, high 80.

A recent hail destroyed all our flowers but the gladiolus, blooming beautifully now: purple and white, cream, yellow with orange centers, the only color in the dusty, gray land.

While George fenced, Father and I went over east this morning, just to check on everything again. He had to drive across a little grassy swale to get to a section of fence needing work, and said, "I hate to drive across good grass."

That's the essential difference between a good cattleman and a poor one (not necessarily between a *rich* and a poor one). Father's careful about even things that seem small, like driving once across the grass. He believes in the old saying, "Take care of the little things, and the big things will take care of themselves."

At dusk George and I took the horse to the prairie dog town, moved the short-eared bull to the pasture on the west side of the tracks, and collected five cows with steer calves that Father wants to sell. I used Oliver as George couldn't catch his Sage. The difficulty we have catching that animal is beginning to get on our nerves.

September 6   Low 54, high 88.

A terrific wind storm struck in the night, with doors crashing open, roaring wind, the attic door raising up and thumping down. I stayed awake for a long time expecting lightning and watching for fires, but George, Phred and Cuchulain slept through it all. Then, just before dawn, I woke because of the silence of the absent wind and wandered into the dining room. To the north, the aurora borealis hung like a waterfall in the sky over the dry land: Mama Nature's little irony.

When we went down to the corrals, we found a fifteen-foot section of plank fence down and had to use the pickup to pull it upright so we could nail it back to the posts.

We went over east again, checking cows and fences, and had several repairs to do because last night's wind piled tumbleweeds against every fence. The neighbors are short of grass and water, and have put what looks like five hundred head of cattle next to our one remaining dugout. We still have good grass so the cattle stick their heads through and push against the fence constantly. Their water hole, only a few feet from the fence on their side, is low and muddy, and they can smell the good water on our side so the pressure on the fence is terrific. They could get in and eat off our pasture practically overnight, but it will carry our cattle for another month if we can keep the fences up.

I received an intriguing letter from my stepdaughter, Erin, today. She's doing a paper for a college class, and wanted me to answer some questions about being a writer and rancher. She asked one question I thought particularly apt: am I considered a rancher, or a rancher's wife?

That's an interesting one, and tricky. I was raised here, of course, and the ranch belongs to my father, so probably I'm thought of first in this community as a rancher's daughter. Even when I was married to Erin's father, I almost had to introduce myself as John Hasselstrom's daughter in order for people to place me.

After I divorced her father and took my own name back, everyone knew who I was, but half of them don't know I remarried because George isn't well known in the community. We don't belong to church, or go to many social events. I'm afraid the thinking is that I'm a rancher's daughter, and George is "that fella she married from out east someplace, like Michigan." If you asked them to clarify that, they'd probably say, "Well, John is sort of training George to take over the place," neatly shoving me back in the kitchen where I "belong." I think a few, people who know me well enough to know I spend almost as much time outside as inside, would accord me the title of "ranch wife." I introduce myself as a rancher.

I imagine that when my father dies, the community perception will be that George runs the place while I run around doing other things. To an extent that's true. He does the chores more often than I do because I also give writing workshops and travel for environmental causes. He's learned a lot about ranching in the last few years, but I know more simply because I've lived here off and on for thirty-one years, and have developed my instincts.

I'm pleased that Erin's becoming aware of women and their problems; she's serious about her college work, but she's also getting married in the fall, as soon as she graduates from college, and I fear for her career plans.

September 7   Low 62, high 97.

Still and hot this morning, more like July than September. Father went over east alone, while George fenced here. I made apple butter; the kitchen is knee deep in apple pulp. It's even on the ceiling.

In the afternoon, we went to Lawrence's beautiful cabin in the hills to cut a load of firewood. Our wood-propane furnace needs about three cords of wood in a normal winter; we'll try to get six. Lawrence was busy, but directed us to a spot he wants thinned. It was cooler in the trees, and except for the noise of the chain saw, a pleasant way to spend the afternoon.

Before Lawrence quit ranching and built his cabin — he cut the trees on his own land and hand-crafted everything inside it — we worked together representing ranchers' interests on environmental causes. When we go to his woods to cut trees, we envy his solitude, and always take time for a tour of his garden or a walk in the woods where he points out flowers he's planted. He's now less publicly active as an environmentalist because he's busy living his beliefs.

I make a ritual of counting tree rings. Today we cut a tree 150 years old: 1836. James Madison was president; Davy Crockett was killed at the Alamo; Indians and a few fur trappers were wandering through these hills.

September 8   Low 65, high 98.

Up early and spent a pleasant half-hour drinking coffee on the porch before heading over east. Phred and Cuchulain came out with me and sat on the steps for awhile, surveying the landscape, before wandering off on their separate errands. I should always imitate their way of beginning the day: sitting quietly, absorbing the sounds and smells.

The neighbors' cows had the fence down at the dugout, and we had hot work separating ours from theirs; good thing we'd left my horse there. It was miserably hot, but I felt a slight breeze as long as the horse was moving.

About dusk we heard shots and saw Ginger, the horse we had pastured in the driveway, racing for the house. We grabbed our pistols, raced to the highway and found a Game, Fish and Parks truck parked there. The driver came back carrying his rifle and wearing a pistol. He'd been hunting coyotes on the pasture north of us, and hadn't seen the horse. He claimed he hadn't fired toward her, but we told him there was no coyote hunting allowed in our neighborhood.

In the evening I canned a half bushel of tomatoes and sliced another half bushel to dry, before falling into bed. I feel like a squirrel storing food. The song of my days in the fall: storing up food, fixing fences, preparing for the long white cold night of winter.

September 11   Low 55, high 98.
The house was full of the rich mingled smells of drying tomatoes, onions and garlic this morning, a fall smell. The air always seems particularly fragrant to me in fall, not only inside, where the harvest is being stored, but outside, as the grasses are cured by cold nights and dry days. And perhaps the richness is heightened by my knowledge that soon the air will smell only of the cold purity of snow with a hint of wood smoke for variety.

When it "cooled down" to ninety degrees in early evening, we went over east. The waterholes are getting low and the grass short; Father says the cattle are as short of water as they were during the Dust Bowl years of the 1930s. But the cattle look good; their hair is long and shiny, their flanks fat.

In the evening I turned the sprinkler on the buffaloberry, plum and chokecherry bushes we've planted north of the house, and stood in the spray for a few minutes. Then I sat on a rock throwing a stick for the dog and enjoying the sight of our house tucked into this spot on the prairie. We have no lawn, but the buffalo grass scraped aside by the bulldozer is slowly coming back. I transplant clumps of grass and wildflowers into the bare ground each spring. Juniper bushes, the fruiting bushes, and cedar trees in a low spot to the north will serve as a windbreak as they grow, and catch the snow to provide their own water, and protect our driveway from drifts.

I take great pleasure in how we made the house fit into the landscape. The gray siding blends with the summer's tawny browns and greens, the tan grass of fall, winter's white skies, and spring's dirty patches of snow. At any season, if you weren't looking for the house, you might miss it. The house is dug into the shoulder of a hill and tilted off the north-south axis to present one corner to the prevailing northwest winds. Nothing obscures the view from any window — there are no tall trees and never will be. We see fires start, cows calving and visitors coming. A deep roof overhang helps shade the windows and part of the deck from summer's sun, and big windows collect solar heat in winter.

Many things are still unfinished: we have no garage, no gravel to park the cars on, no porch furniture. Inside, we have no closet doors or doors on my office. We originally planned to put a greenhouse on the south side. We never seem to have time to work on these things. But the house is comfortable, full of the used furniture we both acquired in our separate lives: a nine-foot couch, refinished oak dressers, fat easy chairs for reading with lights over each one so we can curl up anywhere. We keep the wooden trunks full of rendezvous gear in the bedroom, ranged around the walls, where I can read or the cat and dog can sleep.

September 12   Low 76, high 93. Over east at eight this morning, heat haze already rising from the prairie.

I woke at false dawn, while the air felt slightly cool, and walked barefoot to the garden. I was sauntering along, listening to the blackbirds, when I stepped on something squishy and looked down. I was standing on a snake lying along a row of parsnips. I assumed it was a bullsnake, apologized, and walked up to the tail end — where I discovered it was a rattlesnake. It scared me so much I grabbed the hoe, and then reconsidered and just tossed him out into the trees.

We butchered the crippled heifer today since we'd have lost money on her at the sale ring. George, gritting his teeth, shot her and bled her out. He brought her up to the house swinging from the loader on the big tractor, and hoisted her to a tripod made from three tipi poles. While he skinned and gutted her, I retrieved the heart and liver, and hauled the rest out to the field for the coyotes.

Jim and Mavis, friends from Sturgis, drove down on Jim's new Harley this evening. We met them through the muzzle-loading club, and often travel to rendezvous and camp together. We visited outside, and listened to the coyotes yapping and singing as they feasted on the heifer's remains.

September 13   Low 65, high 79.

When we went over east in the afternoon, we found about fifteen of the neighbor's cattle in the school section, and I had a hard ride to get them out. Their Charolais bull is bigger than the pickup, so I mostly gathered the cows with the horse and ignored him. He rumbled a little, and swung his head at the horse whenever I got close, but finally trailed along after us. As Father says, it helps to be a little smarter than the cows.

Resting, we sat on the rocks by the big dam, drank coffee, and watched the water and the snapping turtles awhile. In spring I'm always tempted to catch the tiny ones, the kind I remember seeing in pet stores when I was a child. Most of them are the size of dinner plates now, sunning themselves on the rocks before diving into the mud to spend the winter. I used to swim in the dams but now that I know about coliform bacteria I've given it up. Knowledge is a terrible thing; the water looked so cool.

September 14   Low 68, high 87.

We'd planned to let the heifer hang another day or two, but yesterday was too warm so we started cutting her up. We decided to can her because canned meat is so handy and tasty for a quick meal, and with that crippled leg she may be tougher than usual.

I was prepared with jars, my big canning kettle, and newspapers spread around the dining room table where we cut her up. We discarded all the bones, and I cut the large pieces of meat into one-inch chunks and stuffed them into jars. As soon as I had a kettle full, I put them on to cook and there the bottleneck developed, because each kettle has to cook for more than an hour and a half. Meanwhile we kept filling jars. We quit cutting when we finished the front quarters. George did some chores and a little fencing, and finally went to bed while I kept cooking until almost two a.m.

September 15   Low 50, high 86.

It was wonderful to see all those filled jars of meat standing on the counter when I got up for breakfast. I hauled them all to the basement before we started again.

I finished cooking around midnight. The jars look very impressive on the basement shelves. Every fall I feel this great need to store up food. A year ago, I even dried summer squash, though I haven't found anything palatable to do with it yet. I did make a lot of pumpkin pies, pumpkin bread and frybread from the dried pumpkin this winter. The onions and garlic hang in net bags from the ceiling, and the potatoes are arranged in wooden boxes I liberated from the trash behind the Safeway store. Two aluminum garbage cans are filled with packages of dried food; canned meat, fruit and vegetables fill the shelves and the freezer. Somehow all this food makes me feel more ready to face another winter.

September 16   Low 50, high 85.

George went over east.

I couldn't sleep, so got up at 1 a.m. and worked on rewriting a story until 5:30, then fell into bed and slept until 11:30.

Father has been plowing fireguards along the highway and around the houses all week. The high grass close to the ranch is our winter pasture, and the fire danger is high.

After supper, I went to Lawrence's and joined the rest of the Black Hills Energy Coalition in addressing envelopes until 3 in the morning. This will be our last mailing before the vote on the initiative to ban the disposal of nuclear waste here, and may win or lose it for us.

September 17   Low 50, high 82.

We both went over east this morning and tried to evict a visiting Longhorn bull. His horns were as wide as the pickup bumper, and he bellowed and swung them around rather suggestively, so we decided to leave him for the neighbors to remove. It was a long hot day, with flies gathered so thickly in the shade of the cottonwood trees we could hardly eat our sandwiches in peace.

On the way home we stopped to check a dam in the pasture where my old red mare Rebel has retired. Father was surprised she survived the winter; she's almost twenty-five years old. Her knees seemed stiff last year, and Father doesn't think I should ride her anymore, but she's so lovely running ahead of the wind. I stopped and called her to the pickup for a few pieces of cake and scratched her ears. She ate the cake, then nibbled my pockets and hair, looking for more. I noticed how sweet her breath is, like fresh grass.

Rebel and I really taught each other about riding when I broke her to ride. Actually, I've never "broken" any of my horses, only gentled them into working with me. She was the first, before I had any knowledge of what I was doing, and she was so patient and understanding. Most people sell old horses for mink feed; I hope she can die painlessly, here where she's always run.

In late afternoon we drove to the hills; among the leaves of gold fire the elk were bugling. We went to Rankin Ridge and had just gotten settled when a group of noisy people arrived. Every time things got quiet enough to hear the elk, one of them would squeal, "I don't hear anything. Let's go home. I'm cold."

Disgusted, we found another turnoff above the canyon where we could hear the elk clearly while we ate sandwiches and drank coffee laced with Kahlua.

September 18   Low 65, high 90. The daytime temperatures haven't fallen below eighty degrees for three weeks, and the dry heat would be exhausting even if we did nothing at all.

We both went over east in the morning to sort cattle. The Longhorn bull is still there, but a cow distracted him until we made our getaway with the cows and calves we wanted.

Hawks and falcons are everywhere now; we saw a tiny, fast falcon perched on a post clutching a huge grasshopper today, and another of the same type cruising low over the pasture, hovering, backing up, swooping forward, and finally pouncing on something in the grass. I forgot my pen and had to use the tip of one of George's bullets to write notes.

September 19   Low 50, high 82.

With George leading in the pickup and me riding, we brought thirty head of cows and calves home from over east to sell. We need to cut down on the number of cattle we'll have to feed this winter because we're short of pasture and feed as a result of the two-year drought and some severe hails this summer.

In the afternoon, we started painting the folks' garage, a hot job we'd have loved to put off. Painting walls and writing poetry are both fun for the first five minutes — splashing color over the walls or a page. After that, it turns into work: covering evenly the structure beneath, with all its flaws, smoothing the strokes so they blend in, so the wall or poem will appear to have been done in one triumphant stroke, instead of in jerky motions.

In the evening, I got to the computer and worked on a story that's been on my mind. Since I've been thinking about it for several days while doing other things, I got a rough draft down in about three hours. Now I hope I can get back to it before the inspiration dries up and blows away.

September 20   Low 65, high 83.

Stretching the kinks of riding the horse out of my muscles this morning, I was thinking how I always dreamed of horses, long before we moved to the ranch. I got horse books from the library when I was five years old, and day-dreamed about the Black Stallion. When I finally climbed on dear old fat Blaze, bought with eighty dollars of my own money, I began to understand what I'd been longing for.

Then my uncle Harold decided Blaze was too old to be much fun, and gave me Rebel, who was less than a year old. Her mother had never been broken. In order to get them to our place, my father and I each put ropes on Rebel's halter and led her between our horses through the pastures. Her wild mother, tail dragging the ground even when it was held erect, circled us whinnying and screaming, and Rebel continually fought the ropes.

My father decided to quiet her by tying her in the barn until he could find someone to break her for me. As soon as he left the ranch, I'd slip into the barn and talk to her and pet her. After she'd quieted down, I'd take her out in the corral and get on her. I never was very good at knots, so I think my father suspected, but all he said when he caught me was, "How long has this been going on?"

After that, he supervised while I rode her around the corral. She was eager to learn, but full of fire. We came as close to being one organism as is possible; I rode her bareback with the reins loose from the first, guiding her by leaning. Sometimes she seemed to know what to do with no direction at all, unless she read my mind. Her gait was the smoothest I've ever felt, a long, loping stride even though she was small and fine-boned.

I still think the sensation of speed is much more satisfying on the back of a good horse than in the fastest car; there's more participation. A car simply whizzes along; on a horse, you're part of the process. The minute I get on a horse, I feel so comfortable I wonder why I ever get off; I slip into the rhythm of the horse's movements as if I were born to do nothing else.

September 21   Low 40, high 71. First day of fall.

While drinking my morning coffee, I watched a coyote hunting in the field south of the house, tossing mice in the air and catching them as they fell, like a puppy playing with a ball.

The truck came at 11:00 for the cattle. I always have mixed feelings when we're loading: pride at the quality of the cattle and their condition, and a sadness at seeing cows I've worked over, and calves I've saved, go off to their fates. The cows will probably be sold for dog food though some of them are fairly young. The calves will be sent to a crowded feed lot, and turned into the overly fat beef the American public seems to favor.

Father always worries about me being kicked when I walk among the cows, but the only times I've been hurt by cattle were when I was, of necessity, hurting or frightening them. When I walk among them, I mentally broadcast a message that I'm just passing through and mean no harm. I find myself absently patting flanks, scratching ears; several cows will eat cake from my hands. This is a great contrast to some ranchers and almost all TV programs, where everything is done at a gallop, with whips. If I try to walk among some of the neighbors' cattle, they bellow and flee by the hundreds.

After the truck rumbled out, we hastily cleaned up, and picked up lunch in town on the way to the sale ring. When we got there, we walked out to the corrals to see if the calves had been unloaded and watered, and ran into a delightful old man. He came meandering out of a corral, one big hand wrapped around the reins of an old horse. He was lean and bony, wearing a ragged, oily scarf at his throat, his old felt hat pinched at one side where he grabs it to settle it on his head.

"Lookin' for yer calves, are ye? What's the name? Hasselstrom? OK, follow me."

While he led us to the calves, he never stopped talking. "I ain't never been around cows before, so I don't know what I'm doing here." He looked over his shoulder at me and winked.

"Ha. I'll bet you haven't been around cows much," I said. "That saddle's older than I am." It was completely black with oil, with the high cantle and swell of an ancient roping saddle; a worn rope hung on the horn.

"So's the horse, honey. How old do you think I am, anyway?"

I knew he had to be at least seventy-five but I said, "Sixty, maybe."

"Humph. Let's see, how old am I? When you're over a hundred, you tend to forget things. Let's see, I was eighty last January. My wife died in eighty-one. I've been alone since then."

"That's tough."

"My name's Hudson. Folks came to Fairburn in 1883. When I growed up I rode at Cherry Creek for the Diamond A Cattle Company. Guess how many we shipped out of the Cheyenne Reservation one winter?"

"Five thousand?"

"Humph. Two trainloads, 23,000 head. Do you know what this means?" and he said a phrase in Lakota. "That means 'them white girls are no good.' I hung out with all them Indians. My dad helped haul in dead Indians in ninety-two, you know, from that Wounded Knee thing. I knew all them Indians up at Cherry Creek. Here's your calves; see you around now."

The cattle sold early, and we were back here by 4:00, so we finished painting the folks' garage and started on their house. After supper, George went to the bedroom to practice on his chanter, the flute portion of a bagpipe. Once he masters breath control and fingering, he hopes to get the air chamber and upright drones that complete the modern Scots bagpipe.

After he'd played awhile, I began to hear other notes beyond the faint sound of the chanter. I slipped out on the porch and listened: all around us, coyotes were howling. When George finished, I told him they thought he was torturing a coyote. Perhaps they feel a kinship with those wild notes; I've always felt the bagpipe had a primitive, shivery sound.

September 23   Low 67, high 95.

We finished painting the folks' house today. Father muttered that we ought to paint the chicken house and barn, but we pretended not to hear him.

Father asked us to walk around to all the bale stacks today and estimate the number of bales. He'll compare our count with his own, and that turned in by the boys who did the work, and come up with the percentage they earned for themselves. It's great to see so many stacks waiting for winter despite the drought and hail. I love bales, because if George's back goes out,

I can feed and load them. And since our tractor with the grapple fork is used by the neighbors who feed the main herd in the winter, six miles away, we don't have it to lighten the winter labor of feeding.

In the afternoon, we had a sudden, vicious hail; it's been two months since the last rain. At that time we had three-quarters of an inch but the hail finished off much of the grass. This time it didn't do much damage to the grass since there's hardly any left, but it banged up the new paint on the garage and the folks' house. Sometimes I think Mother Nature has a nasty streak.

Late in the afternoon, while it was raining after the hail, a big red-tailed hawk perched on the deck railings, looking drenched and angry.

Lying beside George last night, holding his hand, I listened to the trucks and cars on the highway and wondered where everyone was going on this remote highway at 3 in the morning. What's important enough to miss this delight of warmth, cocooned with a lover, secure? Earlier, I had gotten up to write since I couldn't sleep, and my absence woke George, who came downstairs wearing only his tee-shirt, plaintive because I wasn't there, wondering if something was wrong.

September 24

We were up at 6:00 to head for Denver to see George's doctors. Raining lightly; Father says it's more like it's sweating. Fog followed us almost to Lusk, and there were low clouds around the buttes I like there, but no rain. Sunny by Orin Junction, with cottonwood leaves juggling light.

We reached Denver in the light and are tucked into a relatively cheap motel, nice on the outside, but not clean, with hairs in the shower and dim lights, the bane of the reading traveler.

September 25

I'm people-watching while I wait for George in the radiology department. People's walks are so revealing: many here in the city walk with shoulders bent, feet slapping the floor heavily, hips taking the blow, showing depression, shyness, perhaps fear. Those wearing hospital slippers shuffle along like walking death; George says just putting the slippers on can make you sick.

Tests show George has one large lump and two smaller ones in his thyroid. It could be cancer caused by the radiation he had for Hodgkin's disease. We have to come back Monday for another scan, ultrasound and a biopsy. If it's cancerous, the thyroid will have to be removed.

We found a delightful room at the same price as the dump we had last night: nice carpet, huge bed, reading lights beside comfortable chairs.

George put his .357 pistol in the bedside drawer with the Gideon Bible and said, "Thy rod and thy staff shall comfort thee!"

Though people who meet George often think his size and silence are forbidding, his sense of humor is one of his most wonderful qualities. When we first met, I was walking my Scots Terrier; George said, "Hey, lady, where'd you get such a funny-looking dog?" and then blushed. That got my attention.

September 26

Both of us slept well. George doesn't seem to be worried about the possibility of thyroid cancer, but then he never shows his worry as I do; he never chews his fingernails. We took a drive, but agreed these mountains are too bare and rocky to attract us much. Central City was swarming with noisy tourists and shops, and although I was tempted to stop, we went on through and turned off on a gravel road that took us high above the tourists. We passed an old cemetery filled with sightseers so we drove on. I love old cemeteries, but George seemed to want us to be alone. The aspens are lovely, gold and red, with leaves drifting in the riffles and ponds.

We finally parked at the edge of a high meadow and sat on a rock, silent, watching the trees and mountains. I asked him if he wanted to talk, but he just shook his head. I'm trying not to think what more cancer would mean to him. I met him soon after his second battle with Hodgkin's disease had begun, while he was still taking chemotherapy. We'd make these drives to Denver, he'd get a checkup and injection, and then he'd drive like hell to get us out of the traffic before he started the required six hours of throwing up. I'd drive across Wyoming and back home. He once said he'd rather die than take more chemotherapy.

As we were driving back toward the motel, trying to decide where to have supper, we saw an old streetcar converted into a diner. Inside it was 1935: an old jukebox, a sweaty man behind the grill cooking hamburgers for eighty-five cents, old-fashioned malted milk for a dollar.

September 27

We slept late, and had breakfast at our diner, then went to the Museum of Natural History, where we criticized the North American Indian exhibits. Later we went to the zoo and walked around feeling sorry for the animals and watching the children. Then to our diner for supper and "home" to rest and read.

George is wondering if his thyroid has been responsible for the weight loss that has pleased him so much. He also admitted how worried he's been about his continuing exhaustion and breathing problems. It's so hard for him to talk, even with me, and I find that frustrating. I'm always ready to talk out problems, but it's not his way. It pains me that we've known each other for so long and still he can't give me the trust of confiding in me. I also think there's an element of macho reluctance to show "weakness" by talking of fears.

September 28
We both had a restless night, but arrived at the hospital about 8:30 a.m. for George's injection and the scan. Usually the military doctors don't seem to notice his shoulder-length hair and the two silver earrings in his left ear, but the male nurse who gave the injection grinned and said he wished he was retired.

George simply had to lie on the table trying not to move for an hour while the machine looked for traces of Hodgkin's. Later, we were asked to move to a different waiting room because George was throwing off their radiation-sensing equipment. Here I am, fighting radioactive waste, and sleeping with a radioactive man!

Late in the morning, they gave him the ultrasound scan, then probed the nodules and drew fluid with a needle. They let us go then, and will send us the test results.

What would I do if — as the cliché goes — "something happened" to George? I know, having done it once, that I could survive without a husband, but he has brought so many things into my life.

When my first husband and I were divorced, I thought of myself as self-sufficient and independent, and certainly the divorce was a relief after seven years of watching him charm the ladies. But I was still almost unable to function normally for a long time. When I went back to the ranch it was frightening to know I'd be there alone in the winter. Gradually, I learned how to survive alone, to be productive, to work, to thrive.

When I decided to marry George, it was almost as much because I feared what would happen if I spent too much more time alone as because I loved him. I was afraid I'd grow so used to my own silences I could never live with another person, and George seemed like someone easy to be with. Naturally, since he's an intelligent and independent person, it's been much more complicated than I ever dreamed, but we've grown into a trust of each other, a solidity. This thyroid problem is the first for a long time, but it could be very serious. Since he hates pills, and hates to appear sick, he may be harder to live with. But how would I ever live without him?

September 29   Low 25, high 49. An inch of the first snow of the season was on the ground this morning.

A writer friend knocked on the door about 8:00, and came in for coffee. He'd spent the night in his pickup in the park, listening to the elk bugle. I dug the tulip and glad bulbs, and boxed them in the basement for winter. I always feel as if summer is really over when I finish that job.

When the folks came back from town this afternoon, the cats had a young bird down on his back. Mother rushed over to him, and realized it wasn't anything she'd ever seen before. They rescued it, handling it with thick gloves because of its talons, and put it in a box in the garage. I believe it's a falcon, because of the beak, one of those tiny fast ones. They called Game, Fish and Parks, and an officer came out and picked the bird up. He'll be fed and checked for injury, and then released. I can't imagine how the fat, lazy barn cats ever got their claws into him in the first place, but he's not badly hurt.

As we turned to go back to our own house, I casually asked Father how Rebel is doing; I'd been thinking about her.

Father said shortly, "She's gone."

"What do you mean?"

"I dragged her over the hill."

I assumed that was his euphemism for having shot her, and walked away without a word, the first time I can recall being literally too stunned to speak. He'd suggested that we shoot her last winter so she wouldn't suffer from the cold, but instead we kept her well supplied with hay, and I felt sure she was still healthy and strong.

Later, Mother called me, and said he'd spent two of the hot days we were gone burying her, to save me from finding her rotting corpse while riding that pasture. I know he didn't mean to be cruel. I cried after we went to bed. George held me, and told me he pulled the trigger, the day before we went to Denver. Her knees seemed to be giving her pain. Phred licked the tears from my cheeks.

September 30   Low 30, high 45.

I dreamed in the night of riding Rebel. She seemed to float over the ground as she always did, her slender golden-red legs reaching out, her head swinging, ears alert. It was such a wonderful dream I woke up and lay there remembering her. Faithful horse.

Reading Hemingway tonight, I came across this passage: "If you ever have to shoot a horse stand so close to him that you cannot miss and shoot him in the forehead at the exact point where a line drawn from his left ear to his right eye and another line drawn from his right ear to his left eye would intersect. A bullet there from a .22 caliber pistol will kill him instantly and

without pain and all of him will race all the rest of him to the ground and he
will never move except to stiffen his legs out so he falls like a tree."
I hope that's how George shot Rebel; I'm sure it was.

Digging Potatoes

I

We divided it all, but
my grandmother's shoes wouldn't fit
anyone but me.
                       She'd walked years
to the old stove with firewood,
to the chicken house for eggs,
to the pasture to check the cows.

II

We buried her in the fall, dry
grasses blowing on the hilltop.
There were no leaves to rustle; no trees
can grow on that dry hill. The view is clear
to the river, the gumbo hills beyond.

                                  We even
divided the bright spring flowers —
the hothouse roses, carnations — that
blanketed her coffin. I dropped a rosebud
as if by accident.

III

Wearing her shoes, I'm digging potatoes.
The sweet, rotten earth smell reaches up;
soil clings to my fingers, to the red
potatoes I drop in the bucket. I expect
to see her face at the bottom of each hole,
hear her voice answering the question
I've barely begun to ask.

October

October 1   Low 40, high 48. Cold, rainy, with the mounds of the Black Hills to the west fog-shrouded.

We drove to Lawrence's to cut wood. Lawrence is trying to clear enough trees to encourage the growth of grass under the trees that are left so that the deer will have more forage. Right away we got a big dead tree hung up in the branches of another — what the loggers call a "widow-maker." George had to cut two more to get it down — a very tricky and nerve-wracking job, but he seemed calm. We finished filling the 3/4 ton pickup box at dark — a good cord of wood.

While we were having coffee, two turkey hens and their chicks trailed by Lawrence's greenhouse windows. The hens clucked and worried and the chicks darted everywhere, tripping over each other in their nervousness. We all held still so we wouldn't startle them until they'd all had a chance at the bread and other scraps Lawrence had left for them.

When we got home we found that someone had dumped a broken plastic bag of garbage in our driveway and a couple of empty sixpacks in the road ditch. I get angry at having to clean up after such slobs. But it also makes me sad to think that anyone could so thoughtlessly dispose of a mess and assume that "someone" else will take care of it.

October 2   Low 27, high 40. The geese and cranes are going south this morning in great dark skeins and I hear faint honkings and hootings that sound wild — even here on the plains. I lay on the porch for awhile, watching the shifting overlapping vees.

Just as I was about to go inside I noticed a meadowlark sitting on a post about to sing. Suddenly he shot into the air and seemed to explode. Another moment, and I saw a falcon like the one the cats caught, beating back into higher air, clutching the meadowlark in his claws. He struck so fast I didn't see him coming and neither did the meadowlark. A few yellow breast feathers drifted to earth. It was a harsh lesson but fitting — we saved the falcon from the cats so he could go on about his life, which happens to include killing and eating meadowlarks.

In the afternoon I saw the seven deer we watch each winter in their favorite spot, the dry dam below the house, and four antelope on the hillside; they were slow in wandering off. I love their lack of fear.

October 3   Low 43, high 60. Father went over east to check the cattle so we could have another day of wood-cutting at Lawrence's. I love the woods this time of year; the leaves are soft and damp underfoot. Red and gold vines wind around the trees; sunlight flashes among the branches. Cuchulain barks ferociously, running from one tree to the next, following squirrels that torment him from the branches.

Today is my mother's birthday. I gave her some things she wouldn't buy for herself: new lipstick, a tiny vial of the perfume she likes, some bath oil. But I think the best gift I've given her is to ride with her several times lately on drives around the area and keep my nerves under control so she could restore her confidence in her own driving.

I don't know why she suddenly became unsure of herself. She has never been a very confident driver, but she's always insisted on keeping it up. My grandmother didn't learn to drive until she was over sixty, and immediately people began telling her she was too old, so she gave it up and had to depend on others for transportation in the last years of her life. My uncle George was very good about driving her wherever she wanted to go, but she hated to ask him when he was busy. If she had been able to drive, she could have kept up with her Eastern Star and church attendance and perhaps fended off the senility that came upon her ten years before her death.

"I don't want that to happen to me," my mother says grimly, and I agree with her.

October 4   Low 45, high 62.

I dreamed last night I was having a baby. I knew it was George's, so I was happy and relaxed. The worry had dissolved that it would be deformed because of George's radiation. I felt no pain, just amazement as I looked down at the huge mound of my belly. The nurse came in, checked the dilation, and told the doctor I was ready. Laughing and joking with George, I placed my feet in the stirrups while the doctor gathered his tools. In a moment, he handed me the baby — Michael. I began to cry; he wasn't my child after all.

I woke up crying, and George sleepily held me while I tried to explain why. At breakfast he asked me if I'd like to adopt a child. I don't often think of not having children, and I really believe I am happier without them. Yet it seems unfair not to be able to have a child of my own with George — to see what a combination of his calmness and gentleness and my work drive would be like. Usually I can get rid of these maternal feelings by spending an hour with a child in diapers.

Early this morning we saw a young deer alone in the valley below the house, running in circles and sniffing the ground. It must have gotten separated from the rest of its herd. Finally it wandered over the hill, still looking confused.

George went over east while I worked on the mail and an article I'm writing on my status as a part-time stepmother. In the evening I drove to Custer to present the pro-Initiative stance at a debate. I enjoyed the exchange but resented the other speaker's implication that because I am not an engineer, I'm incapable of understanding the technicalities of uranium processing.

October 5   Low 45, high 58, cloudy.

George left early to go over east and didn't get back until mid-afternoon because he found a stretch of fence down and the buffalo back with us. They refused to go back to their own pasture but followed along the fence and jumped into a pasture south of us, getting farther and farther from home.

I started working on a feature story about Tom, the artist who helped us brand last spring. He collected the notches of skin we cut from the calves' ears to earmark them and has made collages with them, using homemade paper as a background. I expected to hate them, but they're delightful: one has two furry notches surrounded by a fence of yarn and is titled, "Calves look over the fence to freedom." Only four inches square, they're filled with bits of nature: bird tracks, leaves, bits of feathers, twigs, all tiny things that make me more conscious of the nature he's depicting.

A true Hunter's Moon tonight — red-gold near the horizon, then shrinking to a silver disc as it rose.

October 7   Low 43, high 46, with light drizzle all afternoon.

To Rapid City for groceries in the morning. I bought extra cases of vegetables to store in the cellar for blizzards when we can't get to town. George noticed a thirty-pound tin of cherries from an orchard in Michigan owned by some cousins of his, near his grandfather's farm. We bought them and I'm leaving the tin out tonight to thaw so I can re-package the cherries in one-pie packages tomorrow.

Reading back through my journal entries for the last month I'm struck by the daily lists of labors, especially storing up food for the winter. These records are how I define myself between poems and stories, I guess, and perhaps have something of the poetry of womanhood in them too — all these things I do in preparation for the season of cold, so I can feed my family good food from our own land, and we can be safe and warm inside the snow-drifts.

Both of us went over east in the afternoon. The cool rainy weather has calmed the cattle down and softened the grass so they graze better. The calves look quite good despite the dry summer; quite a few of the cows look bonier than they should.

October 8   Low 38, high 51, sunny.

George and I went over east this morning, and I had to saddle my horse to collect a wandering cow from the Triple Seven pasture. They've used a ripper to turn all the sod in the flat areas of their pasture, supposedly to improve the grass. But it's so rough a horse can't go faster than a walk when it's dry. When it's wet — which it hasn't been for two years — the horse sinks into it almost to his knees. We've heard a hired man quit rather than ride his horse across it.

In the afternoon we had a light shower, just enough to dampen the dust. Huge clouds have been by-passing us daily but we're hoping for some serious rain tonight.

The radio announcers often speak of the fall colors in the hills this time of year, and people drive miles to see them, but I always appreciate the subtle prairie colors too. The big bluestem seems to become more blue, and a kind of swamp grass becomes a clown green, shading into yellow at the top. After the first frost little bluestem becomes a warm bronze color that seems to shimmer in the sunlight. We have a few fall flowers: aromatic aster, which blooms a vivid blue shading to purple, and white prairie asters. Both look like tiny daisies. A few spiky yellow salsify bloom beside the huge round balls of the mature seedheads. Yellow gumweed, several members of the parsley family, and goldenrod contrast with the deep brown of the seed pods and stems of flowers that bloomed earlier. Pale green stalks of mullein with thick brown seedheads stand like soldiers along the roads. The sage looks soft as down and seems to glow silver-blue, and the fences are outlined in brown tumbleweeds.

In the distance a cottonwood suddenly seems to light a valley when its leaves turn gold, and a dead branch sticking up, pure white, looks like a crack in the blue bowl of sky. If we've had any moisture, the level valleys are

green as new leaves with a fresh growth of alfalfa. Haystacks, shading from
black to light gray to gold, crouch in herds in the stackyards. As backdrop
for these color accents the hills lie like great tawny beasts, with the taller seed
pods of grasses like squirreltail, three-awn and porcupine grass rippling gold
on the surface, and the deeper tan of curing grasses like blue grama and
buffalo grass underneath. I never tire of looking for new color combinations.

*October 9   Low 29, high 40. The wind blew hard all day, with intermittent
rain; three feet of snow fell in the northern hills, and power lines are down.
We're not anxious for snow, but it would cut down on the fire danger here.*

I drained the garden hoses and brought them to the house. Doing these
fall chores is almost ritualistic. Each is another step away from summer and
toward winter; away from wide open windows and curtains blowing in the
breeze toward the stillness of frost outside and unmoving layers of drapes
over the windows.

George finally called the doctor in Denver, since we hadn't received any
written report on his tests. He doesn't have thyroid cancer but his thyroid is
underactive and he'll have to take pills.

This was my grandmother's birthday. We used to have parties for her
down at the ranch in the canyon, with dinner and cake outside in the fall
sunshine. I haven't been to her grave since the day she was buried four years
ago but I feel her presence in my kitchen when I use her bowls and towels and
wooden spoons. Somehow going to her grave would make me really see her
name on the stone and realize she is there. In my kitchen I can visit with her
and ignore death.

I re-read Leslie Silko's *Ceremony* tonight: "the old mule's bones unfolding
in the sun." Dear Rebel is returning to the earth. Yesterday, over east, I
glanced down at my feet and saw what I thought was a bunch of dry sticks.
I looked closer: a deer's foreleg with a tiny hoof and scrap of tawny skin still
attached, and teethmarks on the slender bone.

October 11   Low 40, high 62.

A lovely day, with rain in the afternoon. I cooked in the morning and our
belated house-warming party started officially at noon when Eric, a poet
who moved here from California a few years ago, arrived with Leslie Silko.
I talked only briefly with her; too many people came at once.

The house was full and nobody left hungry. I'd baked a turkey, which we
simply ripped apart with our fingers, and almost everyone brought
something to nibble on. Quite a varied collection of people — I heard my
neighbor Margaret, her teenage daughter listening, talk poetry with Leslie

Silko. I love to create an atmosphere where those meetings can happen.
Everyone was gone by 8:30 p.m., leaving us time to clean up before we
went to bed. The house reeks of cigarette smoke so we left all the windows
open and piled quilts on the bed. We feel that we've had a good visit with all
the friends we'll miss during the winter when the roads are too bad for
visiting.

October 13
Left the house before sunrise with a half-eaten moon and the morning
star in the sky, in dark soft air. Now, as I drive east, the pink clouds are gone
and the flat white light of morning reaches across the hills. A gentle blue haze
hangs over the ridges of the Badlands. Geese going south make tracks in the
sky.

I reached Watertown by noon and had an all-afternoon meeting with
various environmental groups on our final strategies before the election. My
speech went well. The opposition leader told sexist jokes and implied that
women can't be ranchers. When my turn came I talked about some of the
ranch work I've done lately and pointed out that I'm not a paid employee of
an out-of-state company that wants to profit from our inexperience. The
audience loved it, and cheered when I finished. I hope they all vote.

After the speech my throat was sore and I thought I might be getting a
cold, so I dosed myself with cold medications. I still didn't sleep well, and
had one very strange dream. In it, a man was breaking through a flimsy wall
into a house where I was sleeping. I woke, found a knife, and slashed his
hand when he stuck it through the door. When he came in I used the knife
to knock the gun out of his hand. I was completely fearless. When I had
disarmed him, I shoved my pet lynx off the bed, brushed the leaves off the
fur bedspread, threw the intruder down and attacked him! I've never had a
dream in which I was so aggressive.

October 14
On the way home today I saw an Indian walking along the highway.
Whites jog for exercise and do aerobics, but if they can't drive somewhere,
they don't go. If an Indian wants to go somewhere, at least in South Dakota,
he has to walk.

George was waiting up for me when I got home with Cuchulain curled
at his feet and Phred on his lap. George's gentleness with his cats was
certainly one of the reasons I fell in love with him. When I first met him he
had two — Janet and Jacob — who slept on his chest with their noses in his
ears, purring. After they were poisoned he started luring Phred, who belonged

to a friend, to his house for snacks of cat food, and eventually Phred simply moved in.

When I leave for awhile, George always says, "Don't worry about the dishes." Sure enough, when I get home, there they are: dirty, in the sink.

I asked him about it, and he said I wasn't really listening. I *assumed* he meant he'd do the dishes, when he actually said, "Don't *worry* about them."

October 17   Low 35, high 42, cloudy, with a bitterly cold wind.

Up at 5:00 to get ready for the long drive; I'm teaching workshops at a school on one of South Dakota's Indian reservations part of this week, making the 175-mile round trip drive daily since there is no housing for me at the school. I won't mind the drive unless the weather is bad because the reservation is beautiful.

The drive to the school across reservation land is wonderful. Cuny Table rises out of the breaks and then drops abruptly into the Badlands, a maze of gray and pale green on top and dark green cedar skirts. One house is built close to a slash in the side of the table, so one could slip out the back door, down the cut and be lost in a trackless place in minutes.

Lines of cows pace along the fence toward water. The highway seems a fragile overlay on the land. Blue shadows climb pink and tan spires. A green car lies smashed and rusted in a gully; another, then another. Someone told me a sniper hid here once, shooting tires and gas tanks out of cars and burning the wreckage.

Though my visit was scheduled weeks in advance, class pictures are being taken today, so by noon I'd missed two of the scheduled four classes and no one seemed to care. I finally rearranged the schedule myself and marched into the classes I wanted to teach.

Outside on the playground broken glass glitters, a rooster crows by the slides. A black dog trots past the swings, tail wagging, then stops, body rigid as she smells a pile of trash. In the distance alkali pans shine in the sun. Sage plants space themselves almost mathematically, as if they've been carefully planted, in order to use the available water.

October 18   Low 26, high 36, with light snow most of the day.

Nothing is quite as silent as the silence of brown eyes, brown impassive faces. I read James Welch's poem, "Christmas Comes to Moccasin Flat," to the seventh and eighth graders today because it reminds me of Pine Ridge. Later I spoke about living in a tipi at rendezvous; I could tell I had their interest because they all looked down, a sign of respect in Indian culture. Looking at another person is disrespectful, yet most of the white teachers struggle every day to get their students to look up while reciting. They really seem to expect no scholastic achievement from the kids; they just want them to learn normal white behavior. Many of the teachers are wives of white ranchers and dislike Indians. Qualified Indian teachers are reportedly kept away by politics.

When students here want me to come look at their poems they signal in subtle ways: a finger crooked in their hair, a sideways glance, turning their paper over. Other white teachers refuse to respond unless the child raises a hand; after all, they have to learn to do things "right!"

October 19   Low 26, high 32; more snow, and a high wind.

An 8th grade student I'll call Ann Bear Saves Life started to write about her mother and father today and got stuck so I asked her to tell me what her mother looked like.

"I don't know."

"Why not?"

"She died when I was born."

"Oh. How about your dad? What's he like?"

"I don't know."

?

"He left. I've never seen him." Exit poet, devices shattered.

At noon she came up to me with a folded paper, her usual manner of delivering her poems. This one said she loved her mom and dad "because they're nice to me." Perhaps she meant her step-parents. Perhaps she's fantasizing. Probably neither I nor anyone else will ever know for sure how she sees her parents in her mind.

All week I've been driving through the little town of Scenic twice a day and have not seen a single person, only cars parked in front of the bar. Daily I've passed an isolated house near there with no car in the yard, no curtains in the window. I thought it deserted until yesterday, when I saw two people silhouetted in the window, facing each other across a table. As I passed, a hand lifted a cup. Today, with the chill factor at twenty-seven degrees below zero, no one is visible and no smoke rises from the chimney. Are they gone? Have they frozen to death? I am a coward; I do not stop to see.

October 20   Low 23, high 36; no new snow, but windy.

As I was leaving the reservation today I kept checking my thermos, papers, books, sure I'd left something important behind. Then I realized — I'd left the children, Ann and Pam and Shawn and Arnold and Eldene. I'll miss them, even after such a short acquaintance. I cringe thinking of the teacher who saw my attempts to help them communicate with their world only as time lost from discipline and things they "should" know.

But I have a precious folder full of poems, lines that shatter me with their innocent depiction of a stark world. "Grandpa: He looks like all men when they're old and go short." "Grandmother: Her face her wrinkles shadowed her with darkness." "My father looks like an old gray fox. And is like an old wise owl. He also walks like a soaring black bald eagle, thinks like a new computer, and has hands the size of pancakes."

If I was a tree
someone would take me
away from where I was.

"I am the running of the wild horse going through shining screams of the plains."

I had a long conversation with Lawrence on the telephone tonight about education. Both of us learned to read in country schools with several grades in one room taught by one teacher. We learned to think not in school but by working with our hands, doing chores, figuring out how to repair the mower. We decided that those two things, reading and thinking, are the most essential parts of education, all anyone really needs.

October 21   Low 42, high 59, snow melting furiously. The moon, almost full, was setting at 5:30 a.m. in the west when I got up, and false dawn started at 6:30 while I was having coffee on the porch.

This morning we repaired the stretch of fence the buffalo have been abusing over east. I enjoy fencing, partly because when I finish I can see what I've done and it stays done for awhile — unlike cooking meals and cleaning house. We took out about twenty rotted wooden posts, and then George put in a new corner, digging the postholes deep, while I drove twenty steel posts. Then we strung four strands of new barbed wire, stapling it tight. The buffalo can jump it if they want, but they can't just walk through it anymore.

Taking a breather after putting in a post with the maul, I pictured myself in twenty years, wearing the same worn jean jacket, fixing this fence again and remembering this sunny day with George humming in the background. I felt unbearably sad for an instant.

In the afternoon we went to Lawrence's to cut wood. Resting on a log, I watched a hawk soar overhead, planing between the treetops. Lawrence said after his father died: "I wonder which swallow is my Dad."

Later I saw the flock of turkeys slipping between the trees and suddenly thought of my grandmother, how she fiercely tore the tubes from her arms and died. I had a sudden rush of joy in all the life around me, *knowing* she'd gone on in some way. When Father came to wake me at dawn to tell me she was gone, he said, "It's sunrise, and it looks like a good day to die." The force in life, he said, is so strong that it never ends; it simply goes into something else. He rarely speaks of his beliefs so I didn't question him. Did he mean it literally — burial in the earth allows us to become part of the earth and grass? Or more philosophically — as Lawrence's idea that perhaps we go on to another form? Lawrence has said he plans to be an eagle, and I've considered being an aspen.

One of the best conversations I ever had with my father was when I was about twelve and we were haying. We were lying down after lunch, under the trees in the field. He said he wondered if trees were really conscious beings, and aware of us, only living at a slower tempo than ours so we never grasp their consciousness. I've never looked at a tree in the same way since.

October 22   Low 40, high 65; most of the snow gone.

As I was sitting on the porch drinking my first cup of coffee a hot air balloon drifted silently over the hill south of the house like an explosion of sunrise. The dog barked furiously and ran under it, leaping up as if he could catch it. George made oatmeal — a sure sign of fall — before we went over east and fixed a little more fence. We didn't see the buffalo so perhaps they've moved on.

In the afternoon I loaded up the pickup with assorted junk including paper cake sacks left from last winter, huge tangled masses of baling wire from the hay we fed, and boxes of the magazine I once published and took it all to the city dump. It was heartbreaking to load all those magazines — inadvertently seeing layouts I'd been proud of, articles I was sure would gain enough subscribers to make the magazine pay — but I couldn't stand walking past them in the basement, the bunkhouse and the chicken house any longer. When it actually came to throwing them off the truck, however, I felt exhilarated, as though I'd been carrying them on my back. Perhaps this is a sign it's time to stop thinking of publishing for others and concentrate more on my own work.

The corrals are full of bawling cows and calves; George and Father brought them back from over east to wean. George had trouble with Sage again — took an hour to bridle him and then another hour to load him in the trailer. Father finally resorted to the old trick of tying a lariat to one side of the trailer, running it around behind the horse, and using it and a whip to force Sage to move ahead.

George said later his thighs are sore from nervously gripping Sage's sides;

he calls them the "panic muscles" because they tighten up every time he thinks he's going to be thrown.

October 25   Low 32, high 69.

Just after breakfast, while I was brushing my teeth, the shower stall and bathroom cabinet began to rattle. The wind was blowing hard so I asked George, "Is the wind doing that?" A few minutes later the radio announcer, disbelieving, informed us an earthquake had struck Cheyenne, Wyoming, a couple hundred miles away, and we'd felt the shock, 5.6 on the Richter Scale. I immediately called my nearest neighbor, Margaret, and we babbled to each other about our fear.

When I was riding the bus to highschool Margaret was riding it to grade school; she's ten years younger than I am, so we weren't friends then. When she moved back here with her husband and daughter we began to realize we shared some views on the environment. A few years ago I nominated her as a member of a state citizens' board formed to advise legislators on water policy. Later I asked her to join my environmental group, and we often go to meetings together. In many ways we disagree — with good humor. She doesn't consider herself liberated, for example. I tell her she's beyond help and I'm only using her in order to subvert her daughter, who's fourteen. Margaret's a serious Christian whereas I never go to church. Of such friendly disputes are our long conversations made; often I'm furiously angry about some injustice while Margaret is quietly reasonable.

When we went over east to check cattle, we found that three inches of ice had formed on the dam and tank — so we'll have to be going every other day for awhile. We fed cake, since the grass is short.

We went to town for groceries this afternoon and hit a grouse on the way home. I asked George to stop, caught it — it was bleeding — wrung its neck, and then realized I had just committed an illegal act beside a busy highway. We brought it home and Jim and Mavis were here so we added three game hens to the roasting pot and had the grouse for supper. I had to endure a lot of hilarity about eating roadkills but I told them that's the only way we poor ranchers survive.

October 27   Low 42, high 60; sunny.

We drove down to Craven Canyon this morning, had a brief visit with my uncle George, and then went down to the prehistoric petroglyphs — "the writings" as they're known locally. We looked at all the ones I know, from the great painted "floating antelope," fading now from being chalked over so many times, to the mysterious elk-like figures pecked into the rock. Then we just hiked, looking in likely spots for carvings we hadn't seen before, and enjoying the fall air — cool in the shadows, hot in the sun.

Then George called me to a sloping hill, saying he'd found a new carving. He made me hunt: it was almost buried in the dirt and pine needles under an overhang, and obviously goes much deeper in the ground than I could dig with my fingers. I started looking intelligently then, and realized the whole mound where we stood could be debris that had built up in the mouth of a long-used cave. We disturbed nothing, despite the temptation. This canyon has been surveyed by the archaeologists; I hope they excavate that spot.

I always feel as if I'm in a time warp when I look at the petroglyphs. I can almost see the clusters of children playing, women cooking, and the men — or other women — pecking away at the rock. No one has successfully dated the petroglyphs, but no matter how primitive those people were, they shared so much with us; that's obvious from the beauty of the work. The elk leaped then as they leap now, trying to escape the hunters. The people stored food in the fall, and perhaps wondered, as we sometimes do, if winter would ever end.

October 28   Low 36, high 59; some fast-moving clouds in the afternoon.
Several trains passed in the night; added to the usual rumble and roar was a terrible howling from ungreased wheels — made my hair stand on end. Each time, one of us gets up and goes to the front windows to look everywhere for a fire, as the danger is still acute. I stand shivering at the window, straining my eyes, hoping not to see a red glow somewhere along the tracks.

George and I and my horse went over east with seven dry cows this morning — a cold ride but the cows moved well. We bridled and saddled Sage, loaded him in the trailer, and just hauled him along to try to get him used to it. Before we came back we loaded and unloaded him several times, then brought both horses back in the trailer.

October 29   Low 46, high 68, but felt colder because of wind.
I'm still getting calls from voters and a few last-minute brief interviews with radio and TV people; the general opinion seems to be that we're going to win the election.

Mother drove Father to the hospital for his eye surgery today, removal of a cataract and replacement of the lens. We went to town after finishing chores and saw him for just a minute, looking pale, before they wheeled him into surgery. Mother was too nervous to sit so we wandered through the hospital together, talking, something we rarely do. After an hour and a half the doctor called, saying he'd come out of it well, and we talked with him a minute. He was quite jocular — thought he might keep the eye patch.

October 31   Low 32, high 41.
I worked on poetry in a.m., but getting too many calls on election to continue. The wind blew all night over sixty-five miles an hour and most of the morning we had a sleet storm.

Father's eye is red but he says his vision is better. He doesn't seem to be taking it easy, but we have been able to save him from some lifting. He's been getting telephone calls from neighbors asking about his eye, and had a new item of information for us today. The Triple Seven, our big neighbor to the south, is going to try the "cell theory" of range management, which supposedly will allow ranchers in the arid areas to double the number of cattle they graze on any pasture. It sounds wonderful but I doubt that it will change the methods of people who have ranched this country for a hundred years and know its moods.

At midnight, I'm not sleeping, and an owl is hooting steadily and persistently right outside the east windows, perhaps on the porch.

Deer

—for George

They must be out there, in the gray
sagebrush between this rough highway
and the shining, white-topped Big Horns.
I only see them exploded
by speeding trucks. A little hoof
on a bloody leg waves at me
from a mess in the other lane.

This morning, love, we saw thirteen
ghostly does and fawns, one big buck,
go dancing in the blue dawn haze
among trees and sly alfalfa.

November

November 1   Low 23, high 40.
George went over east with feed for the cattle, and I went to town at 7 a.m.
for a news conference at the library. Not all the TV and radio stations were
there, but perhaps it will attract a little pre-election notice. Worked on some
poems in the afternoon but got little done between telephone calls on the
initiative.

Going back over old poems alternately exhilarates and depresses me. I
find good material, things I still want to say, but get caught up in the flaws
of expression that made me put the poems aside in the first place. The
"poems that need work" file has held some of the same stuff, in slightly
different incarnations, for ten years or more. I can never completely abandon
them, but they never satisfy me either; it must be like having children.

*November 5   Low 22, high 31; light snow. Winds sixty-five miles an hour
battered the house all day; with no snow on the ground, the fire danger is
acute. I kept bouncing up from my chair and running upstairs to look out
the windows. The sky leaked a little drizzle in the afternoon.*
Pre-election jitters; I tried to write before breakfast but it wasn't working,
so after George got back from over east we drove to Custer and bought a load
of post ends for father's wood stove. In the afternoon we went to Buffalo Gap
for a load of cake.

Mike, George's fourteen-year-old son, called in the evening. He has only
a short Christmas vacation, and several hockey games, so we may not get
to see him. George was gloomy the rest of the day.

November 6   Low 18, high 28; snowing most of day, winds 30 mph.
George over east. I spent the day writing, with the phone blessedly silent,
but felt guilty about not going over east. Snowfall and brisk winds all day;

hard to tell how much snow we have now because of the drifts, but probably more than a foot. I walked with George to get the feeder calves in, earlier than usual, and went to town about four to vote.

I always feel a surge of — I suppose — patriotism when I go into Hermosa to vote. The fields are brown with drifts of white, haystacks lined up neatly, trees bare. The little town is battened down for winter, with piles of firewood in everyone's yards. Cars are gathered around the little red brick school and neighbors greet each other in a friendly way though they may be cancelling each other's vote.

The women behind the official table in the school gym put down their coffee cups, cookies, and cards, look important, and shout out every name as though there were an audience of thousands. Each of us takes our ballot and self-consciously steps behind the plywood partitions, picks up the stubby pencil tied to the ledge, and marks the ballot. It all makes me feel the intimacy and power of the people's involvement in government, and gives me renewed confidence that things will, eventually, work out.

We went on to Rapid after voting, to the suite the Nuclear Waste Vote Coalition rented at the hotel. Babies of every skin color from purest white to deepest black were tucked into corners of the three rooms. A black man in a three-piece suit, with a single diamond stud in one ear, chatted with several American Indian Movement members who wore headbands, tee-shirts and belt knives. Older members of my group, the Black Hills Energy Co-alition, were dressed in nylons and high heels with matching sweaters and skirts, and sipped coffee beside hippie leftovers from the commune in the hills.

Everyone was gloomy because the national races were not going well for liberals and Democrats, but the early returns on the Initiative were encouraging. Every now and then a newsman would battle his way into the room and stand looking bewildered until one of us went to the hall or lobby for an interview. The refrigerator and bar were mostly filled with fruit juices and decaffeinated colas rather than liquor, so the gathering only looked rowdy. Despite the rather heated differences we've had with some groups — like AIM — everyone was caught up in the pleasure of watching the Initiative march right through party lines and roll up votes.

November 7   Low 10, high 22; brisk winds. George over east.

Slept until 8:15 a.m. before being awakened by a congratulatory call. I take grim pleasure in recalling that TV newsmen appeared here early the morning after the last election — which we lost — to get statements. Today, when we've won, they're content to get them over the telephone. Perhaps the faces of winners are not as interesting as those of losers.

Cranes seem to just appear in the sky. One minute it's empty, the next they're there. Perhaps you have to see in a certain way to see them coming. Perhaps it's a special attention, or caring, some factor in the viewer that suddenly makes them visible — and perhaps that's the answer to why some people see ghosts, and some people see the prairie as empty and dull. At noon we drove to Lawrence's and cut wood in the peace of the trees, then helped him fix supper and gloated over the news reports. We won by more than sixty percent and the opposition still hasn't been located to make a statement. They spent a quarter of a million dollars; we spent $10,000.

November 9   Low 10, high 36; sunny.
I had a terrible time sleeping, still working on stories in my head. Up at 6:45 a.m., built a fire, made coffee, and wrote while watching a coyote take his morning constitutional. No new snow today, and sun shone so we had some melting.

George went to the creek to fix fence. I took lunch down about 1:30 p.m. — cheese, sardines, crackers and sweet rolls. He asked for the rolls; he and his grandfather always had them when they worked in the orchards. I envied him fencing on a nice day like this. It's a job I love despite my innate hatred of fences.

When I got home Father was waiting with Oliver saddled, and we took a bull to the dike pasture. We'd had him shut in the corral recovering from a lame leg. Then he took the pickup and I rode the horse to check fences. Tumbleweeds piled up along the fences this summer and have pulled down a lot of wire; if we let it go, more will go down the first time we have a heavy snow. Some gullies are packed chest deep to a tall horse with them, clear over the fences. I pulled a lot of them away from the wire, but I hadn't worn gloves, and my hands began bleeding.

November 10   Low 5, high 34. Sleet, cold wind and freezing rain all morning, but George went to the creek to fence anyway; said he was sick of it and wanted to get the job done. When he returned in late morning we went to Lindsays for a cow Father wants to sell. I tied Oliver behind the pickup to take him to the pasture and he had a tantrum and broke every rope we had with us, so I dug out the tow chain and fastened him on with that. He behaved fine when I was riding him, though — acted like a real cowhorse for a change.

George went over east in the afternoon while I visited my skin doctor, who had great news: I now have *acne rosaria,* have to avoid caffeine (which I gave up anyway because it was causing breast lumps), spicy foods, and alcohol. What's left?

I got a few groceries, including twenty-five pounds of bananas for eleven cents a pound, and cut them up for the food dryer this evening. Made oxtail soup for supper. I just love it, but George isn't fond of any kind of soup — unfortunate, since I've got twenty-five pounds of soup stock in the freezer.

November 12   Low 13, high 26; sunny, with no wind. Foggy and icy this morning, with a layer of ice on everything, flashing in dim sunlight.

George was grinding his teeth in the night; I can always tell when he's tense, but he stops if I pat him on the shoulder. We have both benefited from working separately the last couple of weeks; being together twenty-four hours a day is only a teenager's dream of love. This morning we went over east to move eight dry cows from the government lease pasture up into Lester's. We traded walking because the snow was too icy to risk riding the horse. Even the grass that had been blown free of snow was slick with ice. On the way back we met Father in the Lindsay pasture. He's decided to sell some old cows, and was walking the whole bunch up to the corrals. We helped, then sorted off ten old cows and their calves and I walked them the mile back to the house.

I pride myself on my perception, my attention to detail — both as a rancher and as a writer. Yet whenever I "report" to my father after a trip over east, he always asks a question I can't answer. How much water was in the dugout? Did the neighbors have bulls next to us? Was the one-eyed cow's calf sucking?

After lunch we went to the creek, where George fixed fence while I loaded wood he'd cut previously. When we got back Father had built a fire in the corral and was ready to brand the two forgotten calves, so we finished that job before supper.

November 13   Low 12, high 32; cloudy and drizzling, with thermometer undecided about freezing.

Father called at 6 a.m. to ask us to take the cows to Sturgis for tomorrow's sale. We'd been planning a full day of shopping, thinking he'd ordered a truck to take them. Then the trailer had a flat and we had no spare, so we had to go to town and get the flat fixed, buy a spare, and then start hauling cattle. Two trips to Sturgis and the day was over for us at 6:30 when we pulled into a truck stop north of town for supper.

We're always a little nervous with a full load on the trailer, since many drivers don't seem to have any conception of how hard it is to stop a truck with a full load of cattle dragging along behind — around ten thousand pounds of beef plus the weight of the truck and trailer. I don't know how to figure that in terms of velocity, but it takes a lot longer to stop, even without black ice like we had today.

I always enjoy the truckers' cafe. George and I have the same habits even though he's not a writer — we listen to conversations. Two ranchers sat down behind us.

"Hell, he's been getting $450 or $500 for those calves until last year; then he only got about $250. I don't see how he's got along. He's renting all that pasture you know."

"And he's never home. His wife does all the work."

"He ain't going to be able to keep it up for long, that's for sure. This dry spell — he told me once he'd borrowed a quarter of a million dollars to buy that one place."

"Yeah, he said he'd never pay off the principal, just the interest, but he can't even pay interest at these prices."

November 14   Low 24, high 38.

Took the horse over east and rode all over the Triple Seven searching for two of our bulls missing the last time George fed. I rode the horse, ducking into all the little narrow canyons, while George drove the truck along the broader gullies. I'd get on top of a hill every now and then to let him know where I was, and he was to honk if he found them. Finally we went north into the Baker pasture. I found the bulls sunning themselves at a little dam and started back with them, and he caught up with me before I got back to the gate. We got them back to the chute in our pasture, loaded them in the trailer with the horse behind, and brought them home. They can stay in the corral for awhile. The cows should be bred by this time anyway.

The wind was "crisp," as the weatherman says, but I felt warm in the sun. The horse's hoofs puffed snow as he trotted, and he swung his head alertly, blowing clouds of steam into the cold air. I love being alone on a good horse miles from highways and houses.

Father has the calves from the cows we sold shut in the corral; all of them are "drouthy." He'll keep them in until they start eating creep feed and cake, then add them to the eighteen other calves we've weaned so far. He wanted to sell their mothers now while they're in the best shape. All of them were over ten years old, thin, and thus a risk to carry through another winter.

Tonight we saw the northern lights shooting up, green curtains billowing and flashing over the horizon, meeting at a point overhead. The lights seemed to pulse in waves, beginning at the horizon and growing brighter and greener as they moved overhead. They lasted for more than an hour while we stood

with our arms around each other, shivering. I called Margaret even though
it was nearly 11 p.m. Normally, no rural person would call another after 10
p.m. because most of us get up so early, but Margaret and I ignore that policy
for natural phenomena. Neighborliness takes many forms.

November 16   Low 24, high 41; sunny.
Over east in the morning to feed cake and chop ice. On the way back, in
the Lindsay pasture, we collected a sick cow Father wanted home. The wind
was freezing so we traded off walking her the two miles home. She is terribly
thin, and so weak she kept staggering.

We put her in the chute and looked down her throat. A huge bone was
lodged against her back teeth, but none of us could get hold of it so we loaded
her in the trailer and took her to the vet. He caught her head and propped
her mouth open. The smell was awful. George had to go outside and throw
up, much to the vet's amusement, but we got a huge chunk of shoulder bone
out. The vet gave her several vitamin shots and we virtually lifted her back
into the trailer. When we got home we parked the trailer in the corral, opened
the gate, and left her there with feed and water.

November 18   Low 18, high 32.
My cousin John called this morning and we went to town to have breakfast with him and his wife Judy. John is taking flying lessons and wanted to
take us up in a little plane, but we both declined with extreme cowardice. My
hands sweat at the thought of height, and both George and I have had awful
experiences in little planes. While we were in town we did some quick
shopping; got a parka for the folks to give me for Christmas, since my old
one is shredded.

In the afternoon we drove to Deadwood to The Trading Post to buy our
winter clothes from their stock of army clothes from all over the world. I got
a pair of Norwegian army coveralls a couple years ago: a hundred per cent
wool nearly a half inch thick, with zippered legs and arms and a high collar
that snaps up above my nose, for $20. Every year we pick up something
much tougher and warmer than ordinary clothing for winter feeding, like
wool German army pants with pockets at the knees. We hardly wear jeans
for work anymore — so much for our "Marlboro Country" image.

November 20   Low 10, high 22; freezing wind, a little snow falling.
Mother called at 7 a.m. to tell us Harold had a heart attack, and we all
roared to the hospital. During the day, while we waited outside the intensive
care center, he had several more. The hospital seemed unable to get hold of
his doctor or anyone who would authorize him to be moved to the Mayo

Clinic in Minnesota, which we all thought would be the best idea. By evening he was too weak to move, and a snowstorm had begun.

I wondered if our rushing to the hospital was some holdover from when people asked dying friends to take messages to the dead. I don't believe there's any great merit in seeing a person in the last few minutes before they die — but I've never had the experience, so perhaps I don't know what I'm missing. I've tried in the last few years to make sure I tell everyone around me how much I love and value them so I won't have to try to cram it into a bunch of other stuff around a death bed on short notice.

George has a bad cold and cough but he went hunting anyway. Said he saw a nice buck and four does, but coughed just as he was sighting and they ran off. I haven't had venison for five years.

November 21 Low 18, high 30; gray and cold, with snow falling and high wind. The roads are almost impassable so we called the county road grader; his two-hour plowing job will cost us $100.

George's cold is worse so he stayed inside. Father and I went to the Triple Seven to pick up a cow and calf of ours they had shut in the corral. She gave us quite a time — jumped over several of their corral fences and tried to climb an iron gate. When we got her in the trailer she banged around all the way back home. We took her to the dike pasture and dumped her out. She's dry, so we brought the calf back. It probably belonged to another cow, and got weaned some time ago; looks like he hasn't had much to eat. We put him in the corral with the little steers we didn't sell.

By evening we had five or six inches of new snow on the ground, and it's still drifting with the winds. Seems every time we have the road plowed we can count on wind and snow until it's filled again.

Harold is much better tonight, sitting up and teasing the nurses.

November 22 Low 10, high 28; cold and snowy.

George was really sick this morning, coughing and sweating, so Father and I went over east. The sun was shining but the ice was thick, about eight inches to chop through with the dull axe.

We also picked up a crippled calf he noticed a couple days ago. It turned into a real workout — he was wild and wouldn't go in the truck, so eventually we roped him, crowded him into a corner, and lifted him into the pickup. Quite an accomplishment, since even hungry he probably weighs 350 pounds. Father and I together don't weigh that much. After lunch I baked three cherry and two pumpkin pies for the freezer.

November 24, Thanksgiving   Low −10, high 7; clear.

George and I went over east, then had chicken and wild rice at home since we didn't want to expose the rest of the family to his cold. My folks and a cousin from Rapid went to my aunt Anne's; no one else made it since the roads were slick and a storm threatening.

We fed the cattle around the place in the afternoon. The snow is so deep everywhere we just assume we're going to be stuck several times a day. We've been lucky to keep the cattle over east so long in this weather, but the drive is brutally hard on the truck and on us, and we can't keep it up much longer. I think Father is waiting for a little better weather, and perhaps some melting. It would be a terrible struggle for both the cows and calves to get home through this deep snow.

In the afternoon we built a big fire in the furnace and read in the dim light from the windows. I always enjoy the family gatherings more than George does, but it was lovely to sit in the silence of our own house, warm, with the storm blowing outside.

Anne called about 9:00 to say she'd heard that our neighbors, Margaret and Bill and their daughter Bonnie, had been in a car accident. I called the hospital and talked to Bill in the emergency room. Margaret has a broken back; they don't know yet if she'll be paralyzed. Both Bonnie's thighs were broken, and her jaw, and she has bad cuts on her face. Bill seems OK but has a bad bump on his head. An elderly couple hit them head-on on the bridge just north of Hermosa, and since they had driven the pickup because of the icy roads, their seat belts weren't fastened. One of the officers at the accident told them if they'd had their seat belts fastened they'd have had only minor bruises.

November 25   Low 15, high 29; clear and still.

Over east in the morning. We saw one coyote alone and then three together, all trotting along in a businesslike way. They stand and listen by a drift, and then pounce and come up with a mouse. I suppose they can hear the little movements in the mouse tunnels under the snow.

All the way over my mind was only partly on the snow, and mostly on Margaret. She's such a warm, loving person, always cheerful no matter how bad things are, and so energetic. She has turned a place that was nearly bare when they moved there into a wildlife haven of trees, flowers, rock walls — much of it by herself because Bill was busy with the ranch work and the bees.

My folks went to town to see Harold in the morning. After feeding we went in and visited him briefly. No one but family was allowed to see Margaret and Bonnie.

Then we met Jim and Mavis for supper and took them to the Willie Nelson concert. It was billed as a benefit for Yellow Thunder camp, and the audience was about half Indian. Many whites had said they'd boycott it because of the benefit aspect but I couldn't see that as a reason to miss Willie. He made no speeches, just played and sang, and the whole audience was united at least in that we loved it. Silent Jim, who seldom shows emotion, got quite excited. During one number where the entire room was jumping up and down, clapping and screaming, Jim actually tapped his finger on his knee.

November 26   Low −6, high 2; real howling blizzard most of the day.

We fed baled hay to the cows in the corral and stayed inside the rest of the day. I got a lot of writing done between going to the windows to watch the drifts pile up.

I was able to talk to Margaret's parents today. They still aren't sure about her back, but she's conscious. Bonnie's thighs will have to be in traction for a long time — weeks perhaps — before they can be set, with the possibility she may not walk well again.

I got my Crazy Horse novel back from the agent as I expected to, but not for the reason I expected. Once I'd sent it off, I felt as though it was just the bare bones, more like an outline than a novel. But the agent praised the writing — except for the depressing end — and said it wouldn't be saleable because there's no national interest in Indian-white relations! If there isn't, there ought to be.

November 27   Low −10, high 4; no wind, about four inches of new snow.

The wind died during the night so we got the hay hooks out of the barn, loaded the 3/4 ton pickup with bales of hay and went over east through snow so deep now it looks blue. By the time we got there the wind had picked up again. The normal trail was buried three or four feet deep so we wound along the ridges. We fed the cattle at the dugout after chopping through ice a foot thick.

The bales we're feeding, bought because we didn't have enough of our own, weigh from seventy to eighty-five pounds each — more than I like to lift, but I can usually use a knee to help move them, and get added leverage from the hay hook. We try to feed about ten pounds of hay to each cow, which works out to around twelve bales, a full load for the pickup.

George's back has been bothering him a little, and I felt full of energy, so he drove while I fed. By the time I'd fed the whole load I was sick of being bent over with wind whistling through my long johns, and had hay in my eyes, my nose, my crotch. My fingers were stiff and my back hurt from bending over, but I'm lucky I didn't fall off the tailgate. The cattle were hungry and they jostled me on the tailgate, long tongues swiping at stray wisps of hay. One ran beside the pickup and jerked a bale off with her teeth so I had to stop George and scatter it.

We were just leaving when we noticed two cows in the Triple Seven pasture close to our fence. They moved their cows out a month ago, so we had no choice but to go check, and sure enough they were ours. We let them in and gave them a little cake. Arrived back home at 3:00, hungry. When will I learn never to go over east without taking lunch!

November 28   Low −10, high 5 above.

Back over east — the drifts are crusted over so we have to choose a route carefully or the pickup is stuck. When we got to the dugout in the school section we found two cows in it, just their heads sticking out. A drift had blown out to the midpoint of the dugout. Ice stays soft under snow. When the cows walked around the drift looking for water, they broke through.

We didn't dare walk out on the ice to get a rope around their heads and one front leg, so we finally just lassoed their heads and tied the rope to the pickup. I gunned it while George stayed outside to holler if they got tangled up or started to strangle.

The first one out was shivering so hard she could barely stand up. The minute she popped out of the dugout the water on her hide froze to ice; she wandered off and I doubt we'll see her alive again. The second one tottered up to the other cows and ate a little cake, so perhaps she'll survive. They couldn't have been in the dugout long or they'd have been dead of hypothermia.

George went down to the other pasture to get some panels so we could fence them out of the dugout, and I stayed and watched them drink one by one so I could keep them out of the drift. I noticed spatters of blood in the snow from the cows' hoofs, splitting from the pressure of walking on ice for so long. We can't do much to treat them, though when we get them in the corrals I can try to squirt on a medicated fluid that hardens and seals the hoof from moisture and manure. This is a tricky maneuver, especially on hind hoofs.

Many of the cows also have swollen knees sprained when they fell on the ice. Several have bloody heads and bleeding noses from trying to eat grass through the snow. They move like heavy old women, slowly, carefully, and when they fall they grunt and groan in pain.

We were cold and wet when we finished putting the panels in so we sat in the truck with the heater on and ate lunch, watching the cows nosing through the snow for more cake. Some of them huddled in the lee of the pickup, looking through the windows at us until we imagined accusation in their eyes.

We drove back to the ranch and told Father about the problem, suggesting that we get the cattle out of there as soon as possible because the panels we put up really won't be very effective to keep them out of the drift and the dugout. He agreed, so after we'd warmed up and dried out we went back over east, moved the cattle down to the lower pasture, and shut them out of the dugout there so they have to water at the tank. We'd hoped to be able to lead them but since they'd already been fed and they didn't want to walk against the wind, George had to walk much of the way behind them.

Neither of us could get warm tonight. We drank hot buttered rum, fed the fire, and wrapped ourselves in blankets, but we were still shivering when we went to bed. The cat and dog, as if helping, curled up between our legs.

November 29   Low 25, high 42; a warm chinook wind blowing from the south.

One deer is lying in the bottom of the dry dam, just her ears showing, while a huge hawk circles overhead.

Over east to feed — the cattle were scattered out grazing where the chinook had melted the snow. The grass is short, but it's a fresh pasture for them and they seem to like a change. We checked to be sure we'd left nothing in the other pasture. The dugout had frozen over but the ice was black and menacing-looking where the cows had gone in. Both of them came to feed, alive and apparently well.

In the afternoon we stocked up on groceries and then bought some fence posts, a real pickup load. When we got home, I made a nightgown out of a flannel sheet that doesn't fit the waterbed, and George made a rosewood handle for his bowie knife. Winter closing in always seems to get us doing these projects.

The moon is huge and silver tonight, with a ring around it, supposed to indicate a change in weather, so maybe it will warm up. We often have these nasty storms in November and then a lovely period of almost autumn weather much of December.

November 30   Low 23, high 31; sleet and freezing rain in the night, so everything is covered with a coat of ice. Fenceposts look as if they've been dipped in wax, and fine casings of ice coat each individual blade of grass, tinkling as we walk through it. I always take a few pictures of ice storms, but the photographs are never lovely enough to convey the beauty and menace of the ice.

Woke up to see one coyote circling the house, then another just ahead of our seven deer down in the field south of us. Every time he got a little way ahead of them he turned and went back, and they followed him a little way before beginning to graze again. We watched them until they all disappeared in the willows to the east of us. I wonder if the coyotes were trying to lure one deer away from the rest; normally coyotes don't attack a healthy animal.

Both of us went over east again this morning. George wanted me to stay home, but I'd worry so much about him I wouldn't get anything done if he went alone.

I often think about what our feeding looks like from the air. One of us drives the pickup, with the other in back shaking out cake or dropping chunks of hay bales. The cattle follow along trampling down the snow. George always drives in a great circle or an S-curve, but I'm always tempted to write a huge message to God or the pilots flying overhead: SEND HEAT. SEND US TO ARIZONA.

The tank isn't watering the cattle adequately and ice completely covers the slope leading to it. So we chopped ice on the east end of the dugout, fenced the cattle out of the west end with panels, and shivered while they drank a few at a time. If they all rushed in together they might walk out on the ice, break through and drown.

The wind was bitter cold and we didn't get back until 1:00. After lunch — I'd left a stew in the crockpot — George brought the tractor to the house and used the grapple fork to push aside some of the drifts around our cars.

Seasons in South Dakota

I

Dirty snow left in the gullies, pale
green spread overnight on the hills
mark spring.
              Taking corn to the hens
I hear a waterfall of redwing blackbird song.
When I open the windows to their raucous mating
I let in something else as well:
soon I'll pace the hills under the moon.

II

Watching struggling heifers birth,
greasing the tractor, I may miss
summer.
               Like spring, it bursts open:
blooming hay demands the mower.
All day I ride the tractor,
isolated by roar.
It's time to turn the bulls out
to the cows, check leaning fences.
Even in summer nights' sweat
I hate to sleep alone.
When I'm too tired to care,
I still hear the larks, feel
the cold flow in each window at dawn.

III

Autumn whistles in some day when I'm
riding the gray gelding
bringing in fat calves for sale:
the air quick-chills, grass turns brown.
Last fall I found two gray hairs;
just as quick, winter came:
I was hurrying to pile fresh wood
from the one-woman crosscut
when the first flakes crowded the sky.

IV

Despite the feeding, pitching hay to
black cows with frost-rimmed eyes,
cutting ice on the dam under the eyes
of sky and one antelope,
there's still time to sit before the fire,
curse the dead cold outside,
the other empty chair.

Winter

Staying in One Place

Riding fence last summer
I saw a meadowlark caught by one wing.
(My father saw one caught so, once;
in freeing it, taught me compassion.)
                                    He'd flown
futile circles around the wire, snapping bones.
Head folded on yellow breast,
he hung by one sinew, dead.

Gathering cattle in the fall
I rode that way again;
his yellow breast was bright as autumn air
or his own song.

I'm snowed in now, only a path
from the house to the cows in the corral.
Miles away he still hangs,
frost in his eyesockets,
swinging in the wind.

I lie heavy in my bed alone, turning turning,
seeing the house layered in drifts of snow
and dust and years and scraps of empty paper.
He should be light, light
bone and snowflake light.

December

December 1   Low −20, high zero. Sunrise: bank of blue-gray clouds lying on the horizon, a single clear pink jewel set in the center. Then the gray closed in: the sun rose higher, glowing red, suddenly ripping the curtain and flaring across the plains.

Margaret is still in the hospital, but I called her this morning. She sounds drugged and tired but as cheerful as ever. I was complaining about getting another batch of poems back, rejected by yet another magazine, and she quoted Robert Frost to me:

> *Do you know,*
> *Considering the market, there are more*
> *Poems produced than any other thing?*
> *No wonder poets sometimes have to seem*
> *So much more businesslike than businessmen.*
> *Their wares are so much harder to get rid of.*

As usual, the poet learns from the beekeeper: I'd read "New Hampshire" years ago but forgotten it. Margaret keeps a copy of the complete Frost on her coffee table and reads him often.

I went over east with George. The ice is getting harder to chop every day — it's more than two feet thick now. The cows bawl and follow the truck as we pour out cake behind it, gobble it down, then huddle with their backs against the north wind waiting for us to chop enough holes so they can drink. We started around 8:00 but the drifts are deep and the going slow, so it was after 1:00 when we got back.

In the afternoon George drove through the drifts and went to Buffalo Gap for more cake; we've fed more than normal because the deep snow keeps the cattle from grazing. I worked on poems.

December 2   Low −28, high −20; wind chill −51. Over east in a.m. to feed in freezing wind.

Every day we get up in the gray light of dawn, wearily climb into the red long underwear and wool pants, fuel our bodies with hot oatmeal, toast, and jelly that looks and tastes like the ripe berries of fall, and go out to battle nature again. Only it's not really a battle; it's a war of nerves, of tactics. If we considered it a fight we could only lose; instead we try to outmaneuver her, to survive, to keep the cattle alive.

We visited Margaret and Bonnie in the afternoon. Plants and bouquets and stuffed animals hang from the traction frame around Bonnie's legs. They're both in pain but calm and making jokes. Margaret's eyes looked tragic and dark in her white face, and an awful cut slashes across Bonnie's fragile forehead. I managed to make wisecracks until we got out of the room, then cried all the way down in the elevator, soaking George's shoulder.

December 5   Low −10, high 15; wind blowing, and lots of drifting.

We went over east together and had to pioneer an entirely new route to get to the dugout. The gullies where our trails run were drifted full so we drove along ridges swept almost bare of snow. When we got to the end of the last ridge, the drift ahead looked fairly shallow. I was driving, and at the last second, worried about the depth of the drift, I gunned the pickup. As we dropped into the drift snow exploded over the windshield, completely burying the truck for a few moments.

The slope above the dugout had only a few inches of snow on it. We chopped the ice and let the cattle in a few at a time to drink so they didn't crowd out onto the ice and break through. After we'd fed, they'd churned up the slope so much the pickup just sat and spun. We tried a dozen times, and were just beginning to face the prospect of walking home — ten miles in snow to our knees, with a cold wind and a chill factor the pickup radio said was close to thirty below zero — when we finally got enough traction to get out. On the way home, slowly thawing out, we decided that if it's a passable day tomorrow we have to bring the cattle home.

The Christmas party for the Thunder Mountain Long Rifles, our black powder gun club, was tonight in Sturgis, but the weather was so bad we decided not to go. We're always afraid of being stuck up there in a blizzard.

December 6   Low −10, high 15; sunny, and felt warm. Called the county shop and asked them to send the snowplow so the propane truck could deliver.

We led Oliver over east behind the truck and moved 168 cows, heifers and bulls home. George was able to drive the truck in the lead much of the way, except where he had to detour around gullies drifted full of snow. It was a real test of his knowledge of the landscape, since all the familiar landmarks are drifted under, but between the two of us we managed to keep the truck out of the worst drifts. The cattle moved along well, but the trip was longer because of the detours and the deep snow wore them out.

At one point, in the Triple Seven pasture, two of the bulls were fighting. The Angus caught the Hereford with his back to a downslope, gave him a boost, and tipped him over. The Hereford rolled over a half dozen times and landed on his back completely buried in a drift. There was a long pause, with the cows looking on, while I wondered how in the world I'd get him out of there if he hadn't broken a leg. Then the snow heaved, and his head popped out. He shook his horns, looked the situation over, picked an easy way out of the gully, and stayed right in front of the cows — a long way from the Angus bull — all the way home.

I've been having diarrhea for several days, which added to my general misery during the six hours it took to drive the cattle home. To hell with laser technology — I'd cheer wildly for the man who invented winter coveralls that would allow a woman to relieve herself in a blizzard without stripping.

December 7 Low −10, high 20; sunny, a little wind.

George and I went to the Lindsay pasture where we'd left the horse, and I had to ride all over to collect everything, the cows we brought yesterday as well as those that were already in the pasture. We brought them all home, as we intend to keep them on feed until we can sell most of the calves. We have less hay than usual, and prices are high so we'd rather not buy any.

I ache everywhere this evening; it's been too long since I spent two solid days in the saddle, and the cold makes tense muscles even sorer. My feet and fingers itch from frostbite.

December 8 Low −10, high 15; nice at first light, then the wind started about 8:30 a.m. and the snow began to drift badly. We are so glad we have the cows home — it was a struggle just to feed them here.

Harold is back in the emergency room with continuing heart problems. The hospital said he had several small heart attacks. I find it impossible to think of the world without Harold's gruff dawn phone calls.

Father talked to our neighbor Al tonight to ask if he'd feed the main herd of cattle in the creek pasture this winter. They started this arrangement while I was away at college and it has gone on ever since. Asking Al to do it each winter has become a ritual they both enjoy. Father drives up to Al's house, drinks coffee and eats cake for several hours, and then just before he leaves, pops the question. Al always accepts. In the spring Al visits my father to bring the carefully itemized bill.

When I was first staying here alone in winter, Al came in for coffee every few days and quizzed me on my political and environmental views, making me defend every stand I took. We both enjoyed our mock arguments. His son Alan and Alan's wife Shirley live in a home they built a few hundred yards from Al's house, and his daughter Margaret and her family live a half-mile down the road. They are our closest neighbors in several ways.

December 9 Low −25, high −10; the wind stopped in the night.

Our first job was to dig the truck out of the barn, followed by digging a trail to the stack of bales and digging through the gates to get to the cattle, which finished the morning.

In the afternoon Father took the 420 tractor, we followed in the 3/4 ton truck, and we managed to get to the Lindsay pasture and feed the fifteen dry cows and eight bulls we left there. We turned them into a small pasture with running water in a tank, and cleared the tank of six inches of ice. On the way home the pickup slid sideways into a hard-packed drift and the muffler was torn off.

Tonight George and I are both lying in our chairs, moving the heating pads from one aching muscle to the next.

December 10 Low −20, high zero; foggy and cold, with almost three feet of snow on the level.

We spent all day struggling through drifts feeding cattle and barely made it to the pasture across the tracks. We ate a cold supper and sat in the living room wrapped in blankets, but seemed to take forever to warm up.

Many western or Great Plains novelists have written about including the land as a distinct character in novels, but it seems to me one also must consider the weather as a separate entity, almost an intelligence. We're especially conscious of it in spring, when the weathermen mention "stockmen's warnings" and urge ranchers to get young livestock into shelter. The observant rancher already knows it by the time it's on the radio. He's seen the smoke rise heavily from the chimney, slide across the roof and drop to the ground, and noticed the low spongy clouds and the heavy silence in the air that means a wet snowstorm coming.

December 11 Low −25, high −12; no wind.

George hauled more cake from Buffalo Gap in the morning after the snowplow came, while I helped Father separate some of the steer calves and give them extra feed.

We spent the afternoon feeding the cows — two pounds of cake and about ten pounds of hay each. Just as we finished struggling out of our coveralls — at 4 p.m. and dark — Father called to say he thought they needed more cake from now on, so we went back down and fed another two hundred pounds. To 145 cows, we're feeding about four pounds of cake each, or six hundred pounds total, and 1450 pounds of baled hay per day, about twenty bales. We load and feed all of this weight by hand since we can't get the big tractor through the drifts to the loose hay stacks yet.

December 12   Low −30, high −15; cloudy, a little wind.

I woke early from a dream in which I couldn't breathe through either my nose or mouth. I tried to get out of bed — in the dream — but fell and lay there trying to make enough noise to wake George. I knew I was smothering and that he'd find me dead beside the bed in the morning. When I actually woke, I was gasping and covered with sweat, my nose plugged — just a cold coming on, but the feeling of panic kept me awake a long time.

The cold temperatures make chopping the ice difficult for George, whose breathing has never been very good. He doesn't seem able to get enough air into his lungs, and we still don't know if it's asthma or something else. In the evening we took a pot of chili to Bill. He says Margaret may be home for Christmas, but Bonnie won't be.

December 14   Low −20, high −10.

After we fed today we went to town and got a few more gifts for Mike, since he will be here at Christmas. It was a rush trip, to get home in time to help Father separate the steer calves again. He intends to sell them first, and each night cuts them away from the cows and shuts them in the corral to feed them alfalfa cubes.

Father spoke today of two particular cows we'd sold at least five years ago, and I asked him how long it had taken him to recognize individual cows. I know some, especially the ones with distinctive markings. He knows them all, every cow, and can usually tell what she was out of, and perhaps who her grandmother was besides. He said he's always been able to do it, since he was a child, which slightly dashed my hopes that perhaps someday I'd learn.

December 15   Low −25, high −10; brisk wind from south rearranged snowdrifts.

The cedar waxwings that visit our cedar trees annually on their migration south are crowding the trees around the folks' house, tippling on the berries and screeching raucously. When they pass through again, headed north in March,

I'll know much of winter is past. They must be hardy birds, to travel after the snow.

We increased the hay to the cattle by a few bales today, as they look terribly thin and weak. Some of them are sore-footed from walking in this snow and ice for so long.

I went to Jo and Harold's this evening to help clean the basement of the old house for the new hired man and his family. In one of the boxes I found an old journal written by my grandfather, Charles Hasselstrom, and borrowed it to read. I never met him.

He used accounting ledgers, recording the money spent in each month on the left hand page, and the money made on the right hand page. For example:

Money Paid Out in Jan. 1928			Produce sold in Jan. 1928		
2	groceries	$1.59	2	15 doz. eggs	7.50
4	bread and castor oil	.80	21	27 doz. eggs	9.45
21	oysters	1.00	31	one can of cream 8 g.	14.49
26	bull from Wm. Snable	250.00			

He didn't record his daily activities, his thoughts or frustrations. But it's a wonderful document because it's so specific. A page in the front lists the work horses by name (Queen, Betts, Beauty, Min, Alkili, Martha, Katie, Bell, Ester, Mary, May and Dolly) and tells when their colts were born. On another page is his inventory for the year 1919, the year the journal opens. He valued the chicken houses and barns at $1000, the fence posts at $1500, and the farm machinery at $1800, and recorded the expenses for the year: $1352. At the end of 1918, he had thirty-five head of cows, twelve heifers, thirty calves, two bulls, thirteen steers, twelve horses, two brood sows, seventeen other hogs, and two hundred chickens, with a total value of $5850.

December 16   Low −30, high −15; radio says chill factor is −60 with a cold wind drifting the snow again.

We had to dig the truck out of the barn again, dig out the stacks of bales, then dig the truck out several times while we fed the cattle. My back and shoulders are getting more used to the shoveling. The snow is so hard we can cut out perfectly square chunks. If we needed to make an igloo, it would be easy.

By noon the wind had dropped, and while we were eating dinner and trying to get warm the cattle from the Lindsay pasture straggled into the yard. All of us rushed out half-dressed and struggled through the drifts until they were all in the corral. So now we have every cow and calf we own standing in the same corral, a situation that makes it hard to feed them properly. The bulls and strongest cows shove the others aside and get most of the feed unless we separate them into several small bunches.

After we collected ourselves, we sorted the cows with steer calves into the pasture around our house and tried to turn the others out into the big pasture. But the wind was up again and they didn't want to go. So we fed everything a little cake and staggered back to the house.

We offered to go to Lindsays to see if all the cattle came up, but Father's sure they would all stay together. That's good, because I don't think we could get there. The 3/4 ton truck will ride up on top of a drift for a ways and then drop through and be stuck as hard as if it was in concrete.

I bought Father a pedometer for Christmas; he's been wanting one so they could measure their daily walks. Today I fastened it to my belt before walking down to the corral to begin feeding, and by noon I'd walked three miles.

December 17   Low −10, high zero.

We cut out the twenty-one two-year-old heifers and put them on the hillside so we can give them extra feed; they'll calve for the first time in March. Now we have three separate bunches to feed and are moving at least seven hundred pounds of cake and twenty-three bales of hay a day — something like 2400 pounds by hand.

Because of the extreme cold the drifts are crusted over and each time you take a step you break through the top crust with a jerk, then hit another crust, and then another before your foot reaches the last layer above the ground, so walking is a real effort. All of us are having sharp pains in our legs.

I was reading Charley Hasselstrom's ledger today. Properly interpreted, it could provide an entire history of the times. Someone, probably my Aunt Anne, recorded $92.50 for the hospital bill when her father was operated on, $9.75 for a dress for her mother and $226.60 for the funeral parlor when they buried him. I went over parts of it with my father but he said it was too hard to look at — "Get it away from me."

December 18   Low −26, high −10; light wind in morning increased to sixty miles an hour by noon, with heavy wet snow falling.

Despite a cold wind, we managed to get feed to everything. In mid-morning when the winds hit sixty, it drove the snow into our clothes so that when we got into the pickup and it melted, we were soaking wet immediately.

After we changed clothes and had lunch, Father called and asked us to feed more cake to the cows. They were humped up with the cold, bawling, and gathered around the truck like sharks. I read somewhere that for every degree below zero they should have another pound of feed, and we're not feeding even close to that much.

Father ordered a truck for tomorrow to haul the rest of the steer calves, the best of the heifer calves and about fifteen dry cows to the sale. He'd hoped to keep more of them through the winter but it's too risky with the small amount of feed we have and the price it will cost us to get more. Also, the way the drifts are building up we soon may not be able to get a truck in here to deliver feed or to haul cattle to the sale ring.

December 19   Low −20, high −10.

We were up early this morning but Father beat us to the corral, and we spent a cold two hours separating the cows from their calves and then sorting off the best of the calves to sell. We picked out 113 to sell, leaving us about seventy to take care of this winter. We left them separate from the cows. Weaning them in weather this cold we risk wholesale pneumonia, but we'll have to move the cows soon, and the calves need more feed than the thin milk they're getting from their mamas.

I usually enjoy the few minutes' calm after sorting calves, while Father looks them over and allows himself a little pride in how they look. This year they look bad. The cold weather the last few weeks has knocked the bloom off them. Some are sorefooted and all of them are bonier than usual. Father looked at them awhile, then said, "We'll be glad we don't have them about February," and walked away.

Of course the ones we're keeping look even worse, the real dregs of bovine society: sick calves, calves born later than the rest, and calves from two-year-old heifers, which are always a little stunted. We decided to keep the dry cows, and hope we can sell them next week, as we have a big load with the calves.

The snowplow had just finished opening the road when the cattle truck came at eleven, and with much shoving and swearing we loaded the calves. We loaded cake onto the Ford pickup to give it more stability on the icy roads, and Father took it to the sale. We had a quick lunch before tackling the feeding. Of course the cows spent a lot of time bellowing and running back to the corral to look for their calves.

Sometime recently I wrote a note on the bedside pad about a title for this journal: "Windbreak: The Journal of a Ranch Woman." I noticed today George has added: "Breakin' Wind: The Journal of a Hired Hand."

December 20   Low −30, high −10.

Father called at 6:00 to tell me gloomily how cold it got last night, and that another storm is predicted, so they plan to leave for Texas today.

"Have you heard about the guy who said, 'Cheer up — things could be worse?' " he asked.

"No."

"So I cheered up, and sure enough they got worse."

Usually he remains pretty optimistic, but this storm is beginning to get him down.

After breakfast I helped them hastily pack the car. We took the 3/4 ton truck and had to tow them most of the way out the driveway. Then at Father's request we followed them to Hot Springs. The road was icy and visibility about one-quarter mile all the way so it was a hair-raising trip. We got back home at 2:00 and had to scramble to finish feeding before it got dark at 4:00.

Checking to be sure the folks' house was secure I found a pad on their dining room table headed, Jottings from an old man to his Children:

"Start calves on one lb. of creep feed and increase to two lbs. as they all get to eating. Maybe there is enough feed bunks to feed them all at the same time. If not, build more.

"If calves start crawling thru fences, FIX the fence and shut the fence crawler in the corral till the fence holds him. Don't get them all to be fence crawlers.

"To conserve energy, when a pickup is not moving ahead, shut the motor off. Starters and batteries are cheaper than gasoline these days.

"Don't keep a lot of horses in the corrals feeding them hay. If there is snow on the ground a horse can get by in a pasture without water. Hay is expensive.

"Get the calves fed and watered before noon. John Lindsay used to say if he didn't get work done in the morning, he might as well go fishing for the rest of the day.

"When you feed cattle cake, know how much you are feeding them; don't guess at it. Remember, every hundred pounds costs $6.85 these days.

"Don't take chances and get caught in a storm. Remember a cow can stand more weather than you can.

"Don't forget I've never kept livestock in a house in which I live. Please observe and respect my way of life. Thank you."

This combination of practical advice and sarcasm (by livestock in the house he means our cat and dog) is typical of him; he always seems to assume we are wasteful and not very bright. On the other hand, he's put seventy years of work in on this ranch and it must make him a little nervous to go away, leaving it in our hands. Destroying it all in one winter would be hard, but others have done it.

December 21   Low −10, high zero, with heavy, wet snow falling, high winds, lots of drifting — so it's a good thing the folks got out.

George and I used every bit of our energy to get feed to everything. The hose at the main tank was frozen. Father's been taking it into the house every night, as the flow of water isn't enough to keep it from freezing, but I forgot. I ran their bathtub full of hot water and put the hose in it until the ice drained out.

We're feeding the calves four thirty-pound buckets of alfalfa cubes in the morning with a hundred pounds of creep feed, and four more buckets of cubes in the afternoon, 340 pounds of feed for seventy calves, or almost five pounds each. My arms are practically pulled out of their sockets when I stagger through the drifts with thirty pounds at the end of each arm. That makes lugging the fifty-pound bag of creep feed seem easy. I bent instead of squatting to pick up the buckets this morning, and strained my back.

While we're pouring the feed into the bunks the calves dash in, butting and kicking each other, and it's tricky not to get kicked. My knees and thighs are a mass of bruises where I've been kicked, nudged and bludgeoned, but so far I haven't been knocked down.

In the afternoon George worked at reinforcing the stackyards, as the cattle had broken in during the night, led by the jumping cow we call Ugly. I spent the afternoon putting up plastic and insulation on the folks' porch and moving Mother's plants into the warmer part of the house. Tried to keep a fire in their wood stove in the basement, but the wood burned fast and my fingers remained stiff.

This evening Margaret called from home; she's in a back brace and probably will have to have a lot of surgery — even possibly have her spine fused — but she's cheerful anyway. Bonnie's thighs are set but the doctor says one leg will probably be shorter than the other. She won't be home for Christmas. I took the truck and went up for a minute to leave Margaret a fruit cake and a pot of chili. Her table was stacked with things people had brought her in the hospital: cards, toys, books. She was amazed at how kind people have been, perhaps forgetting that she's always the first to help others.

She'd decorated their tree. It's covered with things Bonnie made in school, and even some things Margaret made when she was in grade school. What a beautiful symbol of togetherness, of family life. When I got home I put a few decorations on the Norfolk Island pine in the living room. I am always pleased not to have to destroy a tree in order to observe Christmas. It looks bare and scraggly with its few ornaments; our history as a family is still so short.

December 22   Low −25, high −10.

We've been worried about the cows and bulls on the hillside south of the house. They're in the worst shape, thin and footsore. Each night they've been struggling up over the hill to get shelter from the cold north winds, and each day it takes them longer to stagger back down to feed. We've been afraid they'll get trapped on the other side where we can't get to them, so today we turned them into the alfalfa fields. Father cut and raked some hail-damaged hay that he didn't have time to stack and they can clean that up. Unfortunately, a lot of it has drifted under, so we have to shovel to find the windrows, since cattle won't dig with their hoofs like horses.

Instead of bawling and rushing to the gates as they usually do, the cattle stand waiting for us to feed, hip bones sticking up like masts on a ship.

In the afternoon we managed to get out through the pasture — getting stuck twice — to get groceries. When we came back the pasture route seemed to be drifted even worse than the road, so we tried the road — and got stuck three times. This may be our last trip out for a while unless we get the snow plow, and he'll be busy with all the new drifting. Glad I've been laying in extra groceries for the last few weeks.

When we drove into the yard a golden eagle was perched in a cottonwood tree beside the folks' house. I choose to interpret this as a good omen.

We're weaning the leftover calves — the ones not sold — and they stood in the corral bellowing frantically all morning until we fed them ten bales of hay and some cake. They're chewing on the corral planks, a steady gnawing like a million locusts. We got some blocks of mineral but it hasn't stopped them. I told Father about it when he called from Alliance, Nebraska last night and he said, "At the price of feed, it would be cheaper to feed them planks."

By the time George chopped the ice out of the water tank it was almost empty. The chunks of ice were more than two feet thick. We're keeping the pump running full time — if we shut it down to keep the tanks from running over, the pipes and hoses freeze. But when we let it run over, the ice freezes around the tanks and makes the footing hazardous for the cattle, so every day I take a bucket of ashes down and sprinkle it around the tanks. The gravel that usually helps the cows' footing is a couple feet under the ice.

December 23   Low −30, high −7; windy.

The feed store wanted to deliver the twelve tons of alfalfa cubes we'd bought today, so we called the county grader. He got stuck and spent an hour waiting for a tow. We couldn't help, so George got the army surplus tank heaters working, while I checked the folks' house, fed the barn cats, and hooked up the hoses on the tanks. We'd just finished feeding the calves when the semi came, but in spite of the work the grader had done, the driver was unwilling to drive into the yard — he was sure he'd get stuck. We had to dump the feed on plastic tarps in the yard beside the road.

We increased the cows' rations, since they're looking so thin and weak — to five pounds of cubes a day, a pound of cake, and ten pounds of hay each. We had to dig again to get to the bale stack, and shovel more snow off the hay for the cattle we turned into the alfalfa fields.

George said today, "You know, every other winter, I've had to listen to the old-timers talk about how much worse the Winter of '27 was, or the Winter of '49. This year they just shut their mouths and keep shoveling."

December 24   Low −35, high −15.

I called Jim and Mavis and advised them not to come for Christmas. The entrance road is completely closed by huge drifts and the pasture route risky. But their pipes are frozen and they're sick of working on them, so they're coming anyway.

When we got to the corral this morning we found a cow down. We tried to get her on her feet but she was too far gone. She was lying with her head downhill, so I suppose her lungs filled with fluid. She looked so thin I checked her teeth, and found the bottom front ones worn nearly away. All the feed in the world wouldn't have helped her. We can't get through the drifts to the boneyard so tonight she's lying in the driveway looking very small and pitiful.

We are continuing to feed cake, hay, and alfalfa cubes to all the cattle, but they still seem weak and lacking in energy, as well as terribly footsore. The yearling calves look gaunt even though they're getting all the creep feed and alfalfa cubes they can eat. Too much will make them bloat.

Jim tried to come in the main road, got stuck and dug out without us seeing him, and then parked the truck halfway to the house in the pasture and walked the rest of the way. I heard Mavis yell, and opened the door in time to see her teetering through the drifts in high-heeled boots, shrieking, "Damn Christmas! To hell with living in the country!"

We had a good visit around a supper of chili and cornbread, enhanced with scotch for the men, brandy for me and pink squirrels for Mavis, and played cards until late.

December 25, Christmas   Low −25, high 10 above; feels like spring.
I'm keeping Father's journal too, now. He always leaves it for me so he'll know later what the temperatures were during the winter. Naturally I read back through what he's written. Mostly he sticks to the facts: the work done, which cows are with the bulls, how much rain we get. But it will be a wonderful record to have in the years ahead; already he uses it to settle arguments with Harold about exactly how much rainfall we got in a certain year, or how much snow. Mother also keeps one, though I've never seen it. I'm pleased to know we're all recording life in our own ways, though I wish I had children to pass all these journals to.

We all went together to feed, and got Jim's truck in as far as the house at noon before stuffing ourselves on ham and turkey.

Mavis reminded me of the last time we were together on Christmas, a couple years ago. It was the first nice day for awhile so we moved the cows home from over east. At the very last pasture gate I was shouting at George and Jim, who were riding in the pickup in front of the cattle while Mavis walked, and I rode, behind. My horse slipped on the ice and fell, with my right leg under her. My head hit the frozen ground and I was knocked cold.

When I came to, Jim, who has had EMT training, was checking to see if my legs were broken, and Mavis, a nurse, was looking at my pupils and saying I had a concussion. George loaded me in the pickup and we headed for the house. After a minute I asked why Jim and Mavis were here.

George: "Because it's Christmas."

Linda: "Then why are we moving cattle?"

He laughed — said later it was the first sensible thing I'd said all day. I was dizzy the rest of the day — my second concussion from having a horse fall with me. Mother always said my real father's family was famous for having hard heads. Grandmother Bovard fell on her head in a bathtub once and knocked a chunk out of the tub.

December 26   Low −30, high −5, with fifty-mile-an-hour winds most of the day.
Jim and Mavis went back to their frozen pipes. The folks called from Texas; they made it safely and are settling into their apartment, but someone had broken in and stolen their TV.

Started reading Loren Eiseley's *Star Thrower*. Ray Bradbury wrote at Eiseley's death that he "stepped down to lace his bones with ancient dogs and prairie shadows." May we all.

Auden said Eiseley was "a man unusually well trained in the habit of prayer, by which I mean the habit of listening. The petitionary aspect of prayer is its most trivial because it is involuntary."

I like that thought. I've long since given up asking the being we call God for anything, but I often think of Him in appreciation — when enjoying the songs of the blackbirds, for example. I think He must be much more sensible than the Christians insist, and make allowances for people like me.

I remember my father, one Christmas Eve when I was a child, asking my mother and me if we really believed that a child had been born in a manger to take the world's sins on himself. At the time, I believed it passionately, but I was uneasy about my father in relation to religion. Even then he never went to church, but I knew I couldn't respect a God who would condemn him to hell.

December 27   Low −20, high 15.

We're low on propane in both houses but no truck could get up the road, so I called the county road crew again and a grader made a few quick passes through the yard while we fed. He was stuck on the hillside leading to our house for a few minutes, and left a narrow track with walls of snow six feet high on each side.

We haven't been able to get to our garbage dump since early in November, so I've got full garbage bags stacked in the basement waiting for the thaw. My compost pit is buried under five feet of snow so I throw the scraps out on a drift and hope the rabbits and grouse will eat some of them. I save meat scraps for the barn cats.

In the afternoon George made two more trips to the Gap for cake, finishing off their supply. Most ranchers have now used more cake than we usually use for the entire winter, and the feed stores are frantically trying to get shipments in, but the highways are bad in the entire state. Harold says he's heard cattle are dying on trucks and in the sale ring as ranchers sell cows they can't afford to feed, cows already weak from inadequate feed for the past two months.

A story in the paper describes ranchers in Wyoming who have cattle literally freezing to death. They say the cattle are losing patches of hair, and under it are masses of pus. I've never seen anything like that, but I imagine we will.

December 28   Low −30, high −15, with sixty-mile-an hour winds all day.

The cows hunched up behind any shelter they could find and we dumped the hay out in big chunks so it wouldn't blow away. The corrals are piled with frozen manure on top of at least two feet of snow and ice. Cows hate to eat on filthy ground but they're so hungry they pick up every straw. The wind beats at them, and at us, incessantly. It's like a frozen nightmare with no end in sight.

The calves are either weaned or they're too depressed to bawl anymore. They just stand around the corral waiting for feed, or huddle in the shed, or gnaw on the corrals. They have no bare ground to lie on except under the shed. Every night they crowd in there and the heat of their bodies warms up the mud so they emerge covered with filth — which promptly freezes. The poor things spend the time they're not eating just standing, shaggy with winter hair, covered in frozen mud, eyes glazed, looking half-dead.

Since George's son Mike was flying in tonight we thought of getting the road grader, but the road would have blown shut before he could finish. Instead my cousin John met him at the airport, brought him to our turnoff, and George walked to the highway to meet him. When I went out, the moon was shining, casting their shadows huge over the drifts. Mike dropped his suitcase and ran to hug me. He chattered enthusiastically about his Christmas presents and was eager for morning to come so he could help us feed. Lucky boy — what has been a nightmare for us is just a diversion for him.

Since I'm so tired at nights I'm not writing much but doing a lot of reading. I seem to spend long periods poised, thinking about a particular poem or story, as if I'm waiting for some impetus to actually begin writing it. During these times I read, or sew, or even feed cattle, and sometimes I take notes. My mind is working but it doesn't show. If I go to the computer during this phase, I may write a phrase or two and then sit, thinking, distracted by its blinking light, which seems to say, "Let's get on with it — time is money." Then suddenly something will force me to the typewriter or computer and I'll stay there working for hours oblivious to meals, cramp, thirst, or even George. When this happens, he obligingly fixes something to eat. Sometimes he simply comes up behind me, hugs me, and goes away again.

December 29   Low −35, high −25.

Since the wind dropped last night, I called for the snowplow so we could go to town for George's appointment with the doctor and groceries; the road was opened by 9 a.m.

The two of us get gloomy about this time of year, plodding through our work without much conversation. Mike tells jokes, rolls in the snow with the dog, chases the cats, asks the names of all the cows, is open-mouthed with wonder at seeing a great horned owl in a tree by the house, and generally gets us out of our rut. He's also a big help shoveling the alfalfa cubes into buckets to feed.

After feeding we went to Rapid for groceries and bought two more army surplus heaters to use in the stock tanks. George had an appointment at the Air Force base hospital for a checkup. The doctor has finally concluded that George may not have asthma at all, but an obstruction in his throat, possibly caused by radiation. He's making an appointment for us in Denver for further tests by the specialists there.

Even though it made us late with the evening feeding, we stopped for a pizza on the way home — Mike's choice. When we got home we couldn't get the truck up the hill because of the new drifts. We had expected to have trouble; the snowshoes were in the back of the pickup. Mike thought it was great fun making three trips up the hill carrying the groceries and trying not to trip over his snowshoes. It's amazing how high our hill is with a load of groceries and how hard it is to walk on snowshoes when you can't see your feet. Mike and George fed the calves with flashlights while I put groceries away and built a fire.

December 30   Low −10, high 25; no wind. Felt like summer.

George and Mike hauled more cake from Buffalo Gap before feeding, afraid the store would run out again. Everyone's making trips to town while the good weather lasts.

I took a vacation from feeding, and spent the morning making a huge roast with potatoes and gravy, and a cherry pie. Whenever I passed Mike's room I peered in and enjoyed the chaos. Usually it's so tidy. What a delight to see it strewn — overnight — with socks, underwear, and tee-shirts with pictures of faces I don't recognize — teen idols, no doubt. He'd rummaged through the book shelves and piled a dozen science fiction and western books on his bedside table for reading after he's supposed to be asleep. George and I pretend not to notice his nocturnal reading, since we both did it as children.

December 31   Low −30, high −15, with a high wind all day.

We kept the tank heaters burning all night but the ice was still six inches thick on the tanks. Another cow was dead in the corral this morning. Her bottom teeth were broken and stubby — another one we should have sold but couldn't because the cold weather set in too quickly.

We noticed another cow limping painfully, and put her into the corral where she promptly lay down in a muddy hole beside the tank. We couldn't get her up so we put hay and water beside her. Mike stood by her, urging her to eat, and wanted us to call the vet. I told him we just couldn't afford to do that for old cows, and it probably wouldn't help anyway. Once they lie down, it's usually the end. Cows can stand a terrific amount of cold weather and hardship, but when they decide it's over they seldom get up again.

Mike insisted we all make snow angels when we came in this noon, so now there is a hefty snow angel, a skinny tall one, and a short one that rolled all over the hill. Then I spoiled the mood by pointing out that all of us had done the same work all morning, and wondering why they were reading while I fixed dinner.

Alan's wife, Shirley, brought us some cream from their cow and we made ice cream with the hand-cranked freezer in the evening — a treat for Mike, and a strangely appropriate way to bring in the new year.

Bone
—for Georgia O'Keeffe

I am a saguaro, ribs thrust gray
against blue hot sky.
                              I am
a polished jawbone, teeth white
against the grass.
I have become all that I see:
an elegant bone gnawed clean,
leaving only bone the end,
bone the beginning,
bone the skyline mountain.

January

January 1   Low 20, high 58; the sun shone all day.

For the first time we were able to use the tractor and feed loose hay, so we can conserve the bales we bought. We used cake to lure the cows into a smaller corral, and shut them in to finish the cake while we scattered hay. George ran the tractor, bringing big chunks of hay into the corral. Mike and I tore the piles apart with pitchforks and scattered little bundles so each cow has a better chance of getting enough to eat. During the delay while we waited for George we took off our coats, threw snowballs, and giggled like a pickup load of kids.

Huge chunks of manure-covered ice are all over the corral, so you can't walk or drive without crashing into them. In every crevice, melt water mixed with manure is running, and all of us — human and bovine — fell down until we were all covered with it. Mike invented a new game: he threw a chunk of snow into the air and tried to catch it on the tines of the pitchfork as it fell. We both played it between George's deliveries of hay, but Mike was the champ.

After they'd cleaned up the hay the cattle were restless so we opened the gates to the hillside pasture. Most of them straggled out and scattered to graze even though only a few patches of grass are showing yet. They're just sick of standing where they've stood — and eaten and defecated — for so long.

Last night we went out on the porch and set off the fireworks Mike brought with him last summer. Then the grass was so dry and the fire danger so high we didn't dare celebrate in the traditional way, but it was almost more fun to do it now. The air was warm enough so we were comfortable with light jackets on. The dog raced around trying to catch the firecrackers as they fizzled in the snow; the cat remained aloof.

After supper I suggested everyone write New Year's resolutions. George wouldn't do it, but Mike carefully printed a list including doing better on his homework, training his dog, and being more patient with his half-siblings. My list was that I should see 365 sunsets this year, since I'm often "too busy"; say no to every silly request made of me and every request for work that doesn't involve payment; make more time for my writing; and work harder at marketing the things I have written.

January 2 Low 15, high 40; another sunny day of melting.

Clear, bell-like notes of grouse in the icy darkness. The orange moon rises late — the Wolf moon.

The cows on the south hillside didn't want to come to feed so we drove up on top to collect them. The white bull snorted and pawed when he saw Mike. I got between them and told Mike to start backing up the hill. Once the bull saw me he seemed to calm down. He probably just didn't recognize Mike, but we'll have to watch him, as it's not the first time he's acted snuffy.

While we waited for the cattle to gather we had a wonderful snowball fight. I seldom hit anyone I throw at, and both George and Mike throw well, so I'm always soaked when it's over, but I love to see the two of them playing — they have so few chances.

After our break, we trailed the cows back down to the corral and sorted off ninety-five head to take to the creek tomorrow, leaving us with about sixty cows here, plus twenty-one heifers and the bulls. Harold will move his cattle off the route we have to take. Al came down this afternoon and took the big tractor to the creek. Now we must move the cattle, as we'll have nothing here to feed them but bales and those are running low. At the creek they'll have better shelter and plenty of hay; we always winter most of them there.

Cuchulain, our Westy, follows all three of us to the bathroom and waits solemnly, his head on his paws, perhaps believing lavatory hazards should not be endured alone.

I walked out on our hillside to watch the sunset tonight and noticed rabbit tracks. Rabbits' feet never touch the ground; they walk on stilts of fur. The air was warm and heavy, almost soggy, and very still — another storm coming. Mike helped me bring in extra wood, a chore that begins to wear me down this time of year.

In the evening we took Mike to the plane and watched him fly away to his other life. When we came home, our road was filled with calves. The snow melted more quickly where we'd been driving, and it's the first chance they've had to lie on ice-free earth for more than a month. We hated to make them get up, but we couldn't drive around them without getting stuck.

Both of us are silent this evening. Three shrunken snow angels melt in the light of a moon surrounded by an angry red circle.

January 3   Low zero, high 15; snowing hard, tiny crystals of ice that remind me of the saying "little snow, big snow." Tiny flakes mean a lot of snow.

When we saw the weather this morning we wished we could cancel moving the cattle to the creek pasture. But we'd made the arrangements, and if this storm is bad enough we might never get a chance to move them again. So with George driving the pickup and me on the horse, we started out in the worst cold I've ever experienced.

The winds were from the north at over twenty-five miles an hour, carrying snow, with a minus fifty-six chill factor. In human terms this meant I could only ride a quarter mile before my legs began to go numb and I had to get off and walk. The snow was so deep that I'd get sweaty within a few steps, and chilled when I got back on the horse. I'd gotten off the horse and back on again a dozen times by the time we'd covered a mile. The cattle didn't want to go against the wind, and kept trying to turn back, so I had to keep close watch on them and continually ride back and forth getting them back into line. If a cow had managed to turn back, the visibility was so bad that within ten feet she'd have been out of sight. The snow seemed to be more frozen ice than the fluffy flakes of the poets. I had most of my face covered, but the chunks cut flesh wherever they hit.

I began to think of the mountain men, of James Clyman riding with Jedediah Smith's band of trappers over the Rockies in the winter — the "dead of winter" — a strange phrase for this living natural force that seems malevolent, but is really indifferent. When the wind let up for a minute the Black Hills were blue and icy-looking in the west, reminding me that nature simply doesn't care one way or the other. She gives us a certain set of circumstances. What we do with those circumstances, whether or not we survive, is up to us. I realize how easily I could die out here. The horse could fall and I might be frozen or buried in snow before George would miss me even though he watches the track behind him in the rearview mirror. Or I could freeze a finger or foot so severely it would have to come off.

Most people are inside today, warm, watching the blizzard through their window panes. Only fools would even go out in cars on a day like this, and here I am on a horse. For once the horse seems to realize this is serious business and settles down, picking his way over the snow-shrouded rocks without falling.

Why do we do this? No one ranches for the money, and it's not that we're all masochists. It's as though we have a covenant with nature, that we're bound to see it through, to figure out a way, every year, in every emergency, to survive. It's less like a battle than a marriage. The problems perhaps serve to enhance our feeling of accomplishment when we succeed, and the more complex or dangerous the situation, the greater the exhilaration when we live through it.

Several ranchers have mentioned to me that they'd make more money if they sold their land and put the money in the bank on interest — and they wouldn't have to work. But they haven't done it.

By the time we got to the underpass at the highway, about two miles, my feet were so stiff and cold we shut the cows in the corral and I got in the truck and took off my boots for a few minutes. My face was partly covered by a balaclava, with a stocking cap on my head, but my cheeks were white with frostbite.

We only rested a few minutes before Harold's horses came running to the fence and Oliver broke a rein and ran to them. I tried tying the rein to the bridle with my mittens on, but it was ridiculously awkward, so I had to take them off, and then my fingers immediately became so numb I could hardly tie the knot.

The next stretch was worse, going up the long ridge toward Harold's with the wind blowing straight in our faces, but the cattle finally lined out and marched, realizing they were moving to a new pasture. The same cow gets in front of the line every year, but I noticed this year several were trading leadership, perhaps because the snow was so deep.

When we got to Harold's we turned them through the next gate so they could go on if they chose, while we went in to warm up. My feet were completely white by that time, and I ate lunch with my feet on the hearth and a roaring fire in the fireplace, while Aunt Jo brought me second helpings of everything and bustled in with hot coffee.

After lunch the cattle were out of sight and the horse had icicles hanging from his mane, so we trotted and galloped to catch up. The cattle had gone on a couple of miles and spread out to graze with their backs to the wind. It was a job to gather them up and turn them north again, but by that time we were only about a half mile from the pasture. I just counted them in and left the fence-checking for a warmer day.

When I got to the creek the banks were coated with ice and the creek partly frozen over. The horse wouldn't go into the water. I decided it would be safer for me if I led him anyway, so I got off and went ahead. As soon I waded into the creek, the water went over my boot tops and inside.

Just as I got to the opposite bank the horse slipped in midstream, scared himself, and jerked back. I let go of the reins and tried to jump out of the way because I knew he'd be trying to get out of the creek. But my boots were full of water and I fell awkwardly right in the path, which is worn three feet deep. There was nowhere for the horse to go but right over me. I felt his hoofs pounding my left leg several times as I got my arms over my head. It seemed to take a very long time for him to climb over me, and I think he did some unnecessary tap-dancing, but finally he was gone and everything was quiet. I could hear George calling to me. I tried to answer and could only groan.

When he got to me I was trying to move my left leg, but the pain was too great. He asked if it was a sharp pain or a dull one, and I swore at him. He helped me sit up, and I finally got the leg to move. I sat on the ground for fifteen minutes before I wanted to try to stand up, and then the pain in that leg was terrific, but I could put weight on it and was sure it wasn't broken. I hobbled up the slope to the pickup while George unsaddled the horse and loaded him in the trailer. As we drove out of the pasture my leg suddenly gushed with warmth — blood pouring out of broken blood vessels. The warmth felt especially odd because my feet were icy cold from walking in the creek.

Since we had the horse loaded, and the trail was beginning to drift, we took him to the pasture east of the tracks where Sage is, and barely managed to drag the trailer back through the new drifts.

By the time we got home I was afraid we'd have to cut my seventy dollar boot, but George gently worked it off. The leg is a rich purple, with five clear hoofprints up the length of it, another on my back and one on my shoulder. I was lucky as well as clumsy. I prescribed a hot bath and a hot buttered rum, but I couldn't stop shivering for several hours, even in the warm house, and the leg continued to hurt.

In the middle of the night, lying awake because of the pain, I was startled to hear the wind suddenly stop. It was as much a relief as having the dentist stop drilling a tooth.

January 4   Low −20, high zero, with more snow falling.

I struggled downstairs to light the fire this morning in extreme pain and spent the day inside while George fed. I kept hobbling to the windows to try to see him, but the snow was so thick I couldn't even see the corrals. Between hobbles I checked over stories and sent some out to new markets, since I couldn't sit at the computer. My leg hurts too much for me to bend it.

Late in the afternoon George drove to the creek pasture and saw that the cattle had settled down comfortably in the trees. In the evening we went to a party. Mavis was there so I pulled up my pant leg. Nothing startles a nurse;

she said she was surprised it wasn't broken, and it ought to be in a cast.
I couldn't sleep because of pain, so sat in the chair until 3:00 in the morning, reading and sipping brandy, hoping to at least induce unconsciousness.

January 5   Low −20, high zero; snowing hard.

I hobbled around helping George feed, but the pain in my leg was excruciating. It's swollen to twice normal size, and a rich purple, with deeper purple hoof prints. We turned the cows out of the alfalfa fields and back into the pasture with the cripples and elderly left here, and gave them all extra feed.

The calves are beginning to catch on to eating their alfalfa cubes and creep feed from feed bunks on the ground, but they still have to be brought into the corral on foot morning and evening. Because of the deep snow and the pain of my leg I can't help, so I stand at the corral gate and call "C'calf! C'calf!" ("Come calf") while George circles around and heads them in. Soon they'll be trained to come at the call alone. After a few days, any calf that stands off by itself while we feed will be shut in a separate corral and kept there with no other feed but the cubes until he's eating.

It's always a relief when the main herd is moved to the creek pasture. We have only about forty cows, twenty-one two-year-old heifers, eight bulls and the yearling calves to feed. If the snow is deep, as it still is, we feed bales and cake to both bunches. If the snow melts, we feed only cake as a supplement to grass.

This feeding consumes almost as much time as feeding the big herd. We usually move the cows in December and I begin staying inside more to work on my writing. This year, I'm starting later than usual, and am going to be frustrated until I can figure out a way to sit at the computer or typewriter with this leg.

Just before dark we noticed a cow calving on the hillside. George went to check and found the calf ice-covered and shivering, so we brought him in and put him in a bathtub full of hot water to warm up. We dried him off and before we'd finished supper he was lurching around the kitchen, bawling for his mother. I kept him in an hour or so, and had several phone calls. We'd be talking, and then the calf would bawl right beside me and there'd be a long silence on the other end. About 9:00 he was getting so rambunctious George took him to the barn and brought the cow down off the hill so he could get some supper.

I spent most of the evening on the couch with a heating pad on my leg. George has to help me get dressed and undressed, gently peeling my wool pants and sock off while I hold onto the dresser. I try not to groan because he can't help hurting me.

After the wind dropped I saw a hunting owl float past the house, making no more noise than the moonlight. People always say of moonlight that it's "bright as day," but how completely wrong. The light has such a different quality, soft and caressing instead of harsh and revealing.

January 6   Low −10, high 10; a decent day: no wind, no new snow.

George fed alone today since I had another sleepless night, then made a quick trip to Buffalo Gap for more creep feed after I called the county plow again. The calves have stopped gnawing the corrals the last few days when they've been able to get a little grass, but they still look pitifully thin.

In the afternoon we went to town for groceries, then to the Base hospital. The doctor and X-ray technician both whistled when they saw my leg, and were particularly intrigued by the series of hoofprints, which have turned yellow. No bones are cracked or broken but ligaments are torn loose. A smiling doctor assured me this is much more painful than broken bones. He put my leg in a splint and gave me a pair of crutches and a bottle of painkiller. I hope it's strong, because I'm supposed to sleep with the splint on.

January 7   Low −10, high zero; snowing lightly most of the day.

I'm glad the cattle are at the creek. My first experience on crutches is astonishing — I can't imagine how Harold ever learned to maneuver them at the age of eighty. With the splint, I can't even sit comfortably in a chair, let alone in the bathroom. If I bend my leg at all or move my foot the pain is excruciating. George has to help me put on the splint and get in bed — it's degrading. I'm trying to save the pain pills for night. I have to sleep on my back because of the splint, after forty years of sleeping on my face.

George did all the feeding and came in with icicles dangling from his mustache and beard. We both napped a little in the afternoon and then he helped me get to the basement to work on my mail and the environmental newsletter, which I can do standing up as long as I grit my teeth.

January 8   Low 5, high 20; sunny.

A young man and woman from New York stopped to visit today. They're working on a documentary about this region's writers. They couldn't stop looking at the view from our living room windows, several miles of deep snowdrifts to the south and east, and spoke over and over of "isolation," though we are less than a quarter mile from the highway. I told them this was crowded for us. "When we want solitude we go to the mountains and camp among the grizzly bears." They thought I was joking. I invited them to stay a few days to experience ranch life in a blizzard and find out what isolation really means, but they hastily declined.

They did listen carefully to my comments on the state's writers, and seemed to have done some careful research. I always wonder, though, about people who fly out from New York for a few days and then fly back believing that they understand the hinterlands. I've seen so many wrong conclusions drawn by people who think they can understand this simple primitive area in a few days.

January 9   Low 25, high 38; sunny, and snow settling a little.

While George was out feeding today, I disobeyed his orders and got down the stairs on crutches, dragging the dirty clothes hamper. I washed a few things — our long underwear was all dirty — and was glad I didn't have to hang the clothes outside. I thought of my grandmothers, who washed clothes for big families week after week, their hands growing red and raw as they scrubbed on washboards and hung the clothes outside in a freezing wind. I remember Mother bringing in the stiff jeans and long underwear and propping them in corners like some quiet relatives to thaw out and dry.

I tried to prop my leg up on a chair so I could work at the computer but it was too painful. Any leg movement causes pain to flow up my entire leg, deep inside, as if it's crawling along the bone. Still, I think it's improving — it itches, like a scab.

In the evening, George lifted my leg and me into the pickup and we drove to Margaret and Bill's for his birthday party and Bonnie's homecoming. The poor child's legs are in a cast, spread wide as if she were giving birth and fastened by an iron bar under her knees. They'd brought her home in the back of a borrowed station wagon. Bill said, "We were going to bring her in the back of the pickup, but she said it was too cold. Kids aren't as tough as they used to be." George and Bill carried her to the house, then had to turn her sideways to get her through the door. They have a hospital bed set up in the living room, and there she'll stay for another month or so. Margaret is still wearing a back brace, and with my crutches I wasn't much help.

Once Bonnie was installed in her bed Bill brought out a birthday cake Margaret had made and we celebrated, giggling at the spectacle we made: one lying on the couch in a back brace, one on crutches, and one in a hospital bed with her legs in a cast. According to the men, their superiority has now been proven — *they* aren't physical wrecks. We women stuck together, though, and I insisted we are only in such rotten shape because we, being the superior sex, do all the work. It was wonderful to see Margaret laugh again, although she begged me not to say anything else funny because laughter hurts her back.

January 10 Low zero, high zero. The thermometer didn't move all day, and the wind blew hard; according to the radio the wind chill was eighty-five degrees below zero.

All the heat seemed to be sucked out of the house. George bundled up more than usual and still came in cold. We are among those who understand the real meaning beneath the old cliché, "chilled to the bone." Walking through the drifts in this cold makes us perspire, and then the sweat freezes as it runs down our bodies. Anyone who had to walk far in this weather could easily die of hypothermia.

In the evening we sat wrapped in blankets, dozing before the farces that pass for entertainment on TV. We both had headaches and were nauseous.

January 11 Low 20, high 55; sunny, and melting again.

It's ridiculous, but we had a bloated calf this morning. Cattle normally bloat only when overeating on green grass in the spring, but the alfalfa cubes we're feeding can apparently also cause it. I helped George punch a hole in his side with the trocar and put in a plastic pipe to drain off the air. The cold will probably kill him.

On the way back to the house we noticed mysterious swirling marks on the surface of snowdrifts, as if the skirts of some huge robed figure had swept the snow — and realized they are tumbleweed tracks. The wind in the night unhooked some of the tumbleweeds from fences and sent them skittering across the drifts.

When George went to check the electric meter he noticed our vent pipe was plugged with snow, which means we were being poisoned with methane gas and probably accounts for last night's nausea — rather than TV. He cleared the pipe and we'll watch it more closely after this.

Had a good talk with Margaret on the phone this evening, ranging over our usual variety of topics. We agreed it was unusual to be able to talk with someone for two hours and enjoy it. One part of the conversation would puzzle anyone not familiar with this area.

Margaret: "Did you notice the cottonwood tree in the pasture north of us, the one that burned last summer?"

Linda: "No. What about it?"

Margaret: "There's a new one beside it, so maybe it's not lost after all."

Linda: "Well, have you noticed how large the pine tree in David's pasture is getting?"

Margaret: "Yes. I've been watching it for years, and was always afraid their cattle would kill it."

We concluded that only a large bull scratching his horns on the tree could kill it now that it's survived this long.

Here, trees are a rare and precious resource, but even so, it seems strange to know she and I could go on like this, discussing individual trees along the roads we normally travel, for quite some time. One of her greatest fears about her back injury is that she won't be able to resume her tree-planting. She's ordered five hundred little pine trees, determined to be able to plant them when spring comes. I'd hesitate to take on that much planting by myself in perfect health.

January 13   Low 20, high 30, windy; it began snowing hard this morning, then tapered off but stayed cold all day. We have about a foot of new snow and some drifts ten or fifteen feet deep. Both George's van and my little car are completely buried.

George fed the calves but couldn't get out into the pasture to look for the cows. Around noon, with the sun breaking through a little, they appeared on top of the hillside and straggled down into the corral where he'd left their feed. The scene was so stark I took a picture — the shining white hill with a line of black cows silhouetted on the horizon, winding down the side.

In the afternoon a ferocious south wind came up and rearranged all the drifts piled up by north winds. It did sweep some snow off the hilltop, however, so the cows can find grass.

January 15   Low 20, high 48, sunny.

After feeding, George spent the rest of the morning chopping ice off the big tank. We haven't been able to keep the heater going at night because of the wind, and the ice was a foot thick in places. Once the tank was clear, he lit the heater. The calves rushed in and drank a lot; no doubt they've been only sipping while it's been so cold. All of them are coming to feed morning and night now, and George has two shut up learning to eat.

At noon George hauled some of the pumpkins up from the basement and I cut them up, steamed them and put them in the food dryer. In a few days, a twenty-pound pumpkin will be reduced to a quart of orange flakes.

January 17 Low −20; high zero.

Our water pipes were frozen when I got up. We couldn't even have hot coffee. I left the faucets on, hoping the pressure would blow the ice out, and then started to go to the well with George. I couldn't get through the drifts so I stood around and worried while he climbed down inside the cement collar with his propane torch.

Finally I went back in the house, hopped into the basement, and saw a waterfall running down through the heat ducts at the back. The entire kitchen was flooded because the faucets had come on and the sink drains were in. I hobbled out the back door and hollered "Help" at George — scared him — and then ran back and started mopping. Naturally much of the flow into the basement happened to be directly above the tipi and camping gear, but I moved most of it before it got very wet.

January 19   Low 35, high 55; a chinook wind caused lots of melting, with water standing in low spots.

The seven deer were back this morning, inside our fence less than ten feet from the bedroom window. Phred, sitting on the windowsill, woke us with his growling just before first light and we crawled to the window and looked out. The biggest doe looked up at the window, grazed a bit more, and then, like water flowing, jumped the fence and calmly began grazing on the other side. The little buck is lame, wounded by a hunter.

The calves finished eating quickly and moved out onto the grass. They've stopped gnawing on the corrals and their salt consumption has dropped from fifty pounds every four days to fifty pounds in two weeks. I noticed from the window one twitching his tail, however, a sign that perhaps he isn't getting enough salt and water and may be getting waterbelly.

I was feeling too exhausted to do much today, but I did cook a roast for dinner, and made soup tonight. In these days of working couples, I wonder if only farm wives still regularly cook three meals every day. It seems to me I just get well immersed in a story or poem when it's time to cook again. I could stand to eat less but George needs a constant supply of fuel since he's so active outside now.

January 20   Low 38, high 55; melting, with water running in every draw.

The water piles dams of debris, then runs around it in new channels, sweeping along the debris from the summer winds: napkins, fast food cartons, shotgun shells, feathers from birds the coyotes have killed. It's both exhilarating and frightening to see water running six inches deep in our paths. The calves refused to cross the deep draw we call the L7 this morning, so George had to get behind them and scare them into the water.

I stuffed my leg into the pickup and drove for George while he fed this morning, and then he slept all afternoon. I think he's still catching up from the awful weather. It sapped our strength almost as much as it did the cattle's despite our warm house. I hope he's not getting sick, with the shape I'm in.

In the afternoon we plowed through the melting snow to town, where the doctor said I can try walking with one crutch if I'm careful, and put on the splint only when I might fall, as when I'm going outside. He tested my leg mobility by bending it, and nearly had to peel me off the ceiling. My scream brought two nurses running down the hall.

"Good orthopedics always hurts," he said with a big smile. Through gritted teeth I assured him of my delight at getting the best.

George's grandparents called this evening and were surprised to hear our cattle spend the winter outside. In Michigan, I suppose, people have only a few cows and plenty of barn space. Out here, sheltering cattle in winter was apparently never even considered. Talking with Harold later, I asked him when ranchers in this area began to feed cattle in the winter. He said probably about 1915. Before that they simply turned them out in the winter and hoped they'd survive. Some winters they had terrible losses.

"But sometimes the prices were higher in the fall. Maybe we ought to try that again!" he said, chuckling. "Now we save 'em all. But saving the sick ones costs us high vet bills, and then we can't sell 'em for enough to pay what it cost to keep 'em alive."

January 21   Low 20, high 46; sunny. I had my first cup of coffee in the sun on the deck, with the dog curled up on my lap.

Spent the morning on the telephone calling local people about some bad bills in the legislature. While lunch was cooking I ventured out for a brief hobble around our hillside. I found coyote sign less than thirty feet from the house. How lovely if our house simply becomes a part of the natural ecology up here, so that the animals go about their business without noticing us.

I'm worried about the horses. Ginger has been over east alone since we brought the cattle back Dec. 6, and we haven't been able to get to the pasture Sage and Oliver are in since Jan. 5. I called my cousin John and asked him to fly over there the next time he's up and see if he can spot them. I suppose I'm glad Rebel isn't having to struggle to survive in this brutal cold.

I've become convinced that Ginger must be dead, since the snow cover everywhere has been more than forty inches over the grass and too crusty even for a horse to dig through. I keep thinking of her during the long nights, picturing her emaciated and starving, trying to paw through the crusted snow. But we've had no way to get to her; no one near us owns a snowmobile. I'll never stop feeling guilty if she's gone, even though she's old. Harold says it would have been a merciful death but I can't see it that way.

January 24   Low 35, high 52; during the night we could hear water dripping from the roof, and in the corrals we sink in mud to our knees.

I got about six good pages of work on a short story this morning, and realized that I felt better than I have in weeks. It seems lately that I've been full of rage, angry at the daily work of the ranch — taking some of it out on George — gnawing my fingernails, and it's all been because I haven't been writing.

When I emptied the garbage I noticed grasshoppers hatching, tiny ones perched in dozens on the drifts, a reminder of their devastation last summer. When I told Harold he was delighted. "The bastards'll freeze if they hatch now."

In the afternoon I cleaned all the chimneys of the kerosene lamps, getting ready for the inevitable day when the electricity will go off. That job always reminds me of Grandmother, who finally let me clean lamp chimneys when I was seven years old. They were our only light to read by when I stayed with her in summer. We'd sit out in front of the house watching the sun set until it was time to light the lamps, and sit in their golden glow reading all evening. I cherish those nights, and feel sorry for people who have never seen lamplight throw shadows on the walls.

Five tons of baled hay were delivered today. Harold came over late in the afternoon to look at it, as he needs more. I brought coffee to my office downstairs and we visited there. He looked a little oddly at my skull collection — the deer, antelope and owls hung on the wall, the cats, skunks, prairie dogs, fox arranged along the window sills with pieces of rock, bird nests with blue and speckled eggs in them, the chunk of twisted root in the corner — but said nothing. It does look like the den of some demented shaman, especially with the Georgia O'Keeffe prints of skulls, the owl wings and claws dangling from a plant hanger beside a prism, the buzzard and eagle feathers stuck into picture frames above the file cabinets, and the chunks of quartz on the bookshelves.

Late in the afternoon a plane flew over low and circled before flying off east — John, looking for the horses. I'm anxious to hear what he saw.

January 25   Low 29, high 50.

Sent in my garden seed order today. That always makes me feel as if spring were a little closer. We gave shots to six sick calves in the morning, and again in the evening. They act like they have pneumonia, and it can kill them fast if we don't stop it. The bloated one survived that, but he's got pneumonia now; a hard luck critter.

Another five-ton load of hay was delivered at noon; George's back is aching from helping stack. The sight of the neatly piled hay on the hill somehow gives me confidence we'll withstand the rest of the winter.

John called at noon. Sage and Oliver are alive but very thin. He saw no sign of Ginger. After lunch, we slowly walked to the top of the big hill and followed it to the tracks. The cows' trail is slick as a bobsled run and covered with six inches of ice. I had to hobble along in the deep snow beside it. Everywhere a clump of grass sticks out of the snow it's been nipped off by a hungry cow.

As we crossed the tracks the horses came running to the gate, and we led them until we got back to the hill pasture. They ran ahead of us to the corral, their manes shining silver in the sunlight. I was regreting the walk by the time we got home. A few painkillers and a heating pad and I'm propped on the couch smiling foolishly and thinking about poor Ginger. Perhaps she died quickly, but I suppose we'll never know. By spring her bones will be like so many I've seen, picked clean, with perhaps just a trace of pink left deep in the joints.

January 26   Low 19, high 52.

We need wood, so after feeding we went to the creek and cut down a cottonwood, and observed a whole ecology: spiders, frozen ants in the heart of the trunk, frozen baby mice and live adult ones. Cuchulain got one, and George sliced one with the chain saw when cutting into the trunk, but at least one got away. The tree almost hit the dog when it dropped; he was running foolishly from George's warning shouts. The open throat of the tree was tan and beige and shining gold. It will be a shame to burn such lovely wood, but our woodpile has shrunk alarmingly.

The gas company filled the propane tank today, so we feel more secure. Finally the hills we see from the windows are more brown than white — amazing how cheerful brown can be. We still are cautious about driving into drifts, since the warm weather makes the snow crust over, and once the truck drops through the crust you're really stuck, spinning on a slimy layer of mud.

At dusk the gray horse's clear whinny cut through the gathering dark.

January 27   Low 32, high 52; sunny and melting.

Walking in the trees, I saw where mink and rabbit tracks met in the snow. Only the mink tracks went on.

We went to town in the afternoon for some antibiotic we can mix with the calves' feed; several more are sick. A warm spell after extreme cold always seems to give yearlings pneumonia. We haven't been to town often since I got hurt, so I stocked up on groceries, including milk to put in the freezer. I always miss milk when we can't get to town — but not enough to get a milk cow.

Instead of going directly home, we picked up some ice cream, stopped to visit John and Judy, and went with them to a movie. As soon as we turned off the highway at home George switched off the headlights and we used moon-light to get to the house. The moon is surrounded by a huge ring of reddish-yellow — beautiful, but a change of weather might mean more snow.

January 29   Low 10, high 15, with snow squalls and wind all day.

George slept until 10:00 and then fed in an hour and a half while I forged ahead on a new short story. It seems to have taken on a life of its own now, and I'm just recording events — a wonderful feeling.

Late in the day we noticed a cow having trouble calving, and tied her in the barn. Only one leg was out, with part of the head, so we pushed together until the head was back inside. George reached in to try to get the legs together, but she kept pushing his arm out, so I did it, since my hands and arms are smaller.

The pressure a cow can exert is terrific. Very quickly my arm was numb, and I had to keep switching arms. Things are very confusing in there, but I finally sorted out two front legs, and then discovered the head was off to one side. We had to push the legs back in and re-position the head before we pulled it. The cow acted oddly. She bellowed a little, and when we turned her loose her mouth was foamy and she seemed reluctant to lick the calf.

January 30   Low 28, high 60 at noon; sunny and most of yesterday's snow gone by afternoon.

I helped George feed, and then we brought in a huge pile of cottonwood logs and piled them beside the furnace — a golden treasure.

We got the cow out into the corral today but she moaned a lot, in time with her breathing, and vomited. She died late in the afternoon; we must have ruptured her stomach. We have no other cow handy to mother the calf so I called some neighbors who calve earlier than we do, thinking they might have a cow who'd lost a calf. They accepted, and came down this evening to take it, a little heifer.

One of the yearling steers was dead this morning, probably from pneumonia, though he also looked a little bloated. We still can't get to the boneyard through the drifts, so we put him in a gully in the alfalfa field — several hundred dollars worth of coyote feed.

The ground has warmed up enough so we could dig some parsnips out from under the mulch. The fresh earthy, taste is the promise of gardens to come.

Scrubbing Parsnips in January

There's a modern sink just inside the door,
but I always scrub parsnips the old way:
with the hose, outside.
The sun shines, and it's forty degrees.

Icy water fans over my hands.
I scrub the clinging earth from white,
stalky roots, their legs splayed
like a man's.
         My mother washes them
outside to keep the dirt
out of the plumbing.

But there's another reason —
the strong earth smell,
the weak winter sun on my back,
chill wind and cold water, those white
limbs open, a thin trail of blood
where my topping knife slipped
and cut my finger.
         The rich blood threads
between two roots and blends with the clear
water, follows it down into the earth
for next year's crop.

February

February 1   Low 20, high 60; another lovely day — we can almost see the drifts subside.

I estimate we have twelve tons of alfalfa cubes left. We're feeding 390 pounds a day, so we have enough for about sixty-one days, or almost through March at the present rate. We'll bring the cows back from the creek in the middle of March when they're scheduled to begin calving. We may need to feed them cubes at that time, but we're probably safe not to order any more yet. We also have about eight tons of 16 percent protein cake left, and are feeding only seventy pounds a day now, but we're almost out of creep feed for the calves.

I always have Mike figure how much feed we have left when he's with us so he'll realize ranchers have practical reasons for getting education. He seems to think his announced desire to become a rancher exempts him from getting good grades.

Ranch archaeology is a neglected science. As the layers of snow melt, things surface: the handkerchief torn from my hand by a gust of wind in December; the tire that disappeared under the snow in mid-November; the oil slick in front of the garage where we repaired the hydraulic unit on the tractor on a freezing day.

February 2   Low 28, high 50. The house shook all night with sixty-mile-an-hour winds. At dawn a few shingles lie around the yard, but no other sign of the night's wildness.

After feeding, we went to town for groceries, and in the evening went to the annual Ground Hog Celebration at Sue and Leonard's. Originally, Sue reminded me, the celebrations on this date were because it is midway between the winter solstice and vernal equinox, so people celebrated the eventual coming of spring — long before they decided to persecute groundhogs. Though I know a great deal of winter is still ahead it always seems as if we've turned a corner when February comes. We can have vicious storms through April, but we know the worst cold is over.

Water was running in every draw and every wrinkle in the land today, a million creeks where normally we have none. Great pools collected at the bottom of draws still blocked with snow, and slithered under the drifts, melting from beneath, until the drifts collapsed into the flood like icebergs and floated away. Snowbirds have suddenly appeared again, zipping in noisy flocks over our heads as we walked out into the fields to unclog the drainage ditches so the water can spread to the alfalfa fields.

February 4   Low 34, high 75.

The weather has been so warm the parsnips were sprouting, so I spent the morning digging and washing them and cutting some up for the food dryer. I have no idea what one does with dried parsnips.

I went to town alone in the afternoon for groceries, the first time I've tried to drive since the accident. I wasn't a safe driver; the pain of using the clutch with my left leg made my progress jerky. The leg is now a vivid greenish-yellow decorated with purple hoofprints. The hoofprint on my back is finally gone.

George must believe summer is really coming — he spent the afternoon melting lead on the kitchen stove and making balls for his black powder rifle.

Later in the afternoon we took our time walking out to get the calves and enjoyed the sunset. We do so much walking as part of the work that we seldom walk for pleasure. Phred came along, sniffing delicately, while the dog dashed about trying to mark the entire pasture as his territory. We saw where mice had dug miles of tunnels under the snow with little rooms every few feet. Some of the rooms were stocked with tiny piles of grass and some were latrines. An entire mouse city flourished while blizzards raged several feet overhead.

February 7   Low 34, high 48.

A white-breasted hawk with black wingtips floats by the windows, turning his head from side to side to examine us while I search — in vain — for his picture in the bird book.

After feeding today, we both settled in chairs and read without speaking until time to do the evening chores. After supper we returned to our chairs and read until well after midnight. I think the responsibility for the cattle, and being together twenty-four hours a day, just overwhelm us, so that we have to retreat into a cocoon of reading in order to stay friendly.

February 8   Low 30, high 45; cloudy, but no snow.
George finished feeding early, then went to Harold's to help him vaccinate his cows against diarrhea. I had no idea one could vaccinate against that. Perhaps ranchers aren't immune to "styles" in diseases; maybe they see an ad for something and suddenly have to have it. Certainly they follow styles in cattle. A few years ago (well, twenty) Herefords were the only kind raised here. Now we have Chianina, Beefalo, Limousin, and something called Amerifax, which sounds like a computer company.

Just as I was going to bed last night a train went by with fire shooting from one stack. I called numbers until I got an annoyed railroad employee who didn't believe it's dry enough for a fire to start. "It's never that dry until June."

February 10   Low 20, high 50.
After he fed, I went with George to Buffalo Gap to pick up cake. We ought to be sick of looking at cows, but couldn't help noticing how bare the pastures were where the snow had melted, and how eagerly the cows grazed. We saw many looking worse than ours, and huge piles of carcasses beside several barns.

It's our nature to forget. In other species knowledge seems to be cumulative to some extent, but human babies must start from the very beginning in each generation. When we lose loved ones we tell ourselves stories about their peculiarities so we keep them fresh and vivid as long as we can. I began this train of thought in the night after a dream about my cat Blue. I still seem to see her occasionally out of the corner of my eye, and wake up thinking she has just patted my nose, her signal that she was ready to go out. I remember Grandmother spoke mostly good things of people toward the end of her life when she was in the hospital. Perhaps we remind ourselves of the noble attributes of the dead mostly to help the living.

February 11   Low 34, high a beautiful, sunny 60 degrees.
My neighbor Shirley rode a lovely bay mare down in the afternoon — a horse she's boarding — and we had a rare visit. Though we live only about a mile apart we seldom see each other. This seems to me a commentary on the way communities have changed in the last twenty years. People always used to go visiting their neighbors on Sunday after church. Now we rush off to the larger town to shop, or we watch television, or work. The pace of life is more hectic so there's no time for visiting — and yet all our houses and garages are stuffed with the latest labor-saving devices, and most of us are trying to buy more.

To me, this seems as great a danger to the "family farm" so beloved of journalists and politicians in election years as foreclosures — this loss of the sense of community, of belonging, of knowing your neighbors. It has its drawbacks. I really don't want my neighbors, however sympathetic, to know all my business as they did in the days of the party line telephone, but it would be almost worth it to feel the support, which seems to have vanished.

February 13   Low 32, high 50.
George is still doing most of the feeding. I hobble out to drive the truck for him about every other day but pay for it in pain during the night. The calves are enjoying the warm weather. Their hair is shiny, and they bounce and buck and bellow as they come for feed. The two-year-olds, heavy with calf, have a matronly waddle.

I've been visiting Margaret one afternoon a week. She is still wearing the brace and Bonnie's still in the hospital bed in the living room. Neither of them is very mobile but they've had a lot of company and most people bring a casserole or some contribution to make Margaret's work easier. It's frustrating for her, though, because she wants to be able to do her work. And she's determined to get well enough to plant her trees. Meanwhile, to my delight, she's decided to write a book about tree-planting in arid areas like ours because she hasn't been able to find the information she needed anywhere else. I'm so pleased that I can offer her suggestions from my experiences in book-publishing in return for the gallons of honey she's given us and the warmth of her friendship over the years.

February 15   Low 10, high 42.
Some of the cows didn't come in to feed this morning so when we finished we drove down the highway — the easiest way to look at the south side of the big hill in their pasture. We could see them south of us in the neighbors' pasture but couldn't drive there because of gullies full of running water.

So we parked at the highway, walked about a mile into the pasture, and found three cows and a bull feeding on some green grass in the bottom of a gully. It was difficult to drive them out because they didn't want to cross the gullies full of meltwater so we wound around an extra mile or so as they found their own way. Then George went ahead and opened the gate and I hazed them through.

We walked back along the fence and finally found where they'd gone out — a big drift covered the fence in a low spot. The snow is still hard enough on top so they simply walked over the fence. We had no tools or shovels with us so we dug the top wires out with our hands and cobbled them back together with some wire left on the fence. If the melting continues at its present rate, the drift will soon be too low for them to walk over.

On the way back my leg was hurting so we lay down on a south-facing slope so steep the water had drained away and left it dry. The sun was so warm George went to sleep. I just shut my eyes and listened to the whispering grass.

February 16   Low 10, high 20.
The tailgate of the truck dropped on the tip of my finger yesterday, and

this morning it was swollen with pain and pressure. George used his favorite method to relieve it: he heated the end of a paperclip in a flame and pressed it into the center of the fingernail. When the nail burned through, blood and fluid shot five feet in the air, but the instant of pain was worth the relief. In a moment the finger didn't hurt at all.

For this brief time until we bring the cattle back in mid-March and calving season begins, I'm able to devote most afternoons and evenings to writing. I become so absorbed in the characters I'm writing about that sometimes it takes awhile to adjust to the real world when the phone rings. Callers always ask accusingly if I've been taking a nap.

February 17   Low −20, high 5. Clear and cold.

We took extra time to look the cows over carefully while feeding this morning since several more may calve early. We have two cows that are one-eyed because a cancerous eye was removed. Both are getting cancer in the other, and both are going to calve. I suppose I could make a lesson of that, of life going on, but meanwhile I'm concerned that they may be suffering before the calves are raised. They don't seem to be in pain yet, and both of them have gotten used to getting around with only one eye.

Everything is covered with ice this morning. It's six inches thick in the yard and flat fields, and even the slopes of the hills have a sheet of ice over them. The cows and calves tiptoe but slip and slide anyway. Harold said he's heard old-timers talk about eighty years ago when ice from snow melt was thick enough so people skated everywhere. It's not that bad now, but bad enough. Many of the cows are crippled again, as they were in November, and we slip and slide and fall when we go down to do chores.

Our cows at the creek pasture are having a rough time from the ice too. Al shoveled through a four-foot snowdrift on the steep creek bank so they could get to the creek for water, but the meltwater runs in the channel, which gets so slippery they can't get back up the bank. Every time it's warm enough he chips more ice away to widen the trail.

George brought in a huge load of railroad ties and built a fence on the north side of the house to catch some of the snow that piles up around the cars. I've taken off the splint and am getting around the house without crutches except when it's necessary to go up and down the stairs.

February 18   Low −24, high 15.

Helped George feed this morning. We brought in the bobtail cow, who looks as if she might calve soon. She was born in a blizzard that froze all but six inches of her tail off.

Father told me once, "You can never tell what a bobtail cow will do."

I said, "Can I count on that as a rule?"

"Yes."

It's good to know there are some rules in this life.

This afternoon I noticed that the onions left in the cellar are sprouting, so George helped me haul them upstairs, peel and dice them, and put them on the food dryer. I had forgotten that the last time I dried onions the weather was warm enough so I could set the dryer outside and run the cord through a window. Tonight the odor of drying onions is so thick we can hardly breathe. On the other hand, onions are supposed to ward off colds, and we're surely absorbing enough through our pores to kill any cold germ I ever met.

February 19   Low −15, high 10.

After feeding today and dosing the horses for worms we decided to go for a "Sunday" drive. We stopped at the creek pasture and looked the cows over; two calves have been born there now. Then we walked down to the creek and found a dead cow, head down in the water. She must have slipped at the top of the bank and fallen twenty feet. She'd been dead several days. Maybe Al can use the tractor to lift her to the bank.

We drove up to Keystone, enjoying the sunlight flashing on the grass, picked up some fried chicken and brought it home for supper with white wine. It was good to get away from the ranch even for a little while, to look at trees instead of muddy corrals, to talk about the songs and news we heard on the radio, about things we've been reading.

February 20   Low −18, high 10. Foggy this morning with frost everywhere. All the grass blades are outlined in white crystals, and the cedar trees around the folks' house look a deeper green against the white. The cows' long eyelashes are outlined in frost and their eyes look delicate, wise and lovely.

On these cold mornings, as soon as the sun rises the cows line up on a south-facing slope and simply stand, absorbing the heat. They seem to go into a trance, and no amount of calling will bring them in; we have to go get them. They look so warm and serene I envy them. Perhaps I should cultivate the art of simply lying in the sun, letting it slowly warm my bones while I contemplate the day ahead.

The pickup lurched over a frozen cowpile while I was sitting on the tailgate scattering cake to the cows today. I shot off and landed on my hands and knees in front of an astonished bull. My hands are full of cuts from the ice, with a little manure worked in, both knees are skinned, and my left leg is swollen more than usual, but at least I didn't land on my head.

I've been working on short stories lately. I had forgotten how wonderful it is to be working on something seriously. I go to bed at night and scenes start running through my head. When I'm helping George feed I keep hearing dialogue. The story fills my head and I resent every minute spent cooking or cleaning or doing anything but writing. Yet the fact that I *am* writing keeps me in a good mood even when I'm doing dull, repetitive tasks.

February 21   Low −20, high 8.

Our eight bulls line up along the fence, staring greedily at the yearling heifers the neighbors have put in the pasture next to us. We'll have to move our bulls or they'll be tearing down the fences. About this time of year everyone moves their bulls away from their own cows to prevent premature pregnancies, but some aren't considerate of neighbors.

The black bull looks like a satanic spirit with his ridged and scarred shoulders, thick neck, snaky head and shining eyes. He rumbles in his throat threateningly, and then switches to a pleading murmur. The heifers, too young for that sort of thing, graze unconcernedly, but switch their tails and look over their shoulders once in a while, like highschool girls passing a construction site.

This afternoon we turned our yearlings into their next winter pasture, the hay field nearest the highway. Since we didn't cut a second crop there last summer some alfalfa is still standing, and the south side of the pasture, always too rocky to plow, has a good stand of cured grass. They spread out to graze right away and this evening we both had to walk out to get them in for feed.

When it's not bitter cold I enjoy walking after the calves, looking at the tracks in the snow — mouse, coyote, rabbit — noticing the pure line of a single blade of grass against a snowdrift. George seems to talk more freely outside and we often talk about things we'll probably never do, like planting trees around the dam below the house for a picnic spot, or planting a circle of oak trees to create a sacred grove.

I've been walking with George every night, partly to keep my resolution to see each sunset. Each one is different, each lovely in its own way, whether a spectacular colorful one or simply a red ball sinking behind the black line of the hills. Somehow this ritual I've begun seems to round off my day, to send me back inside more relaxed and serene. Such a simple thing to have such an effect.

February 22   Low zero, high 10.

Aunt Jo called at 7 a.m. to say there was a forest fire at my aunt Anne's. Plenty of fire fighters, so I went to Jo and Harold's and helped make sandwiches, which Jo delivered. In the afternoon we visited Anne; 650 acres burned just east of her. The fire was started by a neighbor burning garbage. He filled the barrel, lit it and left, with a wind blowing. It burned to the crest of a hill just above her house but she wouldn't move out. She admitted she had a few of her most precious things in the car, however.

I wonder what they were. If I had to decide, I suppose I'd have to save the cat and dog first, photographs, then copies of my work. What else? Perhaps my journals. I still remember so vividly the pain when my first husband read some of the journals I had kept since childhood. In angry petulance, I burned them all. I was in my twenties then. I destroyed years of work and material out of misguided fury. I should have recognized instead the meaning of that invasion of privacy and gotten rid of the man sooner.

The letter I got from Father today had a check in it and this enigmatic advice: "I'm sending another check for expenses. Spend it like a miser, but keep the cattle doing all right."

February 23 Low 5, high 20. Woke to six inches of fresh snow, fluffy and almost beautiful since we've had none for so long. I wish I could birdwalk over it instead of slogging heavily through it. We find the marks of sudden explosions where grouse have been covered with snow while they slept and then flown straight up in a volcano of snow at dawn. Warmth explodes out of cold, life out of death.

The cat stops in the open door, flips his tail, and returns to curl up on the bed for the rest of the day. I've always believed I'd be reincarnated as an aspen tree, but maybe I should hope for cathood.

The snow fell all day with little wind so it wasn't difficult to feed. Still, we had nearly a foot by dusk, when the sunset turned it gold as far as we could see. The wind came up just after dark, howling nastily as it built new drifts.

February 24 Low zero, high 30. The surface of the snow is shiny, as if it's been oiled, and packed hard by last night's wind. The sun seems to spin, growing hotter in the sky, but the heat doesn't reach us here.

After feeding, we went to Lawrence's to help him burn brush left when we cut firewood there. It was delightful to stand in the sunlight, warming ourselves at a bonfire higher than our heads set safely in a meadow full of snow. Lawrence and George confessed to each other that they're chocoholics — they'd drive to town in a blizzard for a candy bar.

After the fire had been burning for several hours and the heat was so intense we had to cover our faces and run up to toss branches in, George lifted a pile of ash with the pitchfork. Under it was unmelted snow — the cold heart of the flames.

*February 25   Low −10, high 25. The sky was filled all day with gray rolling
clouds. Toward noon they all rushed toward the western hills, as if being
sucked over the horizon.*

Coming back from taking mail to the post office this morning I saw a
pickup parked in our lane. I realized as I drove up it was probably the neighbor's hired man, fixing fence, but I hadn't met him.

He looked up when I stopped. His eyes are a clear glowing blue, and his
pure white moustache is saucily curled at the ends. He's at least seventy but
his classic weathered face is handsome, with a great hooked nose, crinkles
around his eyes, a wide smile.

I said, "Are you Martin _____?"

He hammered a staple into a post before he said, "I'm what's left of him."

After supper I turned on the porchlight when I let the dog out and saw
snow silently falling, thick flakes dropping in the darkness. When I turned
the light off I could still feel them, slowly falling, piling up, and had a sudden
vision of them falling inexorably until the house was covered completely,
smothered in snow, along with the roads, the cattle.

I spent this evening writing letters, clinging by mail to people I seldom
see and with whom I can discuss intimate things I can't discuss with anyone
here. I became close to some of these friends years ago. If we met today we
might have little cause for friendship, but loyalty and knowledge of each
other keeps us close. I've known one woman since before my first marriage.
She's seen me, through letters, at my best and worst — and I have seen her
in rough times. I can write to her on any subject and receive relief. I could
never talk to some of my close neighbors about, for example, my fears for
George's health, or the other strains between us. It would seem like a betrayal
even though they'd never gossip. It would seem wrong to use our neighborliness for that kind of confiding, so my letters are the only intimate conversations I can have on some subjects.

February 26   Low 25, high 34, with another six inches of snow.

We went back to feeding bales today, much to the cows' delight. George
hooks them from the stack and carries them to the truck. I move them from
the tailgate into position, stacking them two or three deep. It's great exercise
for the arm, thigh and stomach muscles.

The snow has drifted deep enough so we have to walk up our hill again,
carrying groceries, mail, everything we bring home. When the UPS man sees
no tire tracks he leaves packages in my car, parked in the folks' yard.

When the wind howls cold around the house-corners it's good to sit
snugly inside, quietly content to read beside George, my closest friend. We're

drinking pots of rose hip tea to ward off lurking colds. We talked of where we ought to build the garage so it won't be buried in snowdrifts. George's suggestion: Arizona.

We also talked about making wills. Neither of us ever have, partly because neither of us have ever had much to "leave" to anyone, a concept that strikes me as bizarre at best. Now we have five acres of land and a house, and George has a growing son, so we feel some effort should be made. Once we began discussing it I thought of pieces of jewelry some of my friends and relatives would enjoy — nothing valuable, but sentimental things.

Jim and Mavis have named us executors of their wills, specifying inexpensive burial. "Just throw us in a couple of boxes."

"George, you can have my guns if you can find them," Jim said. "Only you can't tear the house down." Pause. Grin. "I'll bet you can't find them any other way."

February 27   Low −18, high 10.

Twelve grouse were in the folks' yard this morning, eating cedar berries and scratching under the low branches. When we drove in they flew clumsily off, chuckling to themselves. It's good to see them, but I remember when we'd see thirty or forty in a flock.

My relationship with my injured leg is like that with a close friend who once betrayed you — I don't quite trust it. I jumped off the truck without thinking today and it collapsed under me and now is swollen and sore.

February 28   Low −24, high 15.

Either two or eighty-seven coyotes (it's hard to tell) were howling at 2 a.m. down in the yearlings' pasture — it's their mating season. The yelps and ululations always sound so exuberant, so wild and ecstatic, so unlike the modest gray creature of daylight who trots quietly through the pasture with his tail lowered.

Our neighbor, Al, stopped today. He said he gave one of his newborn calves mouth-to-nose resuscitation the other day, and then "drank plenty of whiskey."

Drying Onions

They hung in the cellar's dark all winter
untouched by wind and snow white as they are,
until long green shoots reached for light.
You helped me slice them; crackling
brown skins thin as dragonfly wings covered the floor.

Sweet bitter fruit of the earth;
spread on racks to dry it became
more a part of us than we knew or wanted.
Our eyes began to burn. Our clothes took on its taint.
When we made love, your tongue and mine, this mound
of flesh and that, all flavors
disappeared in onion.
                    All flesh is onion,
all sweat and juice part of us, fruit of our love.

Outside, the snow has melted, crusted,
sagged toward earth. We hack through it, peel back
layer after layer, searching for the white heart,
for earth warm enough to take our seed.

Spring

Mulch

A mulch is a layer of organic matter
used to control weeds,
preserve moisture,
and improve the fertility of the soil.
You will not find naked soil
in the wilderness.

I started cautiously: newspapers,
hay, a few magazines;
Robert Redford stared up
between the rhubarb and the lettuce.

Then one day, cleaning shelves,
I found some old love letters.
I've always burned them, for the symbolism.
But the ashes, gray and dusty as old passions,
would blow about the yard for days
stinging my eyes,
bitter on my tongue.

So I mulched them:
gave undying love to the tomatoes,
the memory of your gentle hands to the squash.
It seemed to do them good,
and it taught me a whole new style
of gardening.

Now my garden is the best in the wilderness,
and I mulch everything:
bills; check stubs;
dead kittens and baby chicks.
I seldom answer letters; I mulch them
with the plans I made for children of my own,
photographs of places I've been
and a husband I had once;
as well as old bouquets
and an occasional unsatisfactory lover.

Nothing is wasted.

Strange plants push up among the corn,
leaves heavy with dark water,
but there are
no weeds.

March

March 1   Low 28, high 30. Snowed all morning, about five inches, but we feel lucky. North of us a foot or more fell, with high winds, so highways and businesses are closed.

A big brown and white owl lay dead in the corral this morning with no visible wounds. I picked him up, marvelling at the softness, the thickness of the feathers. The ground is frozen, and I dislike the idea of burying him in the dark ground after his bright free flight, so I tucked him into a high cleft in a cedar tree. Wind and rain will perform his funeral rituals.

Had a long conversation with Harold this evening; he's been feeling better, getting back into his routine of calling me every few days. When I lived here alone in the winter he'd call daily to check on me and offer to help — that was before he lost his leg. Now he can only offer advice but it's always sound.

He says to seal a hole in a tube tire, put a little sweet cream inside it. When the cream sours and dries, it will seal the hole and last a long time. "That's how we always used to do it in the thirties. We never had time to mess with fixing a tire, and we never had to. We just used cream."

Some folks may find "non-dairy creamer" acceptable for their coffee, but they can't fix tires with it.

March 2   Low and high, 20. Snowing again.

We put a few dry cows, the bulls and the horses into the Lindsay pasture, tying the horses behind the truck and luring the cattle by shaking a cake sack. Once we turned the horses loose, they raced around the pickup and chased the bulls around on the flat, high-stepping like colts instead of aging nags.

When a cow wants to slip away from a moving herd she displays something close to intelligent reasoning. She'll pause to pee, and wait until the rider's attention is elsewhere, then run. Or she'll become absorbed in grazing, seemingly oblivious to everything, until she gets a chance to dodge down a gully. Even a day-old calf will repeatedly stand in front of his mother, trying to keep her from walking, if he's hungry and wants to suck.

We left the heavy cows here, and put them with the two-year-old heifers into a pasture close to the house where we can watch them day and night.

March 3   Low 15, high 20; snowing hard and drifting all morning, with about five inches on the ground.

We shut the heifers in the barn and yearling calves in the corral so they wouldn't bunch up against a fence in the storm. When we went out to feed the calves at dark we buried our 3/4 ton pickup in a drift at the top of our hill and couldn't get it out, so we walked to the barn to feed, and then had to grope our way back along the fence because we could hardly see. How easily one could become lost.

When I checked the folks' house I found their bathroom floor covered with water and the bathtub running over. About this time of year their sewer pipes always freeze. Used the plunger to get some water running, hauled bucketsfull outside, and mopped for an hour before most of it was cleaned up.

There's a big owl hanging around the trees by the folks' house. I wonder if it's the mate of the corpse in the tree. I picture him sitting beside the dead owl, meditating perhaps.

March 4   Low 20, high 20. Sunny, with south wind.

Al came to tow our pickup out of the drift and says we lost a premature calf at the creek several days ago.

After feeding, we spent the morning collecting from the yard all the cattle we put in the Lindsay pasture two days ago. The Ugly Cow, a proficient fence-destroyer, had broken down the gate and led them all back here — again. We left her here and took the rest back to the pasture — on foot — in the afternoon.

Walking back through the yard we saw a skunk busily heading for the barn, so I followed him cautiously while George got the gun. He managed to shoot him just outside the barn instead of inside, but his memory will be with us whenever the wind's right for some time. He was fat — he's spent the winter eating cattle cake and cat food in the barn. We've known he was there by the smell and piles of his scat left contemptuously in our path.

March 5   Low 15, high 25.

After feeding at home, we headed for Lindsays, and got stuck three times. We were worn out with digging by the time we got there, and the cows paid very little attention to us, preferring the fresh grazing uncovered by last night's wind. The tank was free of ice. That's a good winter tank because the water comes into it from the bottom by pipe from the well, and the flow is sufficient to keep it ice-free except in severe weather.

This afternoon we went to Rapid City for groceries, noting some typical signs of spring: dead skunks along the highway, hitchhiker with a backpack, a couple of Airstream trailers full of tourists, and two motorcyclists.

It had been snowing lightly off and on all day but since the sun was shining we hadn't paid much attention. By the time we finished supper in town, six inches of snow had fallen and the highway was glazed with ice. We'd driven the little car instead of the pickup, and it took George nearly an hour and a half to drive the twenty-five miles home. The blizzard howled all night, keeping us both awake at different times as we worried about the cows calving.

March 6   Low 22, high 34.

The bobtail cow had a new baby calf this morning, huddled by a corral fence; it seemed healthy. Nothing else had calves, though some of the heifers look very near. Father has assured us none of them will calve until April. Feeding was a struggle with nearly a foot of new snow drifting.

We saw geese going north, and George said, "Well, we made it through another winter."

When we checked cows this morning, one of the new calves was prancing oddly in the grass. In front of him, like an audience, sat two coyotes. We shot over their heads to discourage that kind of chumminess. Spent the day feeding, checking cows and fences.

Al called to say that another calf was born at the creek and seemed to be fine. We found another new one here at dusk. He was not up yet but the cow was licking him, so he'll be all right.

March 9   Low 19, high 45; lots of melting.

When we went to look at the cows this morning we couldn't find the calf born last night. The cow hadn't been sucked but wasn't bawling. We went to the spot where he was born but found no sign except a little trampled grass. We drove and walked all over the area. I finally got up on a little rise, saw an area of disturbed grass and snow, and found him dead and partly eaten. George pointed out his tiny hoofprints in pools of his own blood.

From the tracks it looks as if he'd been up, a coyote attacked him, and he began to run, bleeding, while the coyote ran after him, slashing and biting. The trail twisted around like a maze but there was so much blood it was easy to follow. The calf's coat wasn't bloody —as if the cow had licked him clean before he was attacked — but his stomach and hindquarters were eaten. His little face was white and clean, the hair curly, as if he was only sleeping. The coyote, as usual, had started eating in the soft tissue at the rectum, gnawed the hipbones clean and started on the guts.

This is the first time we've ever found the slightest evidence of a coyote actually killing a calf. Every morning at sunrise we've watched a pair of coyotes playing in the field below the house — pouncing on mice and tossing them in the air to catch them in their mouths. In spite of the danger to our cats we've enjoyed knowing they were here. It's as if they've betrayed a code. My father has always said coyotes won't kill a healthy calf. A number of our neighbors say they've had problems with coyotes and calves and most of them kill coyotes or allow them to be hunted. We never have allowed it.

George took his rifle when we went to look over the cows in the evening, and slipped out of the truck near the calf. I drove on home so if the coyote was in the neighborhood he'd think it was safe to come back. I watched George through the binoculars from the house, and just after dusk I saw him fire. He said one instant he was staring at the calf, and the next the coyote was simply there, tearing at it. He is sure he hit it in the shoulder, but it got away. He fired several more times to convince the coyote the place was unhealthy.

March 10   Low 30, high 48; cloudy and warm.

Our wedding anniversary. George's grandmother called at 7 a.m., preventing any in-bed celebration of the event.

After breakfast we put my horse in the trailer, hauled him to the creek, and moved the cattle home. As I counted them out at the gate I watched to see if we had any extras, and was surprised to realize I recognized something about every single cow. Father can pick out one black calf from sixty others, know which cow he's out of, which of six bulls sired him, and probably who his grandparents were. I have to have help: I remember cows with distinct markings, or a head shaped in a particular way, or sometimes the personality.

For example, Old Blue, a cow we sold last fall, was always a leader in the herd, but her calves were always slow-moving, very fat, and looked retarded. I could pick them out of the bunch a year after they were weaned.

I left the cows with new calves in the trees, since the calves could never walk all the way home. I still had a terrible time getting the rest of the cows across the creek. The grass was slick, the creek up, and the banks so icy I couldn't maneuver very well on the horse. We all kept slipping and falling.

Then George took the truck around to meet me on top of the hill since the other route is impassable with the truck. Naturally as soon as he left all the cows turned back and tried to recross the creek. I raced the horse back and forth and screamed a lot, and finally got them started. The snow wasn't deep, but of course the cattle are so heavy they didn't want to move very fast, so the trip took most of the day.

My leg was giving me hell so I sat on a rock in the sun for a few minutes at the top of the long hill, letting the cattle move up at their own pace. The sun was warm but beneath my thighs I felt centuries of cold reaching up from the earth, trying to suck the warmth from me and pull me down into the cold.

We took our usual lunch break at Josephine and Harold's, and got home about 5:00. We took the trailer back twice for the cows and calves we'd left at the creek. While we were unloading, one of the calves kicked me — in the left leg, naturally, so I lay on the couch with the heating pad on the swelling tonight. We spent our anniversary evening reading in the living room and sharing some Benedictine — about all the excitement we could handle.

It was the first time I'd been on the horse since he walked all over me. The leg is stiff and sore but I rode fairly well. It's hard to stand in the saddle when the horse is trotting, and very painful if I twist it. But I had been afraid that I'd be timid about riding, and I wasn't — possibly only because I was too busy to be nervous.

Green crescents on the hills mark where the drifts were deepest during the winter and left more moisture — grass remembers snow. Earlier, the wind shaped drifts to the curve of the grass beneath — snow remembered grass.

March 13   Low 18, high 48; it rained a little in the night.

I got up at six to drive out and check the cows. All the autumn grasses are wet from the rain, and the colors bright and clear: red, pale fawn, tan, shades for which there are no names. A silver moon hung low in the west.

Then I came in and found a cow down on her back in the corral with a dead calf half born. I got George to help me try to roll her over, but she died while we were struggling to get a grip on her. She was a fairly young cow and always a good mother. We dragged her to the boneyard in the afternoon. Father always says, "Never count the dead ones," but if we'd gotten up sooner we might have saved her.

This afternoon we drove over east to settle Ginger's fate, which has been much on our minds. We didn't even take any cake, fully expecting to find her shrunken carcass.

Instead we found her alive! We could have hung a coat on her hip bones, and she simply stood, instead of galloping up to us, but she whinnied softly.

We rushed home and got a bale of hay and a bucket of cake for her and rushed back. She ate the cake and nibbled at the hay, and then threw herself to the ground and rolled in it. I was afraid for a minute she had colic from the sudden feed, but I guess she was just happy. We left her snorting at us and eating. I feel awful for her suffering over the last three months.

March 14   Low 21, high 54; sunny, with gusty winds. The cowbirds returned.

We fed no hay today, just cake, as the cattle have plenty of grass. George made a quick trip over east with more hay for Ginger in the afternoon.

On my 6 a.m. check I found a heifer struggling to have a calf but unable to get the head out. I pulled and he slid right out, getting a mouthful of manure as his introduction to life. Come to think of it, what better preparation can he have? Everything is bound to be better from here on, and he's had a good taste of reality.

We're nearly out of frozen meat. We've been watching one yearling heifer Father said might be calfy. She's much too young to calve, and her ears and tail were frozen at birth, so she was the chosen. Today we shot, skinned and dressed her, and hung her in the yard on a tripod we made of tipi poles.

March 16   Low 21, high 56.

Three redwing blackbirds were in the trees this morning, piping a few notes, scouting for the main flock. George always says meadowlarks are the first birds back. We debate over it each year, but he had to admit he hasn't seen a meadowlark yet.

Despite the snow, it's drier and warmer than usual at this time of year, so we decided we didn't dare let the heifer hang any longer. Jim and Mavis came down to help and by evening we had two hundred pounds of meat wrapped, labeled and in the freezer. By the time we finished, we were exhausted and getting silly. The men had abandoned the meat cutting chart I'd stuck to the refrigerator, and just carved off chunks, and Mavis and I were writing labels like "teeny weeny steaks," "huge steaks," "itsy bitsy steaks."

When we finished, Mavis and I sliced the fresh liver and fried it with onions while the men scrubbed the table and floor.

March 17   Low 30, high 63.

After feeding, we brought in a new calf with its mother from the north pasture, as she was butting it every time it tried to suck. It would get up and stagger toward her, and she'd back up, take a run at it, and knock it ten feet. She did that at least five times while we were getting to her.

We put the calf in the truck, drove her in and tied her up in the barn —

both ends. Both of us got kicked once or twice before we got her stretched out and put the calf up to suck. She didn't care for it, but the ropes stayed tight. A day or two of this and she'll decide to claim him. We might have smacked her once or twice with a rope when she tried to kick the calf but I don't think that qualifies as cow abuse under the circumstances.

One of my talents is the ability to get in close to a cow and get away safely. Sometimes I'm pushing a calf up to her side to suck. She doesn't know that — she just feels threatened — but often I seem to have more success than either of the men. I always think very hard that I'm not going to hurt her, that I'm not there, and that I'm not afraid. Sometimes it's as if I'm invisible to the cow, and I've wondered if it's really true that they sense fear.

In the night the coyotes dragged off the feet of the heifer we butchered, which means they came within ten feet of the house.

March 18   Low 29, high 61.

It's so satisfying to get up at dawn, drive out to check the cows and see what has calved in the night. There's frost on the ground at first and then as the sun rises the frost melts and the grass sparkles and the calves get up and leap around to get warm. A few cowbirds were pecking around the cows today, and I noticed a single tree filled with redwing blackbirds. Their songs are unmistakable, sneering wolf whistles and raucous hoots mixed with notes of pure beauty.

The folks arrived home from their winter in Texas about dark. Father hauled the suitcases in, changed clothes, and immediately walked out in the pasture to look at the cows. Later I saw him with a shovel, loosening the earth around the little trees he planted last spring. He can't wait to get home and get busy again after his idle winter.

March 19   Low 19, high 69.

About this time of year I always begin to feel that I spend twelve hours a day feeding something. After breakfast and before we go out to do the day's work, I have to put something on for lunch because when we come back it will be after noon. Then once we're outside, it's all one big feeding spree: the yearling heifers, the yearling steers, the young bulls, the cows, the two-year-old heifers. Meanwhile we check bags to make sure the new calves are eating, too.

The cats and dog have to be fed, yowling around my legs while I'm trying, at 7 p.m. after a long hard day, to figure out what to fix for supper. The freezer is a wonderful invention but it requires planning — standing in the kitchen with a frozen steak in your hand and a starving husband and animals at your ankles, it's not much help.

Now that the weather is warming up a little my hands are starting to become calloused as I discard my gloves. I wash the slime of a birth from my hands in the bathroom, noticing how corded and hard they've become, the callouses and scars, and I think of my grandmother's hands and the work that passed through them over the years. When we arrived unexpectedly for dinner on Sunday she'd deftly catch a chicken, chop its head off, scald, pluck and fry it and serve it up with biscuits and gravy an hour after we drove in the yard.

I notice age spots on my hands too, and dark bags under my eyes in the morning. Time always seemed to be speeding past me until recently. Now that I'm past forty I feel myself caught in it as if in a river of molasses. I try to cut out all kinds of time-eating projects and really concentrate on the flavor of the time I'm using. Yesterday, driving down the entrance road, I noticed the dusty snow blowing across, and thought that I want to be that dust, haunting the places I love after I die.

March 20   Low 19, high 36, and snowing lightly all day while we fed.

After feeding this morning, we went in to have coffee with my folks and visit about their winter in Texas. They are still unpacking, slowly moving back into their house, and Mother kept diving into various suitcases and bringing out gifts for us: a leather belt for George, a colorful serape for me. They are both tanned and look good. They golfed a lot, and Mother looks stronger than she did when they left.

Father said, "We didn't do anything, really, but waste time. Those old people down there are just waiting to die." He'd be perfectly happy to spend the winter here but knows it's healthier for him to get away, and knows we need to be alone too and practice running this place. Mother said he'd been twitchy for two weeks, ready to start home.

I got back to serious writing in the afternoon and George fixed supper so I could work late. He called me upstairs just at dusk to look at a large bird with a white breast and gray, owl-like head sitting on a post near the house. I couldn't find him in the bird book.

March 21   Low 31, high 59; yesterday's snow melted.

Hawks were dancing in the wind currents over the south hill this morning, the first day of spring. The wind was hard and steady all day. A few blackbirds seemed to blow around the yard, sweeping up into the trees.

Panther calved today, a big Longhorn calf. I shudder at the potential combination of Panther's ferocity with Longhorn size. It's a heifer calf so we'll probably keep it and it will turn into a mean cow.

In the afternoon I was filled with energy for writing, and worked until midnight. George went over east and led Ginger slowly back to the pasture near the tracks, and left her with more hay. She's fattened up a lot. He said he found a tree in a gully with a huge pile of horse manure under it where she must have sheltered during the worst storms. I still can't imagine how she survived, but I'm glad. For one thing, I wasn't looking forward to explaining her death to Mike.

March 23   Low 26, high 40; foggy, rainy, cold, with a little snow mid-morning.

Redwing blackbirds are shrieking in the trees and we heard a meadowlark in the calving pasture.

We both spent much of the afternoon milking out cows with too much milk. Some are cooperative, and George can rope their heads and hold them while I slip up beside them and put in a teat valve. I'm good at putting in teat valves — a job that requires close work. I've learned to tell by the tension in the cow's back leg — the one right beside my face — exactly when the cow is going to kick at my teeth, and get out of there in time. I keep one eye on the leg and use touch to locate the swollen teat. Then the valve has to be inserted gently into the nipple. Often the teat is so sore the touch of the valve will make her kick and bawl, so I gently locate the hole, and shove the valve in fast. If I get it in the first time, I just stand back and let the milk flow. If not, the cow is mad and probably hurting and it gets a little trickier. I consider the cow trying to kick me as perfectly fair, though I may revise my opinion the day I'm too slow and one of them removes a few of my teeth.

The cats sit in a row on the steps of the barn, knowing a pail of warm milk is coming their way. One of these days we'll have a cow without enough milk, and we can put a calf on some of these cows. Lucky calf! He'll spend the summer sucking two cows and be twice as fat as his friends.

In the afternoon I transplanted some asparagus from the old bed, which is thick with grass, to the garden, and planted gladiolus and hyacinth bulbs — my annual promise to myself. Mother came out while I was working and we visited a little. She said the hole-infested pair of jeans I was wearing was disgraceful. I said I intended to mend them. She said, "Those are so far gone you'd be better off to jack up the zipper and run a new pair of jeans under it."

March 24   Low 20, high 60.

Both of us were so tired today it seemed an effort to move at all. We've traded a flu-like bug back and forth for a couple of weeks, and each day has been a struggle. Today George hurt his back pitching bales and spent the afternoon on the couch with the heating pad.

We saw a buzzard circling the calving pasture this morning — just checking.

Having Mother phone me most mornings for a visit has reminded me how much I missed her all winter. We talk about nothing much, but it's good to feel her sympathy and concern. Even though we live so close we don't get into each other's houses much. I'm muddy and tired when we finish feeding at noon, and with the gates shut she has to walk to get here. Her winter letters are always full of the daily things they do, and sometimes I read them impatiently — we have such different priorities and entertainments. Yet just when I despair of her understanding my way of life, she'll make a statement indicating she sympathizes and cares.

She did ask a little uneasily if we'd been careful to keep everything clean when we butchered. I assured her we had. She cleared her throat and changed the subject. I suppose the labels on the meat don't inspire confidence.

March 25   Low 25, high 47; the birds sing while the snow falls furiously; the air feels ominously heavy.

The pain in my ribs from pitching hay — since George can't do it — reminds me of the winter Margaret cracked several ribs coughing but kept right on working. That's average for the women around here but it astonishes me anyway.

In late afternoon, fearing a serious blizzard, we decided to get the cattle in and feed in the corral. Of course the cows all dashed through the gate, leaving the baby calves outside. Several calves immediately spooked and took off into the snow, by this time so thick the visibility was almost zero. We managed to get five back through the gate, then took the truck and went after the other three. We found them along the fence line by looking for the steam of their breath rising through the snow that covered them completely. I lifted all three of them into the front of the truck to get warm. As we drove back, one of them stood up, his head smacked me in the chin, and he peed on the floor.

March 26   Low 25, high 31; about eight inches of snow yesterday. The birds are quieter today, all sounds muffled.

We had to get Panther in to be milked today, as she wasn't accepting her calf. She got her name when we had to tie her up to pull her calf when she was two years old and she put both my father and I up on the rafters in the barn. She hasn't mellowed with age. We hazed her into the barn with no trouble, but the minute she saw the rope she began to paw and bellow. George roped her but we couldn't get her near the post.

Finally I served as the decoy, got her to charge me, and then ducked around the post so George could wrap the lariat around it. Then when we wanted to get her closer, I just stepped out so she could see me and she charged repeatedly until she was tied up. I got a rope on her hind ankle and tied it back to another post. Once the calf began to suck she quieted down, but by that time the dust was so thick in the barn we could hardly see each other. We were both so exhausted we napped after lunch.

In the afternoon I caught up on letters and mailed book orders. From my window I could see Father walking through the calving pasture as he does every afternoon, looking for cows with big bags, indicating their calves aren't sucking and may be sick. If he can't rope the sick ones he describes them to us and we try to catch them.

March 27 Low 30, high 56.

The old irrigation ditches are full of melting water today, and after feeding we took shovels and cleared mud from some of them so the water could spread out over the alfalfa fields. Maybe we'll get a better hay crop this year. Everything smelled like spring: a hint of new grass; the flowing water, burdened with manure so that it's dark as coffee; the warm breeze.

We went to a reading by some young poets in the evening, followed by some interesting discussions over coffee. One writer began asking me very direct questions about how and why I write. I finally had to say, "I don't know you well enough to answer that question." I'd never said such a thing before and it reminded me that, despite the fact that I teach, there are still some aspects of writing that are too personal to discuss with a stranger.

On the way home we ran into a brief shower of hail, unusual at night — the first hail of the season.

March 28 Low 34, high 45, with a cold north wind, winter again.

We started the morning helping a heifer calve. It was a little black calf, and once we got it pointed correctly it slid right out and was up and sucking in ten minutes.

In the afternoon we got most of the cows in from the calving pasture and sorted off the ones that won't calve for awhile. This is always a challenging job, since the corral is slick with mud and the cows with new calves feel we're threatening their babies.

A big black Angus cross, white eyes rolling, wants out badly. She nudges her calf, murmuring instructions, ducks her head, backs off, tries a rush. She slips in the mud, bellows, backs off again and comes on fast. Without thinking I jump in front of her. We splash to a stop, both of us on our knees in mud, eye to mad eye. She whirls away, unwieldy but graceful, goes to her calf and leads him off, glares back at me as if to say, "Next time! Next time!"

March 30   Low 19, high 35.   Damp fog this morning at 6 when I went out. The cows were hunched, backs toward the north. The calves were curled in the grass and melting snow. Occasionally a black eye will open as I pass but they won't move unless I come too close or move suddenly.

When I came back I found one of the heifers prolapsed, her uterus terribly swollen. We've been checking them at 10 p.m. and midnight, and Father checks them at 5 a.m. Last night we skipped the midnight check because we were so tired. I called the vet and then made a halter for the cow and held her down — bending up a front foot — while George and the vet washed the uterus and shoved it back inside. The vet sewed her up and by this afternoon she was up, although a bit shaky, and her calf was sucking.

The young black tomcat sits, fur dotted with snow, chewing on the heart of a dead calf by the barn. He has dug the snow away to get at the calf; under his paws it is bloody.

We finally got in for lunch about 1:00. I was wet, tired, cold, sweaty and covered with slime from loading sick calves in the pickup — and felt better than I have in months. There's something about the struggle when it's really life-and-death that always makes me feel more alive, as if this work I'm doing really means something. I think Gandhi once said, "Everything you do will be insignificant, but you must do it anyway."

Just at sunset a little rain fell and we saw the season's first rainbow.

March 31   Low 23, high 44.

Backwards calf to start the day. The barn is dark except for a little light slanting through the vertical bars of the gate. Outside, meadowlarks and redwing blackbirds are singing in the still-bare branches. The lariat is snug around the cow's neck, twice around a post, and I'm holding the end, braced in case she throws her head but ready to turn her loose if she begins to choke. Father has one arm inside her to his shoulder, trying to find the calf's feet. He is reaching into another universe, birth.

Meanwhile the cow pushes against him, resisting his efforts. To do it her way will kill the calf, if he's not already dead, and yet she's only trying to push him out to life. The cow's eyes are glazed and she's calm from total exhaustion. Finally we call the vet and he delivers a dead calf by Caesarean.

Late March Blizzard

Ankle deep in mud that wants
to suck us down before our time,
we plod through the corral, feeding
cattle, fighting to get heavy cows
into the barn, dragging dead calves
out to the pickup. Snow falls so thickly
it's hard to recognize familiar cows,
and each other's blurred faces.
We are tired and cranky, mud and blood
up to our knees. Our minds squeeze down to
a fire, coffee, dry clothes.

                                        A cry
raises our eyes. Two blue herons
circle. Like a Chinese painting,
their angled breasts prow
against the snow, lifting with each beat
of the mighty wings.

We sail into the falling snow,
twin graceful shapes who know mud — and more.
Our fragile feet are not stuck in clay;
we pose in a cottonwood,
then lift,
disappear into time.

april

April 1   Low 26, high 60.

For almost thirty years Father has managed to fool me with some simple joke. I continued the tradition to fool George this morning.

"Well — look at that cow. Twin calves!"

George said, "Really?" and looked.

I guess the simplest jokes work the best.

Between feeding the cows, watching for and pulling calves, checking the heifers at 10 p.m., midnight and 2 a.m., the days are wearing us down. Yet there's a quickening, almost excitement at being past the waiting and into calving, working hard to get the year's crop of calves on the ground and healthy.

Then just as your bones and sinew adjust to the promise of spring, letting go of winter's tension, you'll see a calf lying too still and know he has scours. A new tension takes over — can you get enough pills into him, enough mother's milk, work hard enough to save him? One spring dead calves were piled at the north edge of the calving pasture like dark snowdrifts. We checked cows for a month with the sweet smell of rotting flesh in our nostrils.

If we can get a couple of pills down them early in the illness they usually survive. But it's easy to miss a sick one while we're feeding, so Father and I take a slow daily walk through the herd. He ropes a sick calf and my job is to jump on it, hold it down, and shove pills down its throat. Naturally this operation covers me with evil-smelling slime.

In early evening we're having tea in the living room with the windows open, reading and not talking after a day spent together feeding, pulling and pilling calves. An April evening in the country is never silent. Killdeer emit shrill questioning notes along the dam below the house. Blackbirds trill, or gather in the trees around the corrals to hoot at the humans working in the mud. Meadowlarks warble from every fence post. Cows call their calves, gathering them close to the herd before dark.

April 2   Low 42, high 74.

After the feeding and pilling today I cranked up the garden tiller and made a few rounds. My hands are blistered and my back sore but a third of the garden is black and smooth tonight, covered with blackbirds hunting worms.

Last night around midnight George and I pulled a calf and walked back to the house under the stars, happy to have saved one. Tonight, around the same time, we had to call the veterinarian, and still lost one. I pumped his little chest and felt a strong heartbeat, but his lungs were full of fluid and he didn't shake his head to clear his nostrils as a vigorous calf will. George grabbed him by the ankles and held him up to try to drain the fluid. When he put him back down, the calf gasped a few times and kicked. George exclaimed, but the vet and I said simultaneously, "It's the wrong kind of kick."

We have about forty-five calves in the pasture now. It's wonderful on a warm day to see them playing, butting heads, switching their tails as they suck. They are such frank and open creatures. If they're curious they simply march up and take a look at you from big brown eyes. As long as you hold still, they'll sniff you, taste your fingers with rough pink tongues, and generally act unafraid. Only later will they begin to scamper away from humans, and when they're branded they learn real fear. The ones we keep sometimes become tame again while being fed before their first calves, but most stay wild.

April 3   Low 24, high 42.

Woke up to about six inches of heavy wet snow, so we were soaked before we were half finished feeding. We came back inside, changed clothes, and then George read while I put a roast on for dinner and went to the basement to work on poems, ignoring the dust everywhere, the muddy human, dog and cat footprints crossing the dining room. The house smells of wet wool, with accents of manure and calf scours. As we read we absently pick hay out of our hair and ears. We shower pretty frequently because sweat in our longjohns tends to get pretty rank, but we smell of cow all the time anyway. None of this is complaining; it's just calving season.

Around here, this time of year, we have an excuse for any social event we want to miss or any amount of mess if unexpected visitors show up: "Well, it's calving season, you know." Perfect housekeepers who would normally condemn you to the flames for dust on the books understand, and withhold judgment.

Outside, the snow seemed to muffle all sound. The birds that were so noisy yesterday seemed to be invisible today, with only an occasional squawk from the redwing blackbirds to remind us it is spring.

April 4   Low 27, high 53; melting.

Two sparrow hawks visited us this morning. One circled nervously while the other landed on the porch railing, turning his head from side to side to peer at us.

One develops what might be called a sixth sense, or perhaps more correctly a heightened awareness, when working with cattle, and after a few years can recognize danger signals in ways that are almost subconscious. A stranger wouldn't understand what made us drive over to look at a particular cow today, and perhaps we couldn't explain it. She was having a calf backwards. Once we got close we saw the bottom of the tiny hoofs pointed at the sky. Only rarely does a cow successfully calve this way without help, so we got her in, pulled the calf, and saved them both.

Any cow alone in the pasture in spring is probably calving. At any other time, she may be sick, because cows are social creatures and generally stay together.

The curse and the attraction of ranching is that it is never routine even though the work sometimes seems repetitive. Cows, weather and nature can surprise anyone. No matter how carefully you plan your day, you can't count on it progressing as your schedule indicated it would.

Just as I turned off the lights to go to bed last night I saw the green flash of a meteor. I'd had several ideas for poems during the day but was simply too tired to care. I'll accept the meteor as a sign that I'll get to them sometime.

April 5   Low 40, high 82; a record for so early in the season.

George's back has been hurting and he's been walking with one shoulder higher than the other so he went to the doctor for X-rays while I stocked up on groceries today. I've depleted a lot of my emergency supplies over the winter, and it's too soon to expect that we might escape another bad storm that would keep us away from town for a week or so. I like to be as prepared as I can; there will be enough ugly surprises.

I love going out at 10:30 p.m. to check the heifers. Even when it's completely dark I leave the flashlight off as long as I can and try to sense the trail and the fences. It's best when the coyotes are howling — a cascade of sound, the wailing of the adults mixing with the juvenile yips of pups. When the night is silent — only the breathing of the wind and a questioning note from a bird — the coyotes always seem very near, almost beside me. I've never been afraid of them, although we've heard of some strange instances lately of them attacking pets on people's doorsteps.

In the distance the big trucks race past on the highway, building up speed for the hill. They glow with ranks of light but seem distant, like ships far from shore. Even the aggressive roar of their engines seems small in the great bowl of night.

Then I'm among the heifers. They lie quietly, chewing their cud and looking unafraid at the pool of light. Some have their calves nestled close on the lee side; others are still waiting to calve.

We feed them at night on the theory that a cow can only do one thing at once. I've heard the pressure of the full belly prevents calving. Anyway, most of our heifers' calves are born early in the morning or during the day.

Then I turn out the light and walk toward the house, thinking of Wendell Berry's poem:

> To go in the dark with a light is to know the light.
> To know the dark, go dark. Go without sight,
> and find that the dark, too, blooms and sings,
> and is traveled by dark feet and dark wings.

Finally I see the window of gold and walk on, listening to the tall grass swish against my legs, hearing a questioning cheep from a killdeer down by the water.

April 6   Low 48, high 70.

Three cows were licking new calves or having an afterbirth breakfast when I checked the bunch this morning.

This afternoon we branded and dehorned eight calves born late in summer, after we had branded the others. They weigh four hundred to six hundred pounds and really rattle the calf table if we can stuff them in it. The horns are several inches long and must be sawed off, a process that makes George grit his teeth. Once the veins are severed, blood shoots out in a steady stream, covering my glasses and sizzling between my lips while I frantically try to get bloodstop powder worked into the wound with my fingers. When we're finished we look like slaughterhouse workers. Then we castrate them, with pincers rather than by cutting them, to cut down on the risk of infection.

Castrating no longer bothers me — which probably makes me a castrating female.

April 7   Low 38, high 78. Foggy at sunrise; the calves were cuddled against their mothers' sides, waiting for sun.

This morning as we struggled to pull a too-large calf from a heifer I was nearly in tears because she kept bellowing in pain. Usually they are silent, just straining to birth the calf, but she literally screamed as the head and shoulders passed. Usually the calf will slide out easily from that point, but the hips caught, and we had to turn him a little before cranking him out, and the cow screamed again. The calf was a crossbreed. Somehow the heifer managed to get impregnated by a bull other than the one we put her with. After we wiped the calf off he raised his head and was ready to go but we had to help the heifer to stand up. One back leg kept collapsing under her, so we held her on her feet, swaying in time to her breathing, until she nosed the calf and began to lick him. Tonight she's fine, though exhausted, and her calf is sucking.

One of the bulls we raised last year has turned out to be the ugliest bovine we've ever seen. He was a beautiful calf, perfectly formed, so we didn't castrate him, thinking to gain an extra bull at no cost. He stayed fat all through the winter, but now he's a pathetic sight. His head and flanks haven't grown at all but his belly has ballooned. I suggested we butcher him but Father thinks we ought to keep him through the summer in case one of the other bulls is hurt. Right now we're keeping him in the corral in order to check on the cows we'd like to sell. If he mounts them, they're in heat, and would calve late. We keep those separate, as we may decide to sell them.

In the afternoon we got in all the steers and gave them shots of vitamin A and E to prevent waterbelly, and treated all the red ones for lice. Father says the black ones don't get lice, and he seems to be right.

Doctor called; George has a fractured vertebra in his back, done a long time ago, probably when Sage fell with him over two years ago. It will simply continue to be painful when he lifts anything too heavy. The only cure is to take a break from lifting, which means I'll have to lift things, which will hurt my back . . .

In the evening when we were checking cows we saw a flock of huge birds circling the trees by the folks' house. We drove closer, and realized as they perched in the trees that we were looking at something utterly astonishing: fifteen turkey vultures. They stayed in the trees for a few moments, jostling, then soared to new positions. What kind of omen is fifteen vultures hovering over your house?

Vultures are the most graceful of birds in the air, seeming never to flap their wings. I love to spot one spiraling across the sky. The sight of several of them perched on the shrunken body of a calf, dusty wings hunched, beaks bloody, is chilling — but they keep the prairie clean. My uncle George often mutters that the animal-rights folks will make us bury dead cattle next. He may be right. I hope not, because without carcasses vultures would not be here. Without vultures and the whitened bones they leave behind, the prairie would have lost something important but hard to put into words.

April 8 Low 40, high 65.

We finally stopped feeding hay to everything but the cows that are calving, at least for now — just gave everything some cake to inspire them to graze.

Like children, calves grow confident quickly. A few days after birth they begin to play, and you may see a calf running happily across the prairie pursued by a bellowing cow, her bag swinging ridiculously as she tries to catch up.

At first a calf will bawl plaintively if he's left alone, as when the cow races off to the feed truck. If he's safe she ignores him. The same calf will lie quietly sleeping when he's been left with a babysitting cow. But if you want excitement, grab a baby calf in the middle of a calving pasture. He'll bawl, and every cow within earshot will gallop toward you bellowing madly, ready to protect him. That's one of the things I like about cows. Their reputation is placid and non-carnivorous but they'll fight anything to protect their calves.

In the afternoon we moved some yearling steers across the highway so we won't have to feed them anymore. This is always tricky. I lead them into the dark underpass, calling and rattling a bucket of cake. When I'm silent, their breathing and hoofbeats echo and are magnified. George follows, to keep them moving and give them no time to notice the trucks roaring over their heads.

This time one got nervous, jumped through the fence, and raced down the barrow pit beside the highway, heading back toward home. I ran after him and as soon as he got away from the other steers he got confused. He looked around but he couldn't see them from the barrow pit, so he trotted up and stood in the middle of the highway, bawling. I could hear a couple of trucks rumbling up the hill behind us and was running as hard as I could to try to get him off the highway when I saw Bill and Margaret's little blue car racing down their road. They'd seen us from their windows and came to help.

Bill jumped out and herded the steer back into the barrow pit, and Margaret got alongside him with the car and honked the horn whenever he tried to get back up on the highway, and we ran him back to the gate. George got there ahead of us, got it open and hazed the other steers out of the way, and the steer dashed inside. Then we all leaned against the car to catch our breath. That's true neighborliness — they could have sat in their living room giggling and watched us run up and down the highway. Every time we have to take yearlings across the highway, we hope not to have trouble, but it can come in a dozen ways. A passing car honking at the wrong time can send the whole bunch through the fence and onto the highway. If anyone hits them, of course we'd be liable — even though if the cars would slow down, the cattle would get out of the way.

The long grass on the hillsides is still brown, rippling like hundreds of tawny animals running. Underneath, it is getting green. The short grass in the fields is almost completely green, and when the cows snap it off the smell of spring comes faintly to our noses. Clouds of blackbirds are hanging around the trees by the corrals, screeching and singing and generally having a great time.

April 9   Low 21, high 38. A cold bleak dawn, with a sky white as snow, no rosy hue. Fierce sleety snow squalls whirled around us all day. Or is my mood affected by the fact that this was once a wedding anniversary for me?

A calf was born dead this morning after a long struggle that started at 6 a.m. The cow was old and should have been perfectly capable of calving by herself, but the calf was a huge Longhorn cross courtesy of the neighbor's bull, and she'd started calving with only one front foot and the head out. The calf's tongue was already black when we got the cow in, but we struggled until we got the second foot out and pulled him. He didn't even gasp, so we dragged him outside, skinned him, and transplanted a heifer's calf. The heifer will bawl for a few days but then she'll dry up and have a chance to grow before her next calf.

Father conveys important information in such casual ways. "That's why it's handy to have the two-year-old heifers calve at the same time as the older cows; you have cows to put their calves on. People never used to calve out two-year-olds, until they started wanting to make more money."

I've suggested letting the two-year-olds stay dry because so often we have trouble calving them, but he says they still have trouble calving as three-year-olds. And then we'd have the problem of keeping the bulls away from them an extra year — which is a little like keeping teenage girls away from teenage boys.

April 10   Low 38, high 56.
This morning I found a cow with her back legs partly paralyzed from having an especially large calf. She couldn't get up, so I "tailed her up." This involves pulling on her tail to give her enough balance to get her back legs up. Then you're supposed to let go and let her stand until the feeling comes back.

Someone had forgotten to tell this cow the rules. The minute I got her up she started lurching across the prairie, staggering from side to side with me hanging on. Every time I let go she'd fall in a heap, legs twisted. The third time, I just stayed with her, and she played Crack the Human until I was so winded I coudn't hold on any longer.

Then I followed her and hazed her back toward the calf until she scented it and began to murmur and lick. I know animal experts say mothering behavior is strictly instinct, but it's hard not to believe in real bovine affection when a cow is "talking" to a calf, and the calf raises its head and tries to get up to find the teat.

April 11   Low 45, high 72, with calves stretching luxuriously in the sun.
We fed quickly today, since everything seemed comfortable, and George went to Lawrence's to hunt turkeys. He took the black powder rifle — and a more modern one, for insurance.

The cows are slipping into their calving patterns. One or two cows "babysit" the new calves close to the corrals while the others spread out over the pasture to graze. The north end of the pasture is the private calving area. The cow lies quietly, chewing her cud throughout the contractions, occasionally getting up and looking behind her as if wondering why the calf isn't born yet. Once it is, the cow efficiently eats the afterbirth, licks the calf clean, and gets it fed before she lies down to rest. I admire the process, the independence of it, the sense of rightness. And yet, reflecting on the struggles we've had over the last few days, I can't help noticing that Mother Nature has needed a lot of help.

April 13   Low 48, high 76. Sunny, with clouds in the west and a chill wind. George called me outside after breakfast to see thirteen deer nibbling the new shoots in the alfalfa field, led by a big buck who looked ghostly with the light of the rising sun behind him.
We pulled a heifer's calf around 2 a.m. and the heifer got right to her feet but the calf had a terrible time. George shook him upside down several times to drain fluid from his lungs, until George was about to collapse. Then I knelt by him for a long time, pumping his chest and rubbing the sack over him. Finally he gave a kind of gasp, shook his head and slung snot all over me, raised his head and bawled weakly. The cow knocked me aside and started licking him, and we staggered up the hill to bed.

We saw a three-legged coyote hopping and pouncing on mice in the pasture below the house at dusk. It must be the one George shot; perhaps he's given up beef for his health. I'm glad he's alive, for reasons I'd rather not have to explain to anyone else.

April 15   Low 46, high 73.
We have about seventy-five calves but have had none for two days, as if the cows are on strike or waiting for a blizzard. We're still feeding hay to the calving cows, loading it on the hayrack with the tractor, then hauling the whole works to the calving pasture and pitching it off. The cows come running, leaving the calves to totter along behind, bawling plaintively.

I get real satisfaction from watching cows eat. They enjoy it so much, wrapping their long tongues around a few stems of green grass, snapping it off and rolling their eyes as they work it back into their teeth. Then after they've grazed awhile, they lie down, look philosophical, and belch, bringing up a cud which they chew with an expression like that of a gourmand savoring a special dish.

Some of the two-year-olds are so tame I can walk among them, patting their heads, scratching their ears, letting them eat cake from my hand. Last year I spent days coaxing one with a heart-shaped white spot on her red forehead to eat; we call her Sweetheart.

George thinks I'm silly to enjoy the cows as much as I do, pointing out they are really rather stupid beasts, but I disagree. They have instincts, and in some cases seem to plot against us. On warm days like this you can almost see them thinking, "I don't think she shut the gate to the stackyard very tight. I'll get it down and then we'll all go in there and pretty soon all the humans will come rushing out cursing and shouting and we won't be bored."

This afternoon I planted garlic, taking pleasure in sliding the papery cover off the bulbs and watching it blow away in the wind. I also put in a few radishes, carrots, lettuce and parsnips and started some pixie tomatoes and marigolds inside.

April 17   Low 43, high 72. Red sky at dawn, making the new green grass glow through the brown cover on the hillsides. I helped George feed. For some reason, the hay was tangled together and terribly hard to tear apart. I finally just shoved big chunks off.

In the afternoon, pulling a heifer's calf, we weren't able to get the feet out far enough for a good grip and pulled the hoofs off at the ankles. It happened so quickly. One minute we were pulling gently, trying to get the legs a little farther out so we could slip the chains up, and the next instant the cow lurched and fell on her side, George fell back, and the little hoofs dropped into the straw. In a few minutes we were able to get a better grip and the calf was born alive, so perhaps he can survive on his poor stumps.

Awful sinus headache all day, perhaps from the dust which hung over the hills like smoke, or the constant dry wind. Everyone is already talking about a hot dry summer. Reminding myself that it's not too late for moisture yet, I planted chives in the garden, and some wild flower seed I collected last fall.

April 18   Low 46, high 75.
George was out at 2 a.m. with a heifer, then again at 3. I got up, made coffee, and we played gin rummy to stay awake until we checked her at 4. She was having too much trouble, and we couldn't get the calf, so we called the vet. He arrived at 5 and did a Caesarean, and gave the calf some colostrum milk before going in to breakfast. I went to Wall to teach a high school class, and when I returned the calf was dead. Father said sometimes that first milk is almost too rich. I think we might have gotten it in his lungs instead of his stomach, even though the vet helped us put the tube down.

George planted some plum bushes and several juniper trees north of the house and then came in to lie down — he got a piece of hay in his eye while feeding in the wind. I washed it and it seemed to improve.

April 19   Low 34, high 68.
George woke at 3 a.m. with a lot of pain in his eye, so I bathed it, and we had breakfast, checked the heifers, and then went to the emergency room at 7. The cornea is scratched but it should heal with an eye patch and some antibiotics.

As we were driving to town, windows wide open, a meadowlark sang suddenly on a post by the road. George said, "Thank you!"

Hitchhiking season has really begun. We saw a guy out on the highway with an army duffle, a smile, and a sign reading "Spokane."

Our new Charolais bull is causing us some trouble with calving — the calves are too large for some of our cows. We've had to pull half a dozen already — unusual with full-grown cows — but it became worse today. The cow was a small one and we got the calf's head stuck in the birth channel, and couldn't pull it any farther. By that time the calf was dead, so we called the vet. He worked a flexible saw inside, cut off the calf's head, and then we were able to pull it as far as the hips, where it stuck again. He cut off the body, then worked his saw inside and cut the calf's pelvis in half, and we pulled the haunches one at a time — each of them nearly as large as a normal calf. The cow survived but hadn't been able to get up by evening; her back legs are paralyzed.

Two blue herons flew over the house right at dusk and landed on the big south hill, where they sat peering around for awhile, perhaps resting, before flying on over the hill. The last heifer calved at just about the time the herons flew over. I was watching both events with the binoculars from the house. The calf without hoofs died; I'm glad. He was so brave trying to walk.

April 20   Low 40, high 69. A black crow circles the ranch cawing at dawn. Still cold and windy, with dampness in the air but a lot of dust blowing because it's so dry. Ten inches of snow at Lusk, I-80 blocked west of Cheyenne, and all roads south of Cheyenne to Denver blocked by snow. We could use the moisture but it's good not to be fighting a storm with all these baby calves. Often the plums are blooming by this time of year, but not now.

George's vision is not much better, though he looks quite dashing with his eyepatch, so this morning we went back to the doctor for antibiotics. Father fed the cattle while we were gone. We spent the afternoon tying up a cow for the orphan calf to suck out, and walking through all three bunches of cows with calves, looking for scours. We caught several and gave them pills.

You can always tell a sick calf. He just lies there, belly bloated, eyes dull, running with diarrhea — until George ropes him. Then he's up and bellowing, running and throwing himself against the rope, until I can grab a hind leg and throw him. By that time every cow in the pasture is gathered around us, bawling, snorting, and swinging their heads at us. We watch them over each other's shoulders while I stuff scours pills down the calf's throat. Today one kicked loose from both of us. As he raced away, George said between gasps, "Let's wait until he gets a little sicker."

We lost another big Charolais calf today. It had strangled by the time we could get the cow in, and we had to cut it up ourselves, something I'd like to avoid ever having to do again. It's not the rather clean, necessary job of butchering, but more like torture. We pulled two others that lived, but the cows look shocked by what they have produced, and the calves don't get up with the vigor we've come to expect from crossbred calves.

April 21   Low 29, high 40; cold and windy.

My aunt Jo called at 6 a.m. but I thought it was 7 so I was nice and tried to sound like I was already up. Fed cows with George all morning.

The orphan calf took most of the black whiteface cow's milk so this evening we got in another cow that had two hindquarters of her bag unsucked. We thought we might have to use teat valves in them to open them up, since her calf hadn't touched them, but the orphan sucked them dry and would have been glad to have more. He's doing pretty well right now since some of the newer calves can't yet take all of their mothers' milk.

In the afternoon, with the wind still blowing, we planted more plum, buffaloberry and chokecherry bushes in two rows on the north side of the house. Some of the cedar and plum we planted there last year have died. I persuaded George to put two burr oak on the southwest side, below the house. He's afraid they'll grow too tall and block the view, but I said "not in our lifetime." The beeches we brought from Michigan last summer look dead, from cold or drought. The cottonwood buds are splitting, there are more blooms than leaves on the currant bush beside the folks' back door, and the willows are a bright orange.

Whenever we plant a tree near the house we know there's a good chance we'll hit limestone, since chunks of it sit on the surface at several spots. Our basement floor is poured on an almost-level slab of limestone we hit at just the right place, and limestone forms part of the foundations — handy for building, but not so good when we're trying to plant something. Today George used the pick to hack through a spot where we really wanted a cedar tree.

Tonight I rode back from feeding on the wagon, lying back on the hay and looking up at the pale blue sky. It didn't seem nearly so comfortable as it did when I was a child. The trees are full of redwing blackbirds. I think they come back this early just to play in the trees and fly around and screech, waiting for the grass to get high enough to hang nests on in June.

April 22, Easter Sunday   Low 38, high 63; a little rain in the morning.
We were up at 7 a.m. to feed and give pills to some sick calves. Father fed most of the other cows. Went to church — our yearly gift to my mother — and then drove to Newell to Aunt Hazel's for Easter dinner. Since she's been ill, we all brought various contributions. Her daughter Pat provided a home-cured ham and a roast turkey.

Every car that passed us seemed to have a back seat full of children facing the ultimate in kid boredom: The Family Gathering. The women talk about who had babies and who died. The men talk about wetter or drier years and worse winters. The kids slump, whine, eat, stare, whine, beg for television, wander outside, eat, slump and whine some more.

After dinner the kids rode the horses at breakneck speed through the yard, and the rest of us wandered out by twos and threes, leaned on the fences by the sheep pens and tried to comment intelligently on the lamb crop. Lambing is about over and most of the sheep have been sheared and turned out to pasture. It is always amazing to me that a scrawny, ugly, insignificant, death-prone beast like a sheep can often raise twins, while a cow rarely can.

April 23   Low 40, high 65.
The dog woke us at 5 a.m. but we let him out and slept until 7. After feeding we took thirty-seven yearling heifers down to the dike pasture. We had to separate them from twelve dry cows at one of the gates and since my riding boots are in town being fixed we did it on foot. Several of them pretended to be afraid of the gate, so it took time and patience. Once we'd gotten them through they followed the pickup until they got the scent of the dead cow at the boneyard, and then they all ran directly to her and stood around bellowing and roaring. I always wonder if this behavior is a kind of mourning. The coyotes had thoroughly stripped the carcass of the cow that died in January but they're letting the yearling that died earlier ripen.

When we got the calves to the dike pasture Sage came galloping up and scattered the whole bunch right at the gate. I found a piece of rope and tied him up, and we managed to get them back into the pasture.

Later we followed a cow out to the pasture to try to find out if she'd calved. Her bag looked swollen, and her belly slimmer than it should, but she wandered all over the pasture, grazing and occasionally looking over her shoulder, without leading us to a calf. So as not to waste the walk, we brought in a cow and calf that seemed to need a scours pill. The cow turned wild when we got her in and it took a lot of running and yelling and a certain amount of cussing to get her in the corral.

When I was fourteen, even though I did a man's work driving the tractor, mowing and raking, Father wouldn't even let the hired men cuss when I was around. I never uttered a swear word in his presence until I was thirty-five and still don't do it much — an occasional "That damn cow is beating on her calf again" slips out. He even reprimanded George on a couple of occasions, which didn't help the natural tension between father and son-in-law. As George says, "He doesn't want you to say 'shit' if you're covered with it."

Father tuned up the little tractor this afternoon and plowed furrows for the trees he wants to plant on the north side of the hayfield.

A ferocious wind crashed in on us about 5:30 p.m. from the southwest, with black rolling clouds that made us think of tornadoes. We took shelter in the basement, feeling a little foolish. When we came out we found a section of plank corral fence down, the hayrack tipped over, and a little building that used to be an outhouse tipped over and smashed. Lots of tree limbs are down too; we'll have a lot of extra work to do cleaning up.

While we fed the heifers, the calf we call Lurch because of his clumsiness came up, butted me playfully, and kept it up until I scratched his ears. Then he stood beside me, head lowered, rolling his eyes and occasionally licking my pantleg. Whenever I stopped scratching, he butted me again.

April 24   Low 43, high 78.

Despite last winter's snow, it's dry now, the ground beginning to crack in the pastures. The temperatures have been abnormally high so the cows are all shedding — which could be bad if we have another storm. But it helps in another way — the dry cows shed first, and as soon as they fatten up, some of them may be on the way to the sale ring.

George saw the first burrowing owl of the season and I saw the first butterfly. George says the calves lying in the grass of the pasture look like daisies blooming.

As a gesture to spring housecleaning — which I haven't time for — I gathered up some of the old dried afterbirths that have collected in the barn and around the corrals and hauled them out to the pasture. The cows usually eat them, but some seem to be uninterested or squeamish. They eventually dry to paper-thin but they still smell foul, and our dog loves to drag them to the house and roll in them. If we don't clean them up, sooner or later one of us will fall down in a rotting one when we're working.

It doesn't bother me to see a cow eating afterbirth because it's quite clean and fresh. But when the cow doesn't clean, when the afterbirth just hangs there, rotting and getting covered with manure, that's disgusting. Eventually it falls away — you just pray you don't have to milk her first. A month on a ranch during calving season would probably prevent a lot of teenage pregnancies.

But it's more than just birth. A month on a ranch, especially in spring, exposes one to every conceivable aspect of life and most of the moral dilemmas. We're very aware of the pain the cattle suffer and we try to minimize it as much as possible. One could say this is simply because the cattle are more valuable if they are healthy, but that's not all of it. All of us talk encouragingly to a heifer when we are pulling her calf. The talk isn't practical because even the sound of our voices is not necessarily calming to her. It is simply a kind of communication, a desire to let her know that we'll stop hurting her as soon as we can. I don't feel any sillier communicating with a cow than I do talking to the average legislator.

As for dilemmas: is it kinder to let a calf without hoofs try to survive? Can we help a cow enough with a difficult birth or should we call the vet at once? If we call him too often, the bills will be worth more than the calf crop. In fact, the vet bill for saving a single calf is usually more than the calf will sell for at the end of the year. If the calf dies anyway it's an even greater loss.

April 25   Low 46, high 79.
Watched a huge coyote cross the pasture north of the house while I was
making coffee this a.m.; maybe he's a coydog. After feeding, I went to town
for groceries in the afternoon. It seemed strange to see people walking
around in light shirts without jackets. We're still dressing as if it were winter,
though we have cautiously begun to leave our long underwear off. I felt
clumsy and awkward, with my callouses and my windburned face, slinging
groceries into the back of the mud-covered pickup between feed sacks and
blocks of salt.

The minute I got back we had another calf to pull from a cow, another big
Charolais. At least we didn't have to cut this one up. Father said with a wry
smile, "You have to expect a few problems when you crossbreed." But he's
promised to put only the large cows with that bull this summer.

Lurch comes to get his ears scratched every night when we feed the heifers
now, butting me to get my attention, and again if I stop scratching. It's funny
now, but it won't be when he weighs five hundred pounds.

April 26   Low 45, high 81.
We were awakened by a knock on the door right at dawn, a man wanting
to use the telephone. George let him in, then stayed in the dining room. I was
lying in bed and suddenly heard the man say, "My car broke down. I'm south
of Rapid City someplace. Hell, I'm going to turn myself in. They're going to
catch me anyway."

I got the .357 and stood just out of his sight, where George could see me.
But when he finished his call he thanked us politely and walked back to his
car, and later we saw it was gone.

Pulled two more Charolais calves today — both are alive, though hardly
lively. They just lie there, awkwardly trying to raise their heads. We're used
to Angus cross calves that leap up three minutes after birth and start hunting
for milk.

We felt as if we were getting to the end of calving when we checked the
pasture today — only a couple dozen cows left. The barn swallows are back,
plum bushes blooming, lilacs just starting, and our hillside is covered with
yellow phlox and daisies.

Cold and clear when I walked to the barn to check on a cow tonight, with
a huge ring around the moon.

*April 27   Low 10, high 28. Woke at sunrise because the light from the win-
dows was so cold and blue. It was snowing hard, with six inches already on
the ground, and wind blowing. The weather report last night had mentioned*

possible light snow for tomorrow but no warning of what is already a
blizzard. It rained during the night before it turned to snow, and the ground
is soaked, so that already it was difficult to move the trucks.

It took us two hours to dig out the door of the barn so we could get the
3/4 ton truck out. We dug into the emergency rations of hay beside the corral
and managed to get the truck into the corral to feed bales to the cows that had
come in. Then we drove to the calving pasture and alternated walking and
driving, searching for calves bedded down and snowed under. We didn't find
any calves, but at least one cow in the corral seems to be alone. By noon we
had everything fed, and the snow turned to rain. The wind was blowing so
strongly the rain was horizontal. We spent the afternoon out in it, chuckling
bitterly at the radio announcers saying, "What a wonderful day for everyone
to stay inside by the fire."

Before we could get our clothes off and get warm we had to bring in
wood; we'd assumed spring was here and let the woodbox stand empty. The
woodpile is almost gone, only about a half cord left. We had plenty for a
normal winter, but we've had snow on the ground for the better part of six
months now. The traditional January thaw cleared most of it, and the first
part of April, but this is starting to get old — it's like having three winters a
year.

After supper the visibility was only a few feet, so we both went out and
felt our way along the fenceline to the corrals to check on the cows due to
calve. The wind was so strong it seemed to blow the air out of our lungs,
making it impossible to draw a breath. By the time we got back we were both
worn out and soaked with wet snow. George looked pale, and finally
admitted his heart had been pounding in a way that frightened him.

Whenever George pulls a calf, he collapses on the floor. When a cow does
that, we kick her, shocking her into getting up before her legs get paralyzed.
Father said yesterday, "I don't know whether to kick the cow, or kick George."

Our neighbor Bill took Bonnie, still on crutches from the accident in
November, to school today. On the way back they got stuck in the driveway,
only a half mile from their house, and where we would have been able to see
them from ours if the visibility was normal. She couldn't have walked; the
wind and snow were so thick it would have been a risk for a healthy person.
Bill dug at the pickup for two hours, making a little headway each time, but
he was almost exhausted. He finally turned on his lights, hoping his brother-
in-law Alan, who lives farther up that road, would see. They came to help
just as he finally got the truck free. We were doing chores about that time
but couldn't see even that short distance — less than a mile. They both might

have died right there.

April 28   Low zero, high 22.
Highway 79 is blocked, as well as the interstate and most other highways in the area. The governor has declared South Dakota closed, and ordered the Highway Patrol to arrest anyone who drives on the Interstate — a good idea, I think. Snow is still blowing and piling up.

By afternoon the cows could hardly move in the corrals, belly deep in mud and snow, so we drove them into the larger corral where there's some drainage. Some of the calves were literally stuck in the mud, and we had to wade in, almost stuck ourselves, and drag them out.

One old cow kept falling down so we decided to put her in the shed where she would have more shelter. Step by step we pushed her that way, but just in front of the shed was a horrible morass of deep muck and manure, and when she stepped into it she fell forward, her legs folded under her, her head and neck stretched out. We grabbed her tail as she fell and managed to get her rear end in the air, and there she stayed, swaying a little. Her frantic calf was still trying to suck, sticking his head down into the mud, trying to tongue up a teat. She was moaning a little. Father thought we might be able to winch her into the shed, and he went for the winch while George and I tried to lift her to her feet.

Suddenly she fell over on my leg. I kept trying to work my foot out from under her, but it was against rock underneath, and the muck was up to my knees. Then she started to bawl — not a normal cow bellow, or an angry bawl, but an awful low moaning with overtones of imminent death. We lifted her another couple of steps and she went down again with her forequarters on solid ground. Father had the winch by then and I tied a rope in a bowline around her neck and hooked the winch to it, and we managed to winch her forward a few feet. Father said, "I just wouldn't feel right if we left her in that muck to die, even though I know she's going to die anyway."

Finally we got a steel fence panel and wired it across the front of the shed so she couldn't roll out in the night, gave her some hay, and put her calf with her. When we left her she had her head up, so there's hope for the old girl yet.

Spent the afternoon putting out bales in the most sheltered places we could find, but the wind blew some of them away before the cows could grab them. No one who has not lived through a plains blizzard could really imagine this. The snow sweeps off drifts shoulder high and the icy crystals sting and cut your face. Even ordinary jobs are twice as hard. The wire is frozen to the bales. Everything is so slick with water or ice that you can't grasp a pitchfork without your hands slipping. You take a step and your foot hits the ice crust, then crashes down into the softer snow underneath, so that after a few steps your calves ache with the strain.

Walking in the corral mud requires a sort of waddle to keep your mud-caked feet far enough apart so you won't trip over them. Ordinarily, we walk several miles a day just back and forth from the house, opening gates, check-ing on cows — but the snow makes regular roads impassable, so we walk even farther, and try to avoid driving into drifts we might not be able to get out of.

Our house is cut off completely by shoulder high drifts so we walk back and forth to all the chores. The sky is cloudy but the glare is terrific, and even though we wore sunglasses our eyes are swollen and burning tonight.

The electricity went off at 3 p.m., having lasted longer than we thought it would. We already had the bathtub filled with water to flush the toilet, water drawn in jars to drink, and the kerosene lamps out. When I called the Co-op they said a hundred poles had been knocked down by the storm, but to our surprise the electricity came back on about 8 p.m.

By lamplight I looked at a catalog with a picture of the latest thing in phones: one made in the shape of gigantic red lips.

The trees in the folks' yard are filled with all kinds of birds — flickers, finches, meadowlarks, robins, bluebirds — all taking shelter from the storm. We even saw a sparrow hawk. They are all nervous, since most of them never come this close to the house. Where Father has shoveled the walk or one of the trucks has dug down to the gravel spinning its tires, the birds gather so thick they hide the ground, frantically picking at gravel. We have no grain to feed them but they flew right down among the cows when we started throwing out hay, collecting the seeds. I wish we could do more.

When I went to the bale stack to start throwing bales into the truck, a dozen meadowlarks flew, one by one, out of a tiny space between two bales. I hope I didn't frighten them so much they won't come back.

We've been reading the papers closely, wondering about the man who came to our door, but have seen no mention of capture or an escaped convict turning himself in.

April 29   Low 20, high 32.

George checked on the old sick cow around midnight and she was still alive, but this morning she's stretched out dead. She'll have to stay right there for awhile, until the corral dries out enough to get a tractor in to hook onto her. The snow has stopped but the wind continues, although the snow is so heavy that it can't blow much. The drifts are already higher than our heads in some places, and the van and our car are completely buried. The temperature continues relatively warm, but this is still a killer storm. The wet snow will chill the cattle, and the deep mud and snow exhaust them.

Father says the drifts aren't as high as they were in the famous Blizzard of '49 when the one in front of the house completely covered both high board fences in the corral. "I couldn't put a cow in that corral for sixty days."

We are wearing longjohns, wool pants and sweaters, and heavy coats, and after a few minutes of slogging through the snow we are soaked with perspiration. Then the wind cuts through and chills us. We try to move slowly to minimize the sweating, and get behind some windbreak whenever we can. We've learned from experience that wool clothes are best because even when they're wet, they're warm, and we've been soaked to the skin several times. Yesterday we changed clothes completely three times because everything was wet. We had clothes drying over every chair and heat duct in the house. The cattle can resist the wet for a while, but once they're soaked they can't get inside a warm house to dry off. We'll probably lose some calves over this, and very possibly some cows as well, since most of them shed early. Most of them are in good shape, but many of the calves aren't as strong as they should be because of the severe storms in November and December.

On the south side of every tree this morning is a dead meadowlark, or two or three or a dozen — I suppose they got so wet in the storm yesterday that when it dropped to twenty degrees last night they froze. Or else they simply didn't get enough food to sustain their speedy metabolisms. The cats aren't satisfied with the slaughter. They're walking up snowdrifts into the trees, trying to catch the birds still alive.

We found one robin in the barn, head tucked under his wing, dead. I chased a cat away from one meadowlark, then saw his foot move and picked him up. He was alive, only his feathers ruffled. I took off my glove and warmed him in my hand and he got quite lively, blinking his eyes, turning his head, clenching his tiny claws on my hand, but making no attempt to get away. I put him in an old barn swallow nest high under the ceiling of the shed where he might survive.

After feeding the cows in the morning we started off to find and feed the yearling heifers. We surveyed our usual route across Harold's open field, but he plowed it last week, intending to plant oats, and with the moisture in this storm there was no way we could get across it, even with the 3/4 ton truck. We went through a rocky pasture and blasted our way through the drifts.

The heifers were clear down in the south end of the pasture, and we didn't dare drive down there — several hills were so deeply drifted we couldn't have gotten back up. We called them but they wouldn't come, so we walked more than a mile and tried to drive them back to the truck and hay, but they scattered. We decided if they are that frisky, they aren't starving.

In the afternoon we crossed the highway and drove along the rockiest ridge in the pasture until we sighted nine steers. We fed them and then went looking for the other twenty-four, afraid that they'd gotten into a deep gully in that pasture and gotten drifted under. We checked the gully first and it was level full of snow, so we thought for awhile we'd lost them all. On the way back we checked a tiny gully we thought too small for them, and they were there, huddled together. We got them out and gave them a good feed of bales and cake, and they didn't look too bad.

As soon as we scatter hay in the calving pasture the calves come running and bed down on it — and the cows gather around and eat it out from under them.

My Aunt Jo was telling me today about what a good milker one of their two-year-old heifers is. "Such lovely tits," she said. You have to appreciate that remark in context.

April 30   Low 15, high 48.

After feeding, we spent the morning tying up a black cow that lost her calf in the storm so that we could transplant the orphan calf to her. We got a lariat around her neck and one around a back leg, and she'd throw herself on the floor, stretch her neck out and appear to be choking until George climbed down off the fence and loosened the rope — then she'd go for him, bellowing. Or she'd gather herself in and when we approached to try to get the rope on a hind leg she'd suddenly throw herself backward at Father and me.

Finally we got her more or less immobilized and Father roped the calf and shoved him up to her side, where he proceeded to fill up while she tried to kill him. We even fed her some cake to try to take her mind off the calf, and she demonstrated the usual cow ability of holding up her milk at one end while the other end stuffed itself. And of course the minute you're bent over, trying to shove a slippery teat between the calf's sharp little teeth, wondering if you're going to get kicked in the face, she lifts her tail and fires a stream of green manure all over the neighborhood.

Then we had to get the ropes off. She kicked the one off the back leg, and George managed to work a stick under the lariat around her neck and get it loose before she rushed him. He swung up on the fence and without pausing she whirled and came at Father and me. We both tumbled into the feed bunk, which is protected by a thick log, but she dipped her head down over it and tried to swipe at us anyway. We finally shut her into the small pen with the calf and left them alone.

In the afternoon we managed to get the 3/4 ton truck out of the driveway for the first time since the storm started, and get the mail and go on to town for supplies. It was warm so there was considerable melting and runoff since the ground is already soaked. The meadowlark I tried to save was dead this morning. We've seen no dead blackbirds.

Every night I watch TV, watch the men with their ties and neat sport coats, the women with perfectly groomed hair, long polished fingernails and success dresses, reciting the list of who bombed who that day, what natural disaster killed thousands, the latest difference of opinion taken into a courtroom, and I wonder if there's any hope for humanity at all.

Then each morning I look at my bitten fingernails as I shove a teat into a calf's mouth and watch his little tail switching as the cow burps with contentment and think, "Well, something will survive. It may not be us, but something will survive."

Calving Time

A living calf,
instructed by mother and instinct,
can hide like a rabbit
behind two blades of grass.
His eyes roll as I walk past
but he knows he's safe
from me, and from the coyotes;
so much a part of earth
he's invisible.
From a distance,
he's deceptively a rock,
a bush, a yucca plant. He's
part of the wildness,
part of the earth.

A dead calf,
disguises gone,
has no defense.
He's suddenly alone,
no options, stark black
or red in the snow
and greening grass.
His eyes grow dusty.

His mother stands awhile,
then moves away to graze.
He's part of the wildness,
becoming a rock, a bush,
a yucca plant;
becoming earth.

May

May 1   Low 20, high 34. No dancing around the May Pole today. A snow squall settled over us at midmorning like a great white hen squatting on a nest. An inch of new snow on top of a couple feet of old snow made everything difficult.

We finally stopped trying to feed about an hour after it started, with our coats and wool pants soaked through and visibility zero. When the storm paused about 4:00 we hurried to feed everything before dark, then collected all the cows with the newest calves and put them in the big corral in case there's more snow in the night.

After I'd gone inside George saw a flock of huge birds with black-tipped white wings circling the dam. In the evening we heard on the news that the sandhill cranes were moving north through the Badlands, so this bunch must have become separated.

It's impossible to feed cake in a storm like this because it would be lost and trampled in the snow. Without hay they have no feed, and cattle won't last long in a storm without it — especially cows who must manufacture a couple gallons of milk for a calf every day.

We have a good supply of hay in the stacks but can't get to most of it with the tractor because of the drifts, so the bales we bought in January are saving our cattle now. We shovel a path to the stack for the truck, then shovel a path to the corral fence and throw the bales over. Throwing a seventy-five pound bale that has picked up another thirty pounds of water is a little like trying to throw a cow. A woman who weighs a hundred twenty pounds and lives on a ranch might not be able to explain the theory behind leverage, but she knows how to apply it!

For the young bulls we're raising, and any sick cattle in the corrals, we're pitching loose hay stacked by the corrals, but first we have to dig a foot or two of snow off it.

We're well started on the characteristic rancher tans — the snow glare has burned our faces but our foreheads are white from stocking caps. I have the added distinction of white goggles around my eyes from my sunglasses. George calls me "raccoon eyes."

This evening I reminded Mother how she helped me make May baskets when we lived in town before she married my stepfather. We'd weave the baskets from construction paper and put a few flowers and pieces of candy in them. Then I'd hang them on doorknobs, ring the bell, and run. It was an outdated custom even then, but I wanted to do it because she talked about doing it as a child, and the memory is sweet.

May 4   Low 30, high 53. Sunny at last, and snow melting rapidly; all the low places are running over, with streams rippling down the hills and sweeping through the gullies.

The redwing blackbirds have been peevish since the storm, not gathering in crowds in the trees as they usually do this time of year. Today they arranged themselves on individual fence posts and sang all day long, as if celebrating or announcing that the storms are over.

After feeding this morning we slogged into the garden and planted potatoes and onions. The garlic is up, and the snow finally melted off the rows of lettuce and radishes. Father plowed several strips near his new trees over the last few days, and today Mother was sowing cosmos seed there for a beautiful bank of color against the lilac bushes this summer. I chose not to have a regular yard around our house but I do miss some of the flowers. We have only the ones that grow wild, plus a few I've transplanted. George growls about my leaping out of the truck and digging up wild plants, but our hillside is increasingly a mini-environment. My goal is to have samples of virtually every kind of native plant near our house.

The first mourning dove of the season was calling today, a lonesome wail, and we heard a lone meadowlark for the first time since the storm. I'd begun to wonder if any were left alive.

All the gullies are running. The dam south of the house is almost half full. (It has only filled up once in its fifty-year history.) The yearling calves refuse to cross the gullies until one of us wades across with a bucket of feed to coax them. The water is deeper than our boot tops so we wade back out with boots full of freezing water. Sometimes they still won't cross, so we find a dry patch of ground and feed alfalfa cubes on the ground and skip the creep feed.

Found a few feathers from a bluebird in a patch of bloody snow today.

I love cats, but a bluebird here is like a rare gem to a lover of jewels. The lower edges of the feathers are gray, vibrating into rich blue on the outer edges.

May 5   Low 34, high 59.

While George was driving the stacker this morning, with me standing on the supports behind him, we apparently strayed into the territory a redwing blackbird has picked for his nest. He squawked and flew at high speed between the tractor and stacker frame, straight at my face. What wonderful nerve! I ducked. Then he spotted a flock of ordinary blackbirds gathered around a water-filled ditch and landed to confront them. He hunched his shoulders and flared his wings and ran at them, screeching. They prudently withdrew.

We dragged the dead cow out of the shed, taking down part of the plank fence in order to avoid driving into the deepest mud, from which we couldn't have escaped even with the big pickup. Father said again that he was glad we hadn't left her in the mud to die. "She was a good old cow." A fitting epitaph.

We hauled her to final rest in the boneyard. My stepchildren from my first marriage gleefully collected skulls and bones there for show and tell at school. I wonder if their mother has ever forgiven me for the suitcase full of bones they dragged home.

May 6   Low 34, high 42.

George went out to do the feeding while I worked inside. Right away I heard that there's a stockman's advisory out for today. They're predicting heavy snow and forty-mile-an-hour winds through tomorrow.

The plight of the rancher in spring: just when you think the storms are over and you can spend the day doing something else (we'd planned to go to the black powder club shoot), you hear a warning like this. It might be wrong, but we don't dare leave because by the time we could get back from Sturgis we might not be able to get the cattle in. Perhaps George will go and I'll stay. My folks had planned to go out to dinner but they cancelled their plans.

May 8   Low 42, high 86. Our hillside is covered with low-growing white phlox blossoms. The calves are panting from the heat.

The barn swallows have been back about a week, and zoom overhead, outlined in dark crescents against the sky like boomerangs. They zip between the wires on fences, between the slats on the gates into the barn. They must surely be the most graceful and agile of the flyers we have here. Two of them were doing loop-the-loops over the garden in the afternoon, courting perhaps.

We turned the two-year-old heifers with calves and thirteen heavy cows into the pasture below our house where we can keep an eye on the calves. The dam has enough water in it now so they don't need to come in to the tanks in the corral, and the grass is getting green.

Cuchulain has been covered with ticks lately and so have we. When I feel one crawling on me I can't stand it. I leap out of the truck and start ripping my clothes off, hoping the neighbors aren't driving past.

Looking out my study window today, I noticed two great circles of green where the grass grows taller and thicker on the south hill. We've noticed circles of green in various sizes before and thought they might be tipi rings, but these are huge — a couple hundred feet across. I stare at them every day, wondering what they are. Perhaps the earth itself is confirming what Black Elk said: "The power of the earth always works in circles, and everything tries to be round."

May 9   Low 42, high 71.

We hear that neighbors to the south lost a lot of cows and calves in the April storm. Rumor says they ran out of hay six weeks ago and thought they could get by without buying more, that the storms were over. Another rancher near here had given his cows shots so they'd all calve at once — and they calved during the blizzard, while trying to get to the home corrals. Dead calves are strung out for miles, and some of the cows died when they did get home.

News reports say ten thousand cattle died in the storm in Harding County alone, along with lots of sheep. In Wyoming, dead cattle, sheep and antelope line the highways. They crossed fences in the storm and got drifted into the road ditches and smothered by the wet heavy snow.

A man north of here lost about thirty cows and twice that many calves when they drifted ahead of the storm into a stock dam. He said, "The ones in back just kept walking ahead, and the ones in front just kept drowning."

May 11   Low 50, high 68.

The lone heron flew over this morning and detoured to inspect us before gliding solemnly on. About six years ago a pair of them nested at our pasture land near Hermosa, and late in the spring we found one dead by the creek, its long fragile bones scattered. Now we see a lone heron almost every day in early spring like this, so we cherish the fantasy that they were a mated pair and he (again, we anthropomorphize) has remained alone.

We've been stocking up on supplies for branding, which must be done soon, but I decided to return the ear tags we bought for the calves the other day — $72 for a hundred ear tags less than an inch square. I was indignant to Father about the price, and he said, "I'm glad you feel the same way I do about it. The other ear mark will be enough, or else we'll just punch a hole in the right ear, because that's pretty visible."

I wonder if it's a relief to Father whenever he sees me agreeing with his ideas about ranching. He never speaks of what we'll do with the ranch after he's gone, and once when I questioned him about it he wouldn't say anything — but so much of what he does involves a future he probably won't see. He's been planting trees for the last two weeks — little pines no more than a foot high, in ground he plowed laboriously in April with the old two-bottom plow.

May 12   Low 72, high 96.

Today we branded, with a crew composed of Tom, the artist, my cousin Sue, and her husband Leonard. George and Father and I got the cows into the corral in the morning, and then separated them in our usual manner — on foot.

It's a pleasure to watch Father work cattle. He stands in the gate with his whip and the rest of us bring cows toward him. He takes a few steps one way or another, points his whip at a cow or waves it a little — he never hits them with it unless they duck away from him several times or try to kick him — and the cow slips through the gate, leaving her calf behind.

Once that's done he disappears, going on to other work, and we start collecting branding tools. George digs the fire pit and starts the fire with pitch splinters while we stack firewood, collect the branding irons, ear tags, scours pills, dehorning equipment and vaccine, and bring out buckets of water in case the fire gets away. Then we choose jobs and begin.

One unlucky soul gets in the small corral with the calves, selects a victim, and pushes him up the chute toward the calf table. The pusher is frequently kicked, stepped on, and showered with fresh manure.

Someone with fast reflexes operates the calf table. The calf's neck is caught, he's tipped on his side and one leg tied back so he can be held fairly quiet to be worked on.

Each calf must be tallied. We keep a record of how many are steers and heifers, how many have horns, and how many are branded with Father's brand — the Bar 99 — and with ours. (I wanted to register the brand the homesteaders put in manure on the hillside, a hat on a rail, but it wasn't acceptable to the brand board. They rejected every brand I submitted for six months so I finally accepted one they assigned, an H with a heart upside down under it. The only thing I've been able to figure out to call it is "Heartbreak Hotel.")

Then each calf is vaccinated against blackleg, earmarked with a slit cut in the left ear, checked for lice and sprayed or vaccinated.

Meanwhile, if the calf's a bull George is putting the castrating bands on. Then each calf is checked for horns and dehorned if necessary, and treated for flies.

Father reminded me this morning of the year maggots got into the horn wounds of about forty calves. We had to scrape the maggots out of each rotting wound and put disinfectant on it. "After the first three or four," he said, "no one was very squeamish any more."

Finally each calf is branded. When the iron is first laid on, a thick yellow smoke rises from the burning hair, and there's a brief delay until the iron burns through the hair and the pain finally penetrates to the calf's brain — then he begins to bawl and struggle. When the skin is burned dark brown the brand is complete.

Once everyone gets into the rhythm of a particular job the work goes fairly quickly, all of us hot and sweating from the nearby fire and the hot sun, covered with dust and blood, and coughing from the smoke. By noon we have a good start and we knock off for lunch and a beer, knowing we still have more than three quarters of the year's calf crop to do.

After lunch my cousin John comes — an experienced branding hand — and the pace picks up. Step into the wrong place at the wrong time and you're wearing our brand. I vaccinate myself for the hundredth time. My cousin Sue, who's just announced her pregnancy, gets into the chute to push the calves in, and everyone is suddenly concerned for her welfare.

By 5:00 we're finished, and all the calves are gathered at the end of the corral bawling for their mothers. The cows outside the fence are bawling back. The din is deafening. The calves have to be kept away from the cows for several hours while the horn paste does its work, and the bawling never seems to decrease in volume.

The day's injuries are comparatively minor. John burned his arm on a hot iron, and several of us have mashed fingers from being kicked by a calf or getting a finger caught in the calf table. Several calves jumped out of the chute and were caught by a wild conglomeration of people jumping on them from all directions, which always results in the calf getting in a few kicks to the ribs of whoever grabs the back legs. None of us are bruise-free. No revenge is taken on the offending calves, though there are threats to brand them twice. Any wounds to the calf are dressed at once, but the humans have to wait until the day's work is finished.

In the middle of one especially silly scramble after a calf, during which I got knocked down and the calf rolled over my face, squashing my glasses, I caught a glimpse of my father standing in the other end of the corral, shaking his head and wearing a strange expression. In his youth most of the young men could rope, and no scrambling was necessary.

Near sunset, after a couple of beers while we add the tally and visit, we return to the corral and turn the cows in. I always feel awe when a hundred bawling cows rush into a corral among a hundred bawling bleeding calves, and each walks directly to her own calf. With a dignified air, she turns and marches out of the corral with her calf trotting beside her grabbing for a teat.

May 13, Mother's Day   Low 53, high 87. Chokecherries and lilacs are blooming.

We did the morning chores, and then I frantically ran the vacuum and dustmop and cooked dinner for Mom and Dad on one of their rare visits to our house. We visited after dinner, enjoying the view from our uncurtained windows. Mother and I wandered through the house and she managed not to criticize the housecleaning or the lack of curtains.

Closing a gate today, George glanced down and picked up an inch-long arrowhead. He spotted the flaked edges. If it had been turned over, he'd never have noticed it among the other rocks. I'm intensely jealous. I've spent hours staring at my feet while walking and never found an arrowhead or a piece of worked stone here. Snell's Luck strikes again.

I hold the arrowhead and think of the hours of careful chipping required to make that edge, the patience of the maker, and his emotions when the tip broke, making the point useless. Anyone who has not experienced the joy of making something with his hands has probably missed an important satisfaction that no amount of intellectual achievement can match. I knocked together a crude woodshed when I lived in the apartment behind my folks' house. Any carpenter would laugh at it (and several have), but the fact that it still stands after ten years satisfies me enormously.

A news item warns that bulls may be "unable to perform" because of the intense cold of December. I've always wondered how they kept their testicles warm at forty below zero!

May 14   Low 43, high 74; hotter and drier than usual for May.

George remarked today that the mourning doves look like mist, and the lesser curlew as if it has been carved of wood, stiff and uncompromising. The greater curlews are all around now, making their eerie cries and landing with their wings pointed at the clouds. Frogs are singing in the damn below the house and killdeers are crying. We heard coyotes tuning up last night, perhaps teaching the young ones to hunt.

I rode Oliver to check the cattle across the tracks and noticed bluebells under his hoofs in the deep cured grass still standing from last fall. Father brought a bouquet of them home to Mother this afternoon after a trip over east to check the grass.

My body has finally begun to feel more as it should in spring — stronger, leaner — except for my leg. It should feel as if it has springs, as the muscles come back. It feels more like two chunks of dead wood linked by a strip of unoiled leather. My calf still has a hollow spot and I limp after a hard day. My right hand is swollen where a calf kicked it against a post during branding, and I seem to have no strength in that wrist. I'm beginning to realize some of these injuries are permanent.

May 15   Low 50, high 95.

Unable to sleep, I sat by the windows a long time in the night, and heard a coyote pass through the herd — all the cows began bellowing. They sound so placid and innocent in daylight, but in the moonlight with their calves threatened they sound wild, brutal, with high weird notes dropping to growling and grumbling as the coyote moves away.

I've always envied old men because they wear bib overalls and look so comfortable so I bought a pair and have been wearing them. They're wonderful — loose enough so every time I sit down I'm not cut in half. I don't have to wear a tight belt, and I love the handy pockets for my notebook and pencil. Today I drove to the post office with mail and was inside before I realized I hadn't worn them out in public before. But I don't care — they're comfortable, practical, and cheap.

Another hail about 3:30 p.m. — just enough to discourage the lettuce, radishes and other early garden stuff, and damage the new alfalfa a little.

May 16   Low 45, high 96.

We gathered thirty-five cows with older calves today and drove them from the hill pasture to the pasture east of the tracks at Lindsays. It felt good to be riding, with time to listen to the birds and look at the grass, but my leg was painful by the time I got back.

Then we drove the fence and found a few spots pulled down by snow and tumbleweeds last winter. We were able to fix everything, though the fence by the tracks really needs to be completely rebuilt. A lot of the wooden posts have rotted, and some of the steel ones are too bent to be much good.

The scent of lavender and yellow mustard is heavy in the alfalfa fields, like dirty clothes in a hamper. In the pasture, the wildflowers smell sweeter. The white daisies, phlox and star lilies cover the ground. I rode into a pocket where the scent of currant bushes hung heavy. Then a breeze brought the cloyingly sweet scent of dead cattle from the boneyard — just a little reminder. As gently green as it is now, this country is not really gentle.

The Wicked Witch of the West in *The Wizard of Oz*, Margaret Hamilton, died today. As a tribute they played her wonderful, evil, shrieking laugh, and I suddenly recalled how hard I had practiced to sound like her. I use The Laugh now to drive cows — scares the hell out of them. I demonstrated for George this evening, and it works on Phred — he left twenty clawmarks in George's thighs as he fled.

May 17 Low 56, high 92. In mid-morning, with the sun shining, clouds suddenly rippled over the horizon on the north. Their line advanced like a cavalry charge until they were directly over us, plunging us suddenly into shadow and cold. In ten minutes they had passed on, taking the chill with them.

This morning I rode in the dike pasture to get several dry cows we want to sell. Among them was a cow we call Whirlaway, after a famous race horse, because she's a fast and wily runner and hates corrals. I knew she'd be trouble so I'd planned to outsmart her. We brought the cows to the gate very quietly, and George stood in the gate while I eased the ones we wanted through. But Whirlaway was wary, and at the end she was the only one we wanted who was still in the pasture.

I tried to move her quietly several times, but she threw her head up, stuck her tail in the air and ran off. I decided if I couldn't outsmart her I'd tire her, so I trotted the horse after her wherever she went. She was annoyed, and kicked my leg hard when I got too close to her. I was sure my ankle was broken. The next time I got too close she was above me on a hillside, and she turned and hit the horse in the chest, trying to knock him down.

We kept after her, and George got on the other side of her with the pickup as she headed for the far end of the pasture. She'd let the horse get right up beside her, then whirl and swing her head at him. If he hesitated she'd slip past. George cornered her with the pickup against the fence and she bashed in the door. By that time she was bleeding from running her nose into the fence, and covered with sweat, but if we'd let her go we'd only have had it to do again. We kept on until she was too tired to run anymore.

Once we put her out the gate with the other cows, she still rolled an eye back toward me as she watched for an opening to escape. First she ran through the boneyard, while the horse and I gagged, and then she ran entirely around the pasture, checking every gate to see if it was shut and looking for a hole in the fence. Finally she gave up and let me drive her toward the corrals. Meanwhile the other cows went on behind the pickup.

We hauled water across the highway to the steers this afternoon — the dam has almost dried up. The sun was so warm, the smell of grass so sweet, the meadowlarks singing so lustily, it moved us to romance, much to the interest of the steers. When the tank was almost full we tossed Cuchulain in and watched him swim happily around, startling the steers again. One of them noisily slurped water directly out of the hose.

May 18   Low 58, high 96.

The first thing we saw as we drove out to check cattle this morning was unbelievable — a herd of buffalo in a pasture east of the tracks. As we drove closer, the bulls slowly meandered out to stand in a line between us and the herd. We counted four bulls, ten cows, five calves, and six yearlings. George said, "Maybe the Indians were right — the buffalo are coming back, springing from the earth."

We did some telephoning and found they came from a ranch ten miles east of us. The owner had put them in a pasture next to ours over east — the same yearlings harassed us last fall. They must have come through a dozen or more fences on the way here, so everyone will have fencing to do. The owner said he'd pick them up as soon as he could.

After our daily first aid to the sick calves our jeans were so impregnated with manure that I had to soak them in hot water for several hours before they were even clean enough to put in the washing machine.

I mended clothes and made some hamburger into sausage in the evening. Our neighbor hasn't come after his buffalo yet, and they've now moved into a pasture with my uncle's yearling heifers. He may have some strange-looking calves next spring! I love watching the buffalo through binoculars, watching the way they move across the grass. Even from a couple miles they don't look like cows but like something wilder, more primitive.

May 19   Low 63, high 97.

I got up early this morning and found the buffalo with binoculars, moving north through a great grassy sweep of pasture. Finally the owner appeared with a pickup and horse and started them toward his place. I was a little sorry to see them go — they looked so right against the tawny grass.

Margaret is going to trade eggs for the poster of my poem "Mulch." What a perfect barter! When I had hens, I traded eggs for paintings; that was the only way I could afford art.

May 20   Low 60, high 91.

Wild onions are growing beside our road from the corrals to the house. I remember how we always made soup of them in the spring in Missouri. As long as everyone ate it, we could stand each other.

I was up at 5:30 a.m. to go to a workshop in Newcastle, Wyoming, in a thunderstorm. The road goes west through the higher hills and a lot of lightning was striking very close to the highway as I bumbled along through heavy rain and fog with about six feet of visibility. The buffalo in the park seemed to be scooping the fog aside with their horns, just as they scoop snow off the grass in winter.

The Newcastle Writers' Club had asked me to do an all-day workshop on writing and had drawn people from all over the state to it. I talked about children's writing, poetry, fiction, self-publishing, sending manuscripts out, copyright — virtually everything.

The first question is always, "How do you find time to write?" I'm always polite, because I know people have varied priorities and most of these women are wives, mothers and/or grandmothers. But I want to shout: don't have children, don't clean the house, tear the telephone off the wall, throw a brick through the TV. Say NO; say it again, all together now: NO! NO! NO!

I will *NOT* bring a hot dish to the Ladies' Aid Society meeting.

I will *NOT* pick up your child or your cleaning.

I will *NOT* serve on a committee, no matter how high-minded its purposes.

I say none of these things because I say yes far too often. But I did, when deciding to marry George, consciously note the fact that he is sterile, and that I would thus not have to decide — again — not to have children. Since then, when we've talked of adoption I've resisted my motherly urges because I know I would find it difficult to write, and I must write — and that's a conscious decision.

May 21   Low 62, high 97.

The thirteen-lined ground squirrels are racing everywhere in the grass, cheeks fat with whatever they eat, and the star lilies are blooming. I always enjoy them — they're so tiny and inconspicuous, but once you get down close to them, as lovely as any domestic lily. The mullein leaves are already three or four inches long, and the phlox is blooming. Mother harvested rhubarb from the garden yesterday and gave us some tart sauce.

Barn swallows and curlews are nesting. The barn swallows fly through the yard trailing horsehair to weave into their nests, and if you get too close they whistle past your head like tiny rockets. The curlews are milder. They fly up with their strange haunting call, glide away, and then settle to earth with their wings high over their heads, folding them down slowly like some prototype flying machine, and crying mournfully all the time. Their cries are haunting and as indescribable as elk bugling.

The last two-year-old heifer finally calved today, and did it alone. In the morning we collected fifteen dry cows, including Whirlaway, from the pasture on the hillside and took them to the sale in Sturgis. She was a good cow but her calves were always just as wild as she is, so I won't miss her. Of course, some of her calves are still with us, to carry on their mom's wild ways.

At 10 p.m. Margaret called to say that coming home from church she'd seen some cattle on the highway. We immediately feared it might be our yearling steers, which are in the pasture west of the highway, and we drove out to look them over. In the dark, looking at them with a flashlight, we made a tactical error. We saw they were heifers and concluded they couldn't be ours, several miles away at the Lindsay place.

So we went to Margaret and Bill's and drank a beer while Bill phoned up and down the highway searching for someone who had heifers in the neighborhood. Finally we decided to be neighborly and put them in a pasture by the highway to reduce the danger to motorists and to the cattle. We collected a crew — a rancher who lives east of us several miles, and Margaret's brother and his wife, all willing to come out at nearly 11 p.m. to help even though they didn't know whose cattle they were.

When we all got back out there, I took another look, and swore — they were our heifers. We bunched them up and moved them around an underpass — tricky and dangerous with trucks thundering past — and put them into the pasture just north of us.

George and I drove south for several miles to make sure there weren't any more scattered along the highway. Then we went back to their pasture, where we found the gate down. We shut it without knowing if any were left inside, then went back to the highway and down the missile base road again, where we found their tracks. Once they got the gate down, they had to cross a good pasture, Harold's oat field, and an alfalfa field to get into the railroad right of way, then wander down the missile base road to get to the highway. They were headed south — back to our place — when we found them, but they traveled an incredible distance considering that they should have stopped to graze at the first alfalfa field, like normal yearling heifers.

We concluded that there were two possibilities: that George's horse Sage, in the pasture with them, ran them through the gate, or that he simply opened the gate with his teeth and they got out. Either way, Sage is in trouble.

May 22   Low 50, high 95.

I saw the neighbor's hired man checking fence just as we sat down to breakfast at 7 a.m., and drove down to tell him about the heifers. He had news for me too: two of their bulls had gotten the fence down in the night and moved into the pasture. That made it doubly important that we get the heifers out before the bulls get to them, or they'll calve next February.

First we went to our pasture and found that twenty heifers — and the guilty horse — were still inside. We tried to call the others out of the neighbor's pasture with cake but they were too busy following the bulls around, murmuring enticements, so I had to get the horse. By that time both bulls had developed strong interests in their own cows, so I was able to maneuver around them, collect the heifers, and get them out of there.

May 23   Low 70, high 96. Hot and dry; the high has been over 90 for the past week.

We fixed fence all day. I saw Rebel's grave for the first time, with a mound of rocks piled high over the narrow ravine. I'll never forget the smooth rocking motion of her gallop, and the way she eagerly stretched her neck ahead, biting the cows if they were moving too slowly, and watching them for signs that they planned to escape.

George reminds me of someone's theory that we never know animals' names for themselves, and says hers must have been Red Feather Dancing.

We turned the rest of the two-year-old heifers and their calves into the pasture south of our house and walked through the bunch looking for sick calves. The calves are small — heifers' calves always are — but feisty and vigorous despite the bad winter. The heifers, now officially cows since they've calved, look thin.

May 24   Low 72, high 90.

Trucked three trailer loads (twelve head) of cows and calves over east in the afternoon, a tedious and sweaty job. Father thought it would be easier than driving them on horseback through the neighbors' cows. It's so dry already that dust from our passing hung behind us for a mile. Burrowing owls crouched in the prairie dog holes and ruffled their feathers as we went past.

We found and fixed several holes in the fence where the buffalo may have come through. Buffalo always move in a bunch, and when they decide to go through a fence they simply run straight ahead, or jump over.

May 26   Low 28, high 61.

All my lovely early garden stuff was frosted last night, the corn and tomatoes ruined. That'll teach me to jump the season. I replanted the corn today, but will have to look for more tomatoes in town. It's already too late to get the kind I like. Nothing will be left but the ones requiring a seventy-five-day growing season — and we won't have that long before the next frost.

This morning we sorted off twenty-five of the yearling heifers and hauled them to the sale in Sturgis, leaving only twelve for replacements. Some of the ones we sold we'd intended to keep; they're so beautiful and fat I hated to see them go. I'd picked the ones I branded for quality as well as for markings I could easily identify.

In the afternoon George drove to Sturgis to pick up the bulls Father bought yesterday. He said he got them cheap — "They were just pounding them out" — meaning they were selling good bulls by the pound, for meat, instead of for breeding purposes.

May 27   Low 63, high 97.

A long hot day. We gathered cows in the morning and treated the calves for lice. Lawrence says if early spring is cloudy, cattle will have lice. Sounds good, but it seems as if we have lice every year. I hate the treatment. The chemical we use is so toxic a neighbor died when he accidentally dumped a gallon of it over himself. We wear masks and gloves and gingerly pour it on each calf's back with a long-handled dipper.

The bulls moaned and bellowed like wild animals in the corrals last night; made my hair stand on end, even though I know they just want to be out with the cows.

It's as if the snow never existed — the ground is dry and dusty. In the garden the cat sinks to his shoulders in fluffy dust. Over east the crested wheat grass got green early, but is dried and useless for feed now. Father says it took all the moisture from the alfalfa and better grasses. A little cheat grass survives, short and thin.

May 28   Low 78, high 98.

By 9 a.m. cattle were standing on the tops of the hills trying to catch a little breeze. We branded the two new black bulls in the morning and tried to put them across the tracks, but they wanted to be tons of fun instead, so we waited until evening when they were thirsty.

In the afternoon we branded the two-year-old heifers' calves and a few more that were too sick to brand earlier.

Father and I have had to work out a schedule for watering the lawn and garden. I'm watering at night, putting trickle hoses along the rows just at dusk.

May 29   Low 65, high 89.

A brief thunderstorm last night, mostly lightning with a few violent minutes of rain. Flying in the middle of it were the first nighthawks we've seen this year. They hover in the wind with rain pounding into their faces. They turn their heads from side to side and look as if they are enjoying themselves.

This afternoon I drove up to see Margaret. Though we talk on the phone at least once a week, I hadn't been up for awhile, and she's still not comfortable driving. She was out on the lawn waiting for me.

"Come over here," she said. "We're going to work while we visit."

"Doing what?" I asked suspiciously.

"Weeding my baby trees!" she said, laughing, and pointed triumphantly to a triple row of pine trees set out individually in milk jugs all along the side of the lawn — the 500 trees she ordered last winter. I scolded her for not calling me to help her set them out, but she just laughed and said it felt good to be able to do it herself.

So we knelt on the grass, weeding and visiting, stopping often to watch a butterfly — she can identify most of them — or a bird, and generally having a wonderful time. Her face looks thin and tired, and she's very cautious about bending, but she was smiling all the time.

May 30   Low 63, high 96.

Though officially Memorial Day was early in the week, the folks insist it was today. We loaded hoes, shovels and trowels in the trunk of their car, and the three of us drove to the cemetery above Hermosa. We pulled a few weeds on the graves, and hoed a few more, but it's really an excuse to wander among the stones. Father pauses before each grave marker and tells me something of the man or woman buried there. We spent a couple hours in the sunshine, then loaded the tools and drove slowly home, where I replanted my tomatoes; maybe now we won't get a frost.

May 31   Low 65, high 71.

Took the two young black bulls and the twelve yearling heifers over east, an exciting venture since they were all feeling good from the green grass. They ran in every direction but the right one until they were tired; the horse and I just followed. After we'd toured the hill pasture they quieted down and strolled east to the little section next to the Lester pasture. The dam is usually dry in spring, but this year it collected enough runoff for about a month if we're lucky.

Then we turned the older Charolais bull with the cows east of the tracks, and left Oliver in the dike pasture where he can't chase the calves. He only wants to play, but he's been known to jump on baby calves and break their legs, so we isolate him from the cattle until the calves are big enough to be less fragile.

Frost warning for tonight. Wouldn't you know! We spent a lovely afternoon driving through the hills. Baby buffalo are everywhere. When we turned into the driveway after dark, we caught a baby rabbit in the lights. George slammed on the brakes and the rabbit leaped straight in the air at least three feet, then stretched out his feet as if he were running, came down in the same spot, and ran off.

Memorial Day

I'm on the hill above the town, with
buffalo grass and graves. Nothing else
grows here. These thrive, deep-rooted, pulling
some thin life from the thick clay soil.

Propriety demands the sod turn
once a year above these ancestors.
They're just bones to me. I'd rather let
buffalo grass grow. There's alfalfa
on Charley Hasselstrom's mound; he'd like
that, says my father, his son.
He worked all his life to grow the stuff,
mow it, stack it, feed it to his cows;
worried about it getting hailed out,
burned out, eaten up by grasshoppers.
Now I have to turn under six plants
that volunteered for him.

Dust blooms below the hill: another makes
the yearly journey. I'll leave the spade
against Martha's rock, try the hoe, hack
at the stubborn roots worked deep in clay.
The shock moves up my arm, down the hoe,
drumming to bones I'll never see, deep
in the earth, deep inside my flesh.

Summer

Haying: A Four-Part Definition

I

When I was fourteen, my father bought a new John Deere 420
for me to drive. I'm thirty-four.

Some summers I've missed:

away at other jobs, married, teaching.

But I'm home for now.

For the twentieth spring he hitches up the mower,
mows the big yard, stops to sharpen sickles, straighten
sections, grease zerks.

Impatient, he begins before he's ready,

plunges in. When he's made the first land
he stops the tractor, grins, says "I usually drive it in third"
(so do I, I growl for the twentieth year)

pours himself some coffee.

I mow around the field in diminishing concentric squares
trying to write a poem about haying.

II

On the first round: alfalfa's purple smell.
On the third: redwing blackbirds fly up, screeching.
On the fourth: the cupped nest swings
from three plants; *on the fifth:* four chicks,
openmouthed, ride the nest down to die.
On the sixth: I remember the first time. They cheeped
while I carried the nest off the field. Two redwings
fluttered where it had stood. They never went near it;
a buzzard did. *On the tenth:* damp heat induces sleep.
On the twelfth: I watch the sickle slashing.
On the thirteenth: remember a story. A neighbor caught
his pants leg in the power takeoff. When his sons saw
the circling tractor he was a bloody lump, baseball-size.

On the fourteenth: calculate the temperature at
one hundred ten. The first hour ends.
On the twenty-eighth round: an eagle circles up the grove,
pursued by blackbirds. I think of the poem again:
seeking words for the heat, the pain between my shoulder blades,
the sweat bee stinging under my arm. For fierce hot time.
On the fortieth: I think of water. *On the forty-second:*
the sickle hits a fawn; his bleat pierces the tractor's chug
like cold water on a dusty throat. He lurches off.
There's no way to see them in the deep grass,
no way to miss. Still, we never tell my mother.
I begin to lose track, listening for loose bolts,
but around sixty my father finishes hitching up the rake,
waves me in for coffee. The second hour ends.

III

hay 1. n. Grass or other plants such as clover or alfalfa,
cut and dried for fodder. Slang. A trifling amount of money.
Used only in negative phrases, especially in "that ain't hay."

IV

Today I mowed ten acres of hay, laid
twenty tons of alfalfa down, raked
it into windrows for my father to stack
this afternoon. Tomorrow he'll gesture
to the two stacks and say, "Well,
we've started haying." In a month
the two of us will put up eighty tons;
by August perhaps one hundred ten.
Hay for the cattle against winter, pitched
out in the snow for their slow chewing, snow
blowing among the stems, drifting on their backs.

June

June 1 Low 45, high 62; only two cows left to calve.

Summer flowers are beginning to dominate the prairie: sweet William, the mustards, lots of death camas; fragile-looking Indian paintbrush grows on stony ground. Many flowers seem small and stunted this year, yet very visible; usually the deep grass hides them. The grass that came up early has turned brown and the young alfalfa is short and shriveled. The birds sit in the shadows of fence posts panting — a sight we usually see in July.

Normally the yearlings would be fat with glossy hair from the new grass. Father said as we were loading bales this morning, "It's a *hell* of a thing when you're still feeding hay and cake on the first of June because there's no grass."

After feeding, we sorted out fourteen yearling steers to sell, leaving only nineteen to sell later. The truck came at noon and the folks took their car to go to the sale. We stayed home to watch for fires.

I've been thinking a lot in the past couple of weeks about the workshops I'm doing in Vermillion next week, especially the panel on feminism with Meridel LeSeuer. I have confidence in the authenticity of my own experiences, but hers extend over more than eighty years; I'm afraid of sounding shallow and young.

June 2 Low 40, high 60; cloudy, but no moisture.

I made the first sun tea of the season for lunch. At sunset I'm sitting on the couch with Phred warming my chilly thighs. Dark clouds passed over about 4:00, breaking up the heat and humidity of the day, and now cool winds blow through windows on all four sides of the house. Lightning flashes on the horizon like a broken promise.

My leg has been hurting a lot lately because I've been walking so much, back and forth to the garden and corrals. As a result I'm having such intense back pain I can't get out of the chair where I read in the evening. George has to gently pull me up and hold me for a minute until the pain dissipates. The leg looks almost normal now except for a hollow on the outside of the calf. Sometimes that spot itches intensely, as if something is trying to get out.

June 4   Low 52, high 90; muggy, but no rain.

I saw Father out at sunrise, filling the barrel in the back of the '49 Chevy with water, driving it to his little trees, and then walking up and down the row, dumping a bucket of water on each tree. He's grown dozens of trees with a bucket of water a day.

Worked late into last night copying the rough drafts of all my unfinished poems. While I'm driving across the state tomorrow I'll get them out, read them, and work on as many as I can. When I'm driving long distances alone I can be sure no one will telephone, or want a meal, or interrupt in any way. I can immerse myself in thinking of the work, and my time is arranged by my own choice. Long drives are some of my best working time. This is, of course, the only logical reason for blighting the landscape with interstate highways: so poets can work while driving with minimum danger to other drivers.

June 5

I spent all morning roaring down the highway, reading poems aloud and making notes on changes, with dry pastures sliding past the window. It's dry all the way to the river that slices the state in vertical halves, and the river is low, turgid with mud.

I've tried several times to write a poem about my friends who died on a tiny highway in the eastern part of the state. I haven't driven it since — almost twenty years — but today the interstate is under construction, and several other routes are flooded, so I have no choice. If my friends hadn't died, they'd have been married for twenty-one years by now. The child who died unborn would be twenty and in college, perhaps.

At the University in Vermillion I checked into the dorm, feeling hot, sweaty and elderly as a young man bounced down the hall past me. My room was hot, tiny, musty, narrow — no different than most of them, but I felt horribly constricted in it. I can't imagine spending an entire week in its dim light with a window that doesn't open. I washed my face and hurried to a talk between Meridel and Frederick Manfred.

Meridel did not disappoint me. "In the 1930s, the twin cities were filled with poor farm women. There was no welfare — in a week you could lose your job, house, land. The soup lines were not for women. I began to go where these women were, to listen to their stories. We had a parade in bathing suits of these emaciated, starving figures. People fainted at seeing us.

"We had no place to go so we moved into the top floor of an abandoned ten-story building and built a fire in the center of the floor. When it burned through, we moved down a floor; those ten floors lasted until summer."

After the talk, I was hovering by the door waiting to see if I'd get a chance to talk to Manfred, an old friend, when I met Phyllis, a weaver I've known for several years. She suggested I stay in her big house, gave me directions, and I gleefully collected my bag from the bronzed young thing (male) at the dorm desk. The scenery would have been fine, if a bit distracting, but I'm really not comfortable with youthful males in shorts sprawling around the halls while I'm looking for the shower. Oh lord, am I becoming a conservative? Prudish?

Phyllis' house is a huge ramshackle place set back from the street under tall cottonwoods; the back overlooks the river. We dropped my bags and went at once to a bar a block away where most of the English Department's younger faculty sat around tables clutching cold beer. From there we went out for supper, and then back to the house, where we were soon joined by some friends of Phyllis' for a sprawling conversation. That's one thing I miss in the isolation of the ranch.

June 6

Delightful to wake up in Phyllis' house amid piles of yarn, looms, and weavings on the walls, to talk over coffee with a circle of women who seem woven together. We talked of our children, our stepchildren, our lack of children, and of our work and how it takes us away from our other "duties."

Phyllis let me wear one of her woven blouses today — rough-textured, soft as spider web, made of silk and cotton. What a contrast to the shoddy, gaudy things I looked over in frustration in the mall last week, wanting something new for these workshops. I'm going to buy it, even though it will become the most expensive item in my wardrobe — unless I count work boots.

Meridel said today that statements are not literature — "That's a patriarchal form, a male form — women don't tell stories like that, but it's taken over our literature. Women's stories are not linear; I've never heard a woman tell a story about *winning*. Men's stories are all about who won, how did it *come out?* We need to get away from this objectivity. Women's stories are circular, they talk about details — gossip, it's called."

She mentioned Sartre's self-hatred, and I ground my teeth, thinking how I struggled to understand and identify with my ex-husband's study of philosophy, especially Sartre, not realizing its destructiveness until much later.

"We were always taught to take care of men; my grandmother always told me that men were sort of retarded. I have two younger brothers, and I still take care of them," says Meridel.

"I have twenty-three great-grandchildren. Sixteen are males, so we're experimenting; we don't drown 'em."

The eyes of every woman in the room shine as they laugh uproariously at this. Many of them are older wives, farm women, women who have spent their lives taking care of men, but they're being radicalized before my eyes by this incredible woman. Even the men in the group laugh, a bit uneasily perhaps. None of them argue.

In appearance she's the antithesis of the other women. They are wearing neat polyester pants suits, perfect makeup, hair freshly blued and permed. She is a glorious mountain, hung with bright shawls, her Zuni fetishes and Navajo turquoise jingling with every step, her hair straight and mussed, her leathery skin brown. Her eyes never waver, searching our faces.

"You young women have a romantic idea of your goodness; you still believe you can redeem a man by your sexual beauty," she drawls. She speaks with no bitterness, no loud anger, just profound wisdom. Even the men love her, and nod without the look of superiority one sees so often.

June 7

I move through my own workshops revitalized by Meridel's presence, and eager to finish so I can listen to her. I have never felt more vital, more alive, more aware of my womanhood — and all because of this aged goddess. Some reference was made to age in today's lecture, and she said, "These categories are just made up for women. At seventy, I wasn't feeling well, and a doctor gave me tranquilizers and a wonderful lecture on decay. I told him I'd do my best work between seventy and eighty, and I did, and he was dead in three years. It's not 'age' — I call it 'ripening.'"

She commiserated with us on how much time is taken by womanly chores. "You have a lot more time if you don't feed anybody," she said. "I won't even feed a goldfish."

She chided all of us through one of the women readers today. "Women never come up to me and say, 'I've written this wonderful thing and you must read it immediately,' as men do. Instead they creep up and say, 'I shouldn't even give this to you.' How do you expect others to like your work if you don't like it? And like yourselves?"

Tonight Meridel read a long poem based on Indian prayer forms and asked us all to hum as background. A sense of power began to build up in the room. Thunder crashed outside and lightning flared in the windows. At the end of the poem Meridel raised her arms, and stood, caught in a cone of light, and no one in the room would have been surprised at anything that happened. Had the floor dissolved, had the roof opened, had spirits of the old gods materialized, none of us would have been surprised.

When the moment was over everyone stood up and silently watched Meridel walk through the crowd and away. No one breathed. No one applauded. I have never had an experience more religious, and never expect to.

June 8

Phyllis and I had a late breakfast, and heard on the radio that a tornado had leaped virtually over her house last night, and struck a farm just below the bluff on the other side of the river. Rain has fallen nearly every night this week, so it's hot and muggy and some of the roads I came here on are now flooded. I wasted a lot of time on detours winding between big earth-moving machines that were trying to divert flood waters.

All day, trying to put four hundred miles behind me, I talked into my tape-recorder, trying to recall everything Meridel said and putting down ideas for poems triggered by her words. Meridel seemed to open me up; I've been feeling old at forty, yet underneath was the thought that it might be a new kind of freedom, an opening out, a celebration of the strength and wisdom of this age, a party I've been afraid to attend.

Almost home, at midnight, I glimpsed a fox, his long bushy tail flashing red in the headlights. They're rare here; may he have good hunting.

George was waiting up for me, wonderful man, with a good strong gin and tonic and a back rub, and we talked — or I babbled — about the conference until 2:00 in the morning.

June 10   Low 67, high 97.

We got out our wide-brimmed hats today (we never refer to them as "cowboy" hats), caught the horses, and moved ninety head of cows with their calves to the east pasture for the summer. Father and George had sorted them while I was gone and distributed other small bunches in the Lindsay and dike pastures. Smaller bunches put less pressure on the grass, though we have more work keeping track of all of them.

Because of the heat the cattle moved slowly and didn't try to break away much. If a calf can't find its mother it will always return to the last place it sucked. I've seen them suddenly take off running when they were almost to the east pasture, and run through every fence all the way back home. So we gave them a break several times to collect the calves and rest. The cows were panting in the heat, and the calves walked with heads drooping and foam between their lips.

When I can relax on the trip over east, I think of the hundreds of times I've made it. Once, when Father was in the hospital with appendicitis, I did it with the neighbors' help, and we ran into four hundred head of wild yearling steers in the middle of what is now called the five-thousand-acre pasture. I tried to chase them out of the way, and instead they all ran over to join our cows. But by the time we got to the gate of our pasture most of them had wandered off. The ones still in the herd we cut out easily because our cows were fighting with them.

On another trip we got the cattle just outside our pasture, and it began to rain. We sat in the truck awhile but it didn't let up, so I got out my slicker. I'd forgotten I was riding Oliver — and he'd never seen a slicker before. I managed to get on him before he figured out the flapping noise was coming from me, and then he bucked all over the pasture until he decided he couldn't get rid of it. Then we plodded over east slowly, with rain trickling down my neck and into my boots. At least it was cool.

I never used to pay much attention to hats. They were necessary to keep from frying my brain on the tractor, but I hated wearing one on horseback because if it blows off, the horse expresses his displeasure in painful ways. But George bought me a nice felt hat last year and I took a lot of time shaping it in a rakish way. It began to seem almost like a mask, telling something of me but concealing other things. When I found the vulture feather I wear in the band, it seemed perfect for what I was trying to express. When I go to workshops in civilized places like Vermillion I always consider wearing the hat and my battered boots as symbols.

June 11 Low 83, high 98. Hot day.

George and I checked cows over east in the morning, then spent the afternoon bombing prairie dogs. Mike, who arrived while I was gone, was great and energetic help, running ahead to each new hole while we dragged and panted behind. Whenever he seemed to take too great a pleasure in the supposed slaughter, we tried to explain to him why we wouldn't indulge in this legal murder if it weren't necessary.

The prairie dogs have almost ruined thirty acres of grass and alfalfa in one pasture. Natural predators kill very few of them. We've invited everyone who wanted to come down to shoot them, but it's hard to get enough that way.

At dusk we treated ourselves to gin and tonic on the porch, and strolled on the hillside to look at the cowslips, sweet William, salsify and yellow daisies.

*June 12   The thermometer read 70 degrees at 7 a.m. and got hotter all day,
to a high of 102.*

Bombed prairie dogs all morning, then again after 6 p.m. when it cooled
off. In between we worked in the garden, and George went over east to check
on the water.

The bombs consist of a cylinder of combustible material, and come with
fuses that must be inserted in holes punched in the ends of the cylinders. A
bomb is lit and thrown down an active hole, and then a person with a shovel
digs like mad, trying to cover the hole. Once that's done, the bomb explodes
and burns, and theoretically it burns all the air in the hole and kills the dogs.

The reality is that some holes are twenty or thirty feet deep, with dozens
of side tunnels, several exits, and several ventilating holes. Because of the
drought and heat, the earth is hard. George, with the shovel, was gasping
for breath after throwing a dozen shovels full of dry earth into the hole, and
sometimes we could hear the bomb still rolling downward when it went off.
We'd frantically try to block off the main entrance while looking for smoke
that marked ventilating holes and other exits, and blocking those.

June 13   Low 72, high 100.

Found some wild onions in the yard on the way out to bomb prairie dogs
this morning. Mike wasn't satisfied until he'd eaten half a dozen; we made
him ride in the back of the truck because of the smell.

Late in the day a short fuse burned Mike's fingers, he dropped the bomb
and set a fire. We all jumped and stomped on the flames; probably looked
funny if anyone had been watching. The grass is so dry it crackles as we walk
through it and crumbles when we step on it. Usually even dry grass would
have enough moisture to spring back.

In the afternoon we had a classic June thunderstorm. First the air became
completely still and heavy — even the birds stopped singing. Then the clouds
boiled up from behind the Black Hills — great mounds of white on top,
glowing in the sunlight, shaded below with purple, gray, and black, spread-
ing across the sky in minutes. Then the wind began to blow gently toward
the clouds, as though they were inhaling, building strength. On the fringes
we could see lightning flickering. Slowly the front eased across the sun, and
shadows raced across the hills.

The first serious lightning struck — a glowing bolt of blue-white that
seemed to vibrate between the hilltop and the black cloud above it, making
the grass glitter. The horses in the neighbors' pasture whinnied and raced
along the fence. At the same time we heard the *whock* of the first hailstone
hitting the roof. Pause. There's always a pause. Then *whock whock.*

Another pause. Then the hail began drumming steadily, pounding the roof as the rain crashed into the windows. In brief pauses we could see curtains of rain hundreds of feet high sweeping across the hills, and water beginning to run into the ruts in the road and cascade off the roof too fast for the gutters.

For fifteen or twenty minutes the hail continued, until it began to get on our nerves like fingernails screeching on a blackboard. I always pace from window to window, trying to see, even when it's too wet for the lightning to start a fire. One bolt struck a fence post just below the house; we saw splinters fly, and later saw that the wire was blackened. Between gusts of wind sixty or seventy miles an hour we caught glimpses of the folks' house, and the great tops of the old cottonwoods sweeping back and forth.

Then it was over; the clouds swept past and the sun shone. To the east, the clouds towered over the Badlands, glowing gold and black as the sun began to set. We put on our boots and went outside to look for damage: a few shingles in the yard, flowers and grass cut by the hail, branches blown down beside the corrals. The hail was small and very little damage was done — we were lucky.

We took Mike to the plane after supper; he has to go home for a couple of weeks.

June 15   Low 80, high 102.

This morning the folks noticed a cow lying on her side in the pasture beside the highway. Father called me, and when we got there we discovered she'd been trying to calve for a long time. The birth fluids were dry on the calf, and it was dead, with one leg back so she couldn't get it out.

Father and I both got down on the ground behind her to try to push the calf back in far enough to get hold of the leg. We struggled for over an hour, both of us twined together behind the cow, his face against the cow's flank and mine against his shoulder in a kind of parody of intimacy. His hands were too big to get far enough inside. I could reach inside and get hold of the leg but didn't have strength enough to pull it out.

We tried pushing the calf's head back in, hoping to be able to turn it to a different angle and get a better grip on the leg, but the head was too badly swollen. I even took off my wedding ring because the pressure of the cow's muscles was making it cut into my flesh. The calf's teeth cut my hands in several places.

Finally we gave up and called the vet. I had to hold the cow's vulva out of the way while he sawed the calf's head off and then help him pull it. He gave the cow extra antibiotics because he said the calf had begun to rot within an hour or so in this heat, and she'd been in labor several hours. He suggested

I get a tetanus shot to guard against infection from the cuts on my hand. I haven't had a tetanus shot since I was a child.

When he finished he helped me get the cow up, and I walked her back to the tank. She was so weak that she kept staggering. Then I'd rush up on one side or the other, hold her up, and grab her tail to give her an extra boost.

June 16   Low 88, high 101.

I rode today, moving the cows out of the dike pasture because the dam has gotten too low. A storm had been building up all afternoon, and just as I reached the top of the high hill south of the house I felt the hair on my head and arms lift up, and electricity flow around me. I've always been warned that horses attract lightning, but I couldn't leave Oliver. I lay on his neck and we ran down a gully and waited until the worst of the lightning had passed. The clouds rolled on, withholding rain.

On the ride home, I kept my eyes on the flowers. The grass almost hides delicate scarlet gaura, a complicated name for a flower so fragile it reminds me of childhood and fairies. The tiny blossoms are trumpet-shaped, with narrow insignificant leaves.

At the overflow from the well I picked handfuls of spearmint to dry for tea, chewed some, and rubbed some behind my ears. Beside the yellow salsify blooms are the great white seedheads, ready to blow away in the first breeze. For some reason, penstemon is especially evident this year; whole hillsides show a pale lavender from a distance, more than I've ever seen. Only a couple of weeks ago the same hillsides glowed yellow from the western wallflower, which we incorrectly call sweet William, but they seem to have disappeared now, along with the tiny phlox that are often the first flowers we notice. Purple coneflower is just starting, the round spiky heads becoming almost beautiful as the petals edge out around them. The yucca stalks shot up without us noticing, and now they are covered with creamy blooms. From a distance they look like crowds of slender people. The drought seems to have encouraged more thistles; I've been hating them in the garden.

My favorite, sego lilies, are more evident this year, whole crowds of them, one to a stalk. Though they resemble tulips in shape they're much more graceful, with creamy, slightly pointed white petals marked by brown or magenta arcs at the base of each. The roots are supposed to be good to eat but I've never tried them because the plants have always been rare; perhaps this year I can.

June 17   Low 85, high 98.

I'm sore from cowboying again today. We collected and moved to the dike pasture some cows too small to be bred by the Charolais bull. It had rained a little in the night and the ground was slick; the cows didn't want to come. For each one, I had to ride a mile down to the dam, pick her out, cut her away from the rest, and drive her, dodging and twisting, another mile back to the gate. After two trips, the horse was so tired he started bucking, and then he'd slip on the mud around the dam and I'd think of the month I spent on crutches.

Panther was the worst. She'd bawl ferociously and duck back every time she got close to the gate. I took her through the prairie dog town at a gallop three times, and somehow the horse missed the holes every time. Oliver is a lazy bum most of the time, but when he gets mad at a cow he really turns into a cutting horse.

Those are the only times he reminds me of Rebel. She was a cutting horse all the time — the minute she'd figured out what cow I wanted, she was on her tail and the cow never got away from her. Horse experts say Arabians can't be cutting horses, but she was the best I ever saw, neat and quick on the turns. All I had to do was hold on.

June 19   Low 89, high 103.

George and I and my horse got in the rest of the heifers this afternoon for the sale tomorrow; they are slick and shiny, if not fat. We'd intended to keep these as replacements for older cows, but Father has reluctantly decided we won't have enough feed for them. Never in my memory have we sold the replacements.

June 20   Low 76, high 94.

The "caretaker" at the sale ring is on duty, a fragile-looking retarded man who moves among the pickups wiping windshields and smiling foolishly when someone gives him enough money for coffee. Most people speak to him, or nod, and he bobs his head and grins.

Inside the sale ring, the auctioneer's voice blares off the walls. The farmers wear caps and overalls, the ranchers jeans and wide hats, but they sit together. The women used to wear print dresses. Now they're stuffed into jeans, and wear belts with their names on the back.

The atmosphere is always quiet, with friendly conversation. A visitor wouldn't know the entire year's profit or loss is being decided in minutes by a few bidders — who may or may not have connections to price-fixing stores. In a few minutes a rancher will hear a price he must accept, or take his cattle home; he has no voice in setting the price. Those few minutes will cause endless conversations over the next few weeks: Did the auctioneer try hard enough to sell the cattle?

"Why, I remember in '82, my calves topped the market. . ."

"I'm so dry I had to sell. There ain't enough grass on me to feed a bird." (This is typical; they *are* their land.)

Cows that grazed quietly in the morning run in scared, covered with manure. The ringmen snap whips unnecessarily until the cattle are walleyed, looking for an exit; they are trying to move on, but don't know where to go.

A young Brahma bull makes a determined effort to tip the ringman's horse over, ignoring the whip; nothing stops him until the horse whirls and begins kicking him.

A baby calf cringes under the whip until a girl who works for the sale barn holds out her fingers. It begins to suck and then follows her eagerly outside. If a rancher loses a cow, it's often simpler to sell the calf at birth than to try to raise it. But this also encourages rustling — since baby calves aren't branded yet, anyone who can catch a calf can put it in the trunk of his car and make a fast fifty to seventy-five dollars at the sale ring — if the cows or the rancher don't catch him.

We stopped calving in a pasture near the highway after missing several baby calves one spring. The cows will act threatening, but most of them are domesticated enough not to really attack. Of course, there's always the exception. I'd love to see someone try to steal Panther's calf.

In runs a three-year-old buffalo bull, 1150 pounds. No whip snapping here; both ringmen stay behind barriers. One tosses dirt at the bull, who ignores it except to lower his head a little. I urge George to buy it, reminding him how good the meat is; he reminds me we'd have to haul it home in Father's new trailer, and then try to keep it in the corral, or else butcher it immediately. The bull sells at 51 cents a pound for $575 — very cheap. I tell Father we bought it, but he's not fooled.

Our heifers sold pretty well: ten averaged 512 pounds, at $59.25 a hundred pounds; six averaged 538 at $62.75; one weighed 410 at $55.52. This gives us a little over $3500 for twelve head, and doesn't seem like much when we think about the days we struggled to feed them in below-zero temperatures and how hard we worked at their births in the middle of the night.

June 23   Low 85, high 94.

The wild pink roses are almost finished blooming, dusty and small by the roadside. The yellow ones still cover the bushes beside the folks' house. I wish we had some on our hillside. The fields are purple with blooming alfalfa. Many of the usual flowers seem dried up, smaller and fewer than usual in the heat.

George and I had a vigorous ride this morning, using Sage and Oliver to bring a black bull back from the neighbor's pasture, and picking up one from our pasture on the way. Neither bull wanted to go, and we split up and did some fine riding and cutting before we got them home.

My bull was apparently overheated, as he jumped in the dam, swam to the middle, and looked over his shoulder with a triumphant gleam in his eye. Oliver hates water, but he was mad and hot, so he jumped in. The water came just over the tops of my boots. The bull was so surprised he floundered out.

By the time we got to the prairie dog town, the bulls were tired and quiet. I noticed a dog hole with six tiny, downy burrowing owls stacked one on top of the other at the entrance. Their wings were no longer than a couple inches, yet when they saw the horse loom over them they hissed defiantly, beaks clicking with fury.

A towering black cloud stood on the western horizon at sunset, crowned with white where the sun struck it.

June 25 Low 89, high 96.

George went over east alone while I gardened in the a.m., and picked the first salad of the season: radishes, mustard, lettuce, asparagus and peas. I noticed how bees can sit on the water without breaking the surface tension, delicately drink, and fly away.

In the afternoon Father got the mower ready and I mowed hay. It's a hot job, but satisfying, to see the blooming hay go down in long rows — even though it's thinner this year than I've ever seen it.

This is the anniversary of Custer's meeting with the Sioux and Crazy Horse at the Little Big Horn. I was thinking today, in the heat, of the men lying in little hollows scooped in the tough dry soil, parched, waiting for a bullet or an arrow. They followed orders, and their blood paid the price of their leader's foolishness.

George nobly shucked peas for supper at 9:15 p.m., while I fixed hamburgers. Summer is definitely here when we start having supper that late.

June 26 Low 50, high 91.

The rake tractor wouldn't start this morning, so Father worked on that, and George serviced the stacker while I mowed another field. The sweat bees are with us; one always stings me under the arm while I'm making a tricky turn.

My most frustrating job while mowing is watching for fawns hidden in the hay. There's never any way to see them before the mower hits them, but I always try. It seems that I hit at least one a year, and have to hear it go screaming off through the alfalfa on three legs. I've never seen a three-legged deer, so I doubt they survive.

A noisy thunderstorm struck in the afternoon with enough lightning to get me off the tractor but only a few drops of rain. We went over east to check the cattle while it was grumbling around, and then put up hay until late. A writer friend dropped by about 9:30 and was astonished to find us just eating supper.

June 27   Low 86, high 98.

Haying all day, starting at 7:15 a.m. From now on, Father will make most of the trips over east, help us service and repair the tractors, and fill the water tank on the pickup every day for watering trees or cattle.

The complex torture of haying is being done, this year, in a rolling cloud of dust because of the drought. Instead of green alfalfa that reaches the tops of the tractor tires, I'm mowing scrubby shriveled plants, gray with dust, dry before they hit the ground. I can follow George's progress in the next field by watching a cloud of dust, and when we meet at the truck our faces are streaked black with sweat.

Normally, even with our rather slow, old-fashioned equipment, we'd put up at least two hay crops, harvesting several hundred tons of hay. This year, unless it rains within the next few days, it will be too late for the alfalfa to make enough growth to be worth cutting. The hay we're putting up is all we'll get, and we'll certainly have to buy hay or sell cattle before winter.

June 29   Low 47, high 100.

During the night a little rain fell — just enough to wet the hay too much to cut today, so we drove to Spearfish to haul gravel for the driveway of George's house there, at the request of the renter. We figured hauling it ourselves would be cheaper, and it was — but shoveling it out at a hundred degrees cost more than money. I kept telling myself I was losing weight.

After lunch — we treated ourselves to beer with our pizza — we drove home on some obscure little back roads in the hills, enjoying the coolness under the trees. The wildflowers are wonderful: wild iris, blooming strawberries, currants, yellow and white violets, deep purple larkspur, butter and eggs, black-eyed Susans, blue-eyed grass, deep orange tiger lilies, clover, pussytoes, the graceful and poisonous water hemlock. I know George misses living close to the Black Hills, but he won't talk of it.

We stopped at Roughlock Falls. A water ouzel was collecting bugs, walk-

ing up the slick mossy walls with her wings spread for balance, a spot of blue
against the green. She'd hop in the water, float down a few feet, then hop to
the bank again, almost invisible to the watchers.

June 30　Low 65, high 102.
Father and I went over east to sort out more cows and calves to sell. He
said since it's looking like a dry summer, he's getting rid of any cows "that
are fatter than their calves." He pointed out a horse fly sitting exactly in the
middle of a bull's back — just where the tail wouldn't reach him. Every now
and then the bull would roar and swing his head, but the fly stayed put.

I used the horse to drive the cows into the corral, and then tied him up
while we sorted the cattle on foot — a hot, dusty job. We sorted out eighty
cow-calf pairs to put into the government pasture on July 1, and ten pairs to
sell. The dust settling on us seemed to make it even hotter than it was. Both
of us were black-faced as coal miners when we finished, except where sweat
drew lines.

George stacked all day. Late in the day, when it began to cool off, I hoed
part of the garden, and we both cooled off in the sprinkler before walking
up the dusty path to our house.

Tapestry

—for Meridel Le Sueur

She stretches, sighs, begins untying knots,
loosening the threads
that bound her to this day,
seeking the strands
knotted over the door
to sleep.
　　　　　　In the darkness,
the rumpled velvet hills are stitched
with silver threads of grass.

Ripe grain and rough brown silo walls
carpet the earth, a tapestry ancient as Europe's finest.
This mat was not woven by the tender white
fingers of virgins, but by the scarred, broken
hands of farm wives. It was created, warp and woof,
of their blood and bones.

They planted children in the earth,

to tie the weaving to the loom.
Plows ripped the seams apart;
patiently, they stitched them up again.

Their weaving blanketed the earth,
supple and strong.
                    Then one and another of the shuttles
stopped; the tired old hands lay still,
were planted in the earth they patched and tended,
made sacred by their work, their burial.

Their children moved on; the towns closed in.
Deserted farms sag and sway:
dropped threads, loosened knots.
Tornadoes spin destruction
that will never be repaired.

                                    Above the worn out land
birds swoop like phantom hands,
weaving the clouds.

July

July 1   Low 78, high 103.

Up at 5:45 a.m., collected the horses, and moved eighty cows and calves from school section into east pasture, leaving two unpaired calves that had gotten separated from the cows, and a calf with a broken jaw. I remember branding him. He slammed his head into my nose when I was notching his ear. When I grabbed his nose to hold it steady, I heard a crunch. Poor thing has probably been unable to suck since then.

We have so few trees or sizable bushes anywhere on our land that I've had to get used to waiting a long time to relieve myself in privacy. If I had an Indian name, chosen for its descriptive quality, I'd be Iron Bladder.

Terrible wind and lightning in the evening set several fires in the hills, but none near here

July 2   Low 75, high 110.

Back over east for calf with the broken jaw, but he was dead. It had rained a little there, enough to settle the dust, and we convinced ourselves we saw a faint tinge of green in the buffalo grass. But the crested wheatgrass on the south end of the pasture is dry; the cattle won't eat it unless we get more rain.

Turned the other two calves in with their mothers; cut out ten cows and calves to sell, and brought them back. Because of the heat they moved hard every step of the way. By the time we got them to Lindsays, the horses were too pooped to care when we tied them both on behind the pickup — usually they fight and buck.

In the afternoon, we went back to haying and worked until nearly 9:00. After that we didn't want to go to bed because the air had finally cooled off and we were comfortable for the first time all day, so we sat on the porch drinking iced tea and watching the distant lightning.

July 3   Low 75, high 110, and muggy.

We hayed all day; took a long lunch break, from 1:00 until almost 3:00, drinking ice tea and napping, and then stayed on the tractors until 8 p.m.

Every day Father fills the three-hundred-gallon tank in the back of the truck with water. When we finish haying we still have to haul it to the steers in the pasture across the highway. I put up some steel posts in the garden for the peas to climb on. After the long hot day in the fields, it was a pleasure to spend a few minutes in the green, damp garden. I turned the sprinkler on low so it could run all night; it's too hot to water in daylight.

The yellow and black spiders have arrived to protect my tomatoes again. Every year I expect them, and then suddenly, as I'm looking among the leaves or snapping off a blossom, I see the vivid inch-wide body, the long legs, the funnel-shaped web from which hang neatly-wrapped grasshopper corpses. Spiders terrify me, but I leave these alone and hope I don't find one climbing up my arm.

When we got in the house, we were both covered with sweaty, gritty dust, so we had to shower before eating, and then neither of us felt hungry. We had sandwiches and drank almost two gallons of tea.

Late in the afternoon while I was raking I heard a shout from George. He was pointing behind me at a young coyote who was catching mice as I turned over the hay. He followed me for a couple hours, with a break to trot to the gully for water. At times he was no more than ten feet behind me, and at first I studied him closely, afraid he might be rabid. He sat down and waited patiently whenever I stopped the tractor, and studied me back with yellow eyes.

July 4   Low 85, high 104.

The folks went to the family celebration, but we elected to continue haying. A brief thunderstorm with lightning came conveniently at noon, cooling things off a little but making us wary of lightning-caused fire. We also watch the highway constantly; one careless cigarette butt could burn us out in ten minutes. After the storm was over we hayed until 9:30 and fell into bed.

One lovely picture stayed in my mind until I had to get up and write it down. I saw a dozen brilliant orange butterflies perched on a cluster of purple coneflowers today. The purple and orange were wonderful, a change from the usual gentle greens and browns. Prairie punk.

July 5   Low 92, high 110.

Haying again, from 6 a.m. until 9:30 p.m., with a short break for lunch. It's so hot, windy and dusty that we both make stops at the van where the water jug is, soak a handkerchief, and hang it over our heads under our hats. George, with his huge black silk kerchief, looks like some mad, misplaced Arab.

I carry a notebook and pencil in a pocket of my coveralls, but though I have a lot of time to think of poems, I seldom stop to write them down. Once in a while when I'm on a straight stretch I hold the steering wheel steady with my knee and scribble. One of the reasons I've always loved haying is that it gives me so much uninterrupted time to think, once I get used to the noise of the tractor hammering in my ears.

Rules for haying:

1. Stop when it's too dark to see baby rabbits.

2. Do not use mind-altering substances while driving a tractor — except iced tea, which has been known to cause hallucinations of falling into an arctic pool even when the thermomenter reads a hundred degrees.

3. Check all bolts daily. The one you forget will cost you a fifty-mile trip to town, where the parts man will say gleefully, "We'll have to order that — take about three weeks unless the truckers go on strike again."

4. Take earplugs out before blowing nose, or you'll blow your mind.

We have to be clever and resourceful to keep our old machinery running. The last time we tried to buy a new part for our newest tractor, the John Deere man laughed at us. That one was new on my fourteenth birthday.

Father has several mowers the same general model as ours, bought at auctions, and when we break a part he digs around in the weeds on top of the hill and comes up with something that will work. I used to let him do most of the repairs. But as sure as he heads over east to be gone three hours, that's when I break a section, or shear a bolt, so I've learned to do a lot of fixing. We keep cans of gas oil, water and hydraulic oil in the van with our drinking water so we don't have to go clear back to the house to refill.

July 6   Low 93, high 110.

Haying from 8 a.m. until 9:30 p.m. again today, with a half hour for lunch. We don't dare lie down for a nap, or we'd sleep all afternoon. Every muscle aches, and our ears ring in the silence after we shut off the tractors.

Today a buzzard landed just a few feet from the tractor while I was gassing up, then waddled like a duck over to a pile of hay and peered into it, his wrinkled red neck stretched out. Finally he pecked and brought up a blackbird chick in his beak, gulped, swallowed, and then grabbed another.

A forest fire still out of control in the southern hills and a prairie fire at Kyle are making the prairie smoky and hazy. We work tensely in the smell of the smoke.

I've kept my resolution to watch every sunset, even when I have to prop my eyelids open with my fingers. Tonight, smoke from the fires made the western horizon gray and the sunset turned it all to red. For a few minutes it looked as if the entire world was on fire — or that, as I've sometimes suspected, hell really does exist right here on earth.

July 7   Low 90, high 109.
Worked 6 a.m. until 9:30 p.m. on the tractors, and we both feel as if we've been torn apart and put together by an amateur builder. Our foreheads are white, and then a line of grime outlines the sunburn. I've been wearing sleeveless tops, trying to even out my tan a little, but when I slather on lotion I sweat it off within minutes, and the wasps and bees seem to be attracted to it. We feel dry as two old bones.

Tonight after getting in bed I was wide awake and restless. I went to the basement with a gin and tonic, and a poem emerged, almost as if someone else were writing it. I believe it's in the voice of a pioneer woman homesteader. Or perhaps my subconscious has been thinking how brutal this land and the job we've been doing was before such amenities as showers, when a woman worked over a wood stove to cook meals for men who'd been haying with horses in temperatures like these.

This Is

a day to be pleased with small
clean places. The wash basin glitters
white; the mirror reflects my face, clean and pale. The kitchen
smells of cooking beef, onions,
carrots. I busy myself
with hot water, white suds. On
the rough brown board, the knife blade
waits, glowing.
                          Leaves brush the window.
I stay in, mop the floors, stare
at the red picture frame
around a prairie scene,
polish the lamp.
                          Everywhere the plains
crawl toward me. I suck
them in, slice off neat
rounds, simmer them all day

in the black pot, steam rising
into the still air of small rooms.

At suppertime I lift the lid,
let out a ferocious storm.
A thunderhead rumbles in the bedroom,
lightning flashes among the plates.

I feed.
　　　　Left in the pot: bones.
I throw them out the door
for coyotes, buzzards, grass.

July 8   Low 75, high 100.
　　Haying from 6 a.m. until 9 p.m. While I mowed this morning, George
went to the airport for Mike. After lunch we went back to the field, and Mike
stood behind George on the tractor for a few rounds. Then I showed him
how to drive the rake tractor. He's taken a course in how to drive the monsters
his stepfather uses in the Red River Valley of North Dakota, but that didn't
help him much with our antiques.
　　This was Father's birthday, and he said having it cool off a little was his
reward. We went to their house after supper — around 9:30 — for cake and
ice cream and to take him his present. Ever practical, I gave him a bolt cutter,
since it's the thing we've been needing most. Mother got him fire extin-
guishers for the house and truck.

July 10
　　We were up early, while it was still cool. While I fixed breakfast, George
and Mike loaded the rendezvous gear. Going to rendezvous is our primary entertainment in the summer. The idea is to recreate, for a few days, the atmosphere of the gatherings held by the fur trappers in the years preceding 1840.
　　The tipi poles are tied on top of the van, and inside are arranged the tipi,
liner, cover, trunks of clothing and food, cast iron pots, tripods, guns. When
we finished, the four trunks and the tipi filled the van, with blankets and
hides spread over them to make a comfortable surface for Mike. The rifles
hang along one side, and several five-gallon water jugs and two coolers take
up all but a tiny corridor along the other.
　　I feel terribly guilty leaving with the haying unfinished; we put up only
ten stacks. Our neighbors will cut and bale the rest and stack it, and receive
half the hay as payment — which will leave us short of hay next winter.
Father said not to worry, that there wasn't enough hay left to be worth our

staying to do it, but I hate to have to barter any away when we're so short. We both need to get away, though, and we couldn't enjoy Mike's visit much if we were haying every day.

Mike dozed for the first part of our drive, I read *The Monkey Wrench Gang*, for the sixth or seventh time, and George drove silently, seemingly unaffected by the heat. When Mike woke up he began asking questions about the mountain men. We obliged, taking turns, each of us telling our favorite tales.

As we drive down the highway George's hands occasionally move as though he's motioning to someone to get out of the way. For a long time I didn't know what he was doing, and then realized each time he does it, a bird is sitting on the road or flying across. He admitted, blushing, that if he doesn't push them out of the way, the van invariably hits them; if he does, they go on. So now we both wave the birds to safety as we drive.

We stayed at Rock Springs, Wyoming, a bellowing, dirty mining town with railroad tracks beside every motel; we're too tired to care. I walked Cuchulain through the cool dark alleys where nothing moved, while George and Mike showered. The air conditioner roared too loudly for us, but when we turned it off the room rapidly became like a steam bath. The dog sprawled on the carpet, panting.

July 11

We headed south this morning along Flaming Gorge reservoir, passed through Manila, Utah, population eight hundred, filled the van with gas, and took twisting gravel and dirt roads, climbing higher into the Uinta mountains, following the tipi drawings used to mark the trail.

When I was first introduced to buckskinning I thought it a rather elaborate way to play childhood games. To some extent that's true, though now I think it's no more elaborate or silly than many other adult games: tennis, boating, skiing. All require a costume and equipment. Most rendezvous participants also get caught up in the actual history of the times, and try to recreate in their costumes and shelters specific periods of time, or even actual fur trade characters.

George and I also consider our yearly visits to rendezvous a kind of survival training, and we try to live as we would if we had no comfortable home waiting for us. Also, it gives us uninterrupted time with Mike. It seems to us we achieve a level of communication with him not possible in a home filled with telephones, television, and tape recorders, where he is so easily distracted.

A good part of our social life centers around the weeks we spend at national rendezvous. We see many of the same people every year, and have developed some close friendships that are maintained primarily by visits in camp. I enjoy getting to know people without being categorized as a writer and publisher, or even as a rancher. To these people, I'm primarily George's wife and Mike's mother, and I enjoy the different role.

A valley suddenly opens up, and below us, looking as it might have a hundred fifty years ago, is rendezvous camp: tipis crowded along a winding stream. Cars are parked discreetly out of sight behind a hill. George stops, and we duck behind convenient trees, pulling on our period clothing. Without it, we won't be admitted.

We pay dues at the gate, and read the camp rules while driving up the dusty road between the tipis, looking for the red, black and white cone of Jim's lodge. Camp rules require that we unload and have the van out of camp in a half hour. We manage it with the help of Jim and Mavis and two other families, piling everything at the side of the spot they've saved for our lodge.

Then, while George takes the van out and begins the long walk back, we tie the tripod poles and catch up on the news: who is in camp, who isn't, who came without his wife, the rumors that not even animals should drink the water because of some strange bacteria. Mavis' nursing skills have already been used — one teenager cut himself while sharpening his knife, and several children have had sunstroke from the high altitude.

By the time George comes back, Mike has disappeared. He's supposed to be getting firewood, but the giggles and shouts from the woods indicate otherwise. We begin leaning the poles against the tripod for the lodge framework. Everyone rests or grabs a beer while George makes the required run to wind the tripod rope three times around the gathered poles. He puffs in the thin air of ten thousand feet. The lodge cover is tied to the lift pole, and Jim stands on the butt while George lifts it into place. Then Jim grabs my legs and hoists me up to tie the front edges together, commenting loudly on how well I wintered.

Inside the lodge, Mavis helps me arrange the liner and tie it to the poles. Next we put down the canvas floor and cover it with hides and blankets. The sleeping bags go down next, concealed with a buffalo robe. The coolers, food trunk and clothing trunks are arranged around the perimeter, near the door, with a space left for the axe, shovel and firewood. We toss extra blankets over everything that doesn't look like it might have been made in 1840, and tie the candle lanterns to the poles.

When everyone has stepped outside, I put on my medicine pouch, hang my knife on my belt, pour a cold beer into my tin cup (camp rules prohibit cans being visible in camp) and go outside.

Friends we haven't seen since last year are sprawled on the grass, on logs and stumps. Mike appears, dragging his first stick of wood. George and Jim get out the crosscut saw and begin converting firewood into short lengths to be stacked inside.

I spread a blanket, lean back against the lodge in the sunlight, and breathe deep. We're back in camp. I feel the tension of the hot days of haying begin to drain away.

July 12

George, as usual in rendezvous camp, is up before dawn and has coffee made. By the time I rouse Mike and wander out, the fire is surrounded by visitors. Some are friends, and some have merely smelled the coffee and wandered by with their cups — standard custom. We all visit casually. Perhaps we know each other's names, but more often we know only a camp name: Buffaler Jack, Whiskey Woman, Crazy Bear.

I fry bacon and scramble eggs while we watch the camp come awake. Early morning is one of my favorite times, as cooking fires start to smoke, and sleepy people stretch and smile. The sounds are much as they might have been in a real fur trade camp: horses neighing and squealing as they're taken to water, dogs barking, kids screaming and laughing, the occasional argument between a husband who had too much fun last night and his wife, who didn't.

After breakfast Jim and George wander off with elaborate casualness, muttering something about guns. Mavis and I, used to this, put on our earrings, tuck our running-away-from-home money in our possible pouches, and head for traders' row. Mike has orders to increase the woodpile, but he's headed for the creek, swinging his tomahawk.

At least a hundred businesses are set up along the dusty "street" that has become traders' row. All goods for sale must be authentic — something one might have purchased during the fur trade era. We buy Indian tacos, which bend the rules since it's doubtful they were available in 1840, and lean against a friend's lodge to eat, knowing the men won't be back for lunch.

After a satisfying stroll and visit, we return to our respective lodges for afternoon naps. I never nap at home; I have too many things I "should" do. Here, though I have my notebooks, some unfinished poems and stories, and books to read, I drift off to sleep with the sunlight sliding down the lodgepoles, listening to the comfortable voices of camp.

When we go to the same rendezvous, Mavis and I split the task of cooking supper. Tonight I dig a large roast out of the rapidly-disappearing ice and make a stew while George builds the fire and takes over the task of insisting that Mike get more firewood. In a day or two the ice will be gone; we'll finish the beer, and switch to canned meat, dried vegetables, and whiskey, rather than break our mood by going to town for more ice.

Mike's wet to the hips, one moccasin seems to have disappeared, and we have no firewood. George promptly decides his camp name will be One Moccasin. Since we don't have a spare pair, he'll go barefoot until he can make another moccasin. He limps off toward the woods, the picture of abused childhood.

Soon a line of young girls appears from the woods, each bearing one or two pieces of wood. I've never seen any of them before.

"What are you doing?" I ask a little blonde.

She giggles. "Helping Mike get firewood."

"Why?"

"Because his mom told him once he gets the wood he can play with us." The "mom" disarms me, and I keep my mouth shut.

After supper we check on where Mike will be, and then wander through camp, listening for music. At some fires it's old buckskinning songs, like "Ashley's Men." At others people play bluegrass, beat on drums, or sing sea chanties. Somewhere in the darkness a bagpiper plays. We eventually settle in the shadows around a fire where a fiddler and a guitarist are singing fur trade songs. George accompanies them on his mouth harp, and I bring out my nose flute, an instrument from the early 1700s played by exhaling. I can't sing, but I can exhale.

Slowly the fires burn down, camps go quiet, and people drift off, lighting their way with candle lanterns. When we go back to our lodge, the way is lit only by the glowing cones of the tipis and a flash of moonlight. The silence is deceptive; fire a gun, or scream for help, and from those lodges would erupt men armed with knives, tomahawks, muzzle-loaders and modern weapons.

July 13

George and Jim spent about six hours today at the rifle-maker's lean-to. I haven't bought George a gift for some time, so I wandered up there this afternoon, sat in the back of the lean-to, out of sight, and talked it over. Instead of the copy George ordered, I bought the original rifle but left it there because the riflemaker wants to take orders and it's the only rifle of that model he's made.

I persuaded George to take us "out" to lunch today, down to the Indian taco stand. Then I insisted that he walk traders' row with me so I could point out delectable items I'd like to get for my birthday.

We were just heading back to the lodge when we heard a POP! and saw a column of dense smoke rising just outside of camp. George bellowed "Fire!" and ran that direction, and I ran to the lodge, set our water jugs outside for anyone passing by to grab, and took one for myself.

In seconds, several hundred people were racing toward the fire. I stopped and began yelling for the children to go to their lodges, and for everyone to get a shovel or water before approaching the fire. Then I ran until I was too out of breath to carry the jug any longer. A young man took it from my hand and raced away.

Just at the edge of the trees I realized I was wearing several strings of beads, my concho belt and knife, all likely to be damaged or lost, so I stopped at a lean-to where a young woman was nursing a baby and left it in a pile. She said she'd take care of it until I got back.

Twenty yards farther, a lodge was burning in the center of a clearing, and one man was up in a tree frantically trying to chop off burning branches before the fire crowned in the trees. Some people were dragging flaming brush out of the fire, so another man and I began shouting to throw everything burning to the center, and start digging a trench around the outside. A few more experienced fire fighters arrived, positioned themselves around the outside of the fire, and soon we had an efficient system going. Men and women fought side by side, and it seemed a very short time until the fire was under control.

We all stopped, gasping, and passed the remaining water around the circle. Anyone who'd seen us right then would have concluded we are a tough and nasty bunch: faces red and streaked with soot, clothes ripped and wet with sweat and water, gasping in the altitude and smoke. My dress split most of the way up both sides as I was digging, but no one seemed to notice. Not the sort of individuals you'd want to meet in a dark alley, but our efforts saved the camp. Had the fire gotten among the closely-packed lodges, two hundred might have burned, and lives would probably have been lost.

The pop we heard was a can of lighter fluid blowing up. Someone had dragged a chest out of the burning lodge. We opened it and found enough black powder to have blown us all off the map.

The family that owned the lodge lost everything. The camp booshway passed his hat for donations to the family; by this evening they had collected over $5000. One young woman had to be taken to the hospital for smoke inhalation, but no one else was seriously hurt.

I found the lean-to again, and the young mother gave me a cup of water.

Dog soldiers had passed by and wanted to take my jewelry back with them
to the lost and found, but she told them I'd be back. We remarked to each
other on the trust in camp; I never doubted my things would be safe with her.
Back at our lodge, Mike was waiting nervously. We told him to take all
his friends up to the burned-out lodge and show them what a fire can do.
The last few nights we've noticed people nearby building huge fires.
Tonight, fires are so small you need two candle lanterns to get through camp!

July 14
The district forest ranger visited camp today, and commended us on our
fire-fighting. At the time the fire broke out, a helicopter was over camp. The
observer reported in amazement that he didn't think the Forest Service
needed to send fire-fighting equipment because "it looks like about ten
thousand people are running toward that fire."

The fire had other benefits. Over the last few days the women who are
dog soldiers have been hearing remarks about the "squaw soldiers" and
"pemmican pounders." Since the fire, all such remarks have ceased.

This afternoon we formed a latrine-digging company and provided three
new ones; again, several of the men were surprised to see me digging right
along with them. When we were finished, we agreed solemnly not to tell
anyone that we'd dug new ones — let them hunt.

A latrine in buckskinning camp is a fascinating affair. In this camp we
have very modern ones: a toilet seat over a hole in half a fifty-gallon drum
set in the ground between three trees. Canvas is wrapped around the outside
from knee to neck height for minimal privacy, and toilet paper hung on a
branch.

Several camps we've attended have featured slightly more primitive
styles, such as a log tied horizontally between two trees, over a hole. I prefer
to arrange my own facilities. I walk until I'm far enough from camp to avoid
casual strollers, hunt up a good digging stick and a convenient and comfortable log. When I finish my morning meditations, I cover everything; no sign
of my visit remains.

After the latrine detail, George and I collected our towels and biodegradable
shampoo and walked to the designated bathing hole, downstream from the
designated drinking water. The official hole was full of people, and we don't
like crowds, so we wandered downstream until we found a deep spot.

The water is icy cold; we can see the snowdrift it comes from. We're in
grizzly country here, so we scout the area before starting to undress. It seems
to me it would be especially intimidating to confront a bear naked, though
I doubt it would make any difference to the bear.

After supper, just as I'm about to point out that no one has remembered my forty-first birthday, a couple of friends invite us to their lodge for a cupcake bearing a single lighted candle, and everyone sings "Happy Birthday." I'm presented with my own shovel in honor of having had to dig latrines today. George's gift is a single large amber bead, and Mike has made a card with my mountain name, Sunflower. A group gradually collects in the lodge, and we poke sticks into the fire, pass a jug of whiskey, and visit comfortably.

July 15

I was walking the dog in the woods this morning when I saw two boys about nine years old energetically chopping down a live aspen tree. I marched them back to our lodge, where Jim and George were leaning in the shade. I told them all three of us were dog soldiers, and we were going to put them on trial. Jim looked fierce — he's better at it than George — and asked them if they realized they were killing a tree.

"I didn't wanta do it; I told him not to do it," wailed the one with a runny nose, abandoning friendship and loyalty at the first hint of danger. His buddy was silent, head down.

We took turns explaining why they were in trouble because we kept breaking down in giggles and having to step behind the lodge for a minute. The wailer with the runny nose spilled his guts: not only had they cut the tree, they'd been stealing canvas from the latrines and smearing fecal matter on the seats and canvas. We'd been wondering about those little items.

The other boy didn't say a word, but tears crept down his cheeks, leaving tracks in the dust.

Finally we ordered them to lead us back to their respective lodges, and made them repeat their confessions to their own fathers. Judging from the wails we heard as we walked away, the punishment was just starting. Later we saw the wailer follow his father into the woods and come back with an armload of dry wood.

We joked about the dubious pleasures of being camp police, but I suppose we might have done them good. Perhaps they really didn't know about the trees; a lot of adults don't seem to, and anyway green wood doesn't burn well.

July 16

I woke up this morning thinking guiltily of home. No doubt it's still a hundred degrees down on the prairie, and Father is still struggling to get a few dry stems of hay in the stack, and checking the waterholes over east every day or two.

I treated myself to a long walk just to look at the flowers this morning;

the varieties up here are so different than at home. Clutching my wildflower book, I found dogtooth violets, wild hyacinths, sego lilies, alpine buttercups, blue columbine, cinquefoil, lupine. I finally gave up identifying and simply wandered along, staring at all of them.

Coming back toward camp, I met two little girls about seven years old. They saw the book and shyly asked if I knew what plants were safe to eat. I showed them onions growing only a few feet from their lodge, and they stared up at me, eyes huge.

"But couldn't that be death camas? Mom told us to watch out for that."

Carefully, I explained that death camas has no smell, and bit into an onion to show them how pungent it tasted and smelled. I helped them dig and they went happily off to their mothers, clutching several bulbs in grubby fists.

An hour later they were back, each with a plant she'd pulled up, wanting to know what it was. I told them, and then explained why they shouldn't pull the plants up. Then I took them on a walk and showed them a few more edible things — watercress, a currant bush, lady slipper. I tried to tell them a few basic rules about wild eating, like tasting a tiny bit of something first and waiting awhile to see if you get sick before eating any more. They were wildly enthusiastic, and I felt like a medicine woman. As they walked away, holding hands, I imagined them my spiritual daughters, learning such things in the years ahead because of the time I spent with them today.

July 17

Traffic into camp has worn the stream crossing so deep it became impassable today. Dog soldiers were summoned to build a bridge. Dozens of men and women trooped to the ford with axes. Then we paused while most of them argued over the best method; I had no idea so many theories of bridge-building existed.

I'd just gotten back to camp and settled down with my notebook when George returned, carrying Mike slung over his shoulder. Blood dripped down George's shirt. Mike had whacked his ankle with a hatchet. Once we'd washed the wound it didn't look too serious. Mavis said it had to be sewn up within a half hour to prevent a scar, and the nearest hospital was too far for us to get there in time.

"I can sew it up," George said, getting out his three-inch leather needle. It was a joke, but Mike just bit his lip and looked manly.

"No self-respecting man should be without a scar anyway," I told Mike as I taped the cut. "Think how you'll enjoy telling your friends at home about this."

July 18

I easily lose track of days in camp, slipping into the comfortable routine of breakfast, a walk with the dog, visits to friends. Even the routine chores — cooking, bringing water from the creek to wash dishes, sweeping the lodge — seem less routine than they would at home, where they'd actually be easier. This timeless relaxation is why we're here, though it's hard to explain to people who ask, "But what do you *do* at rendezvous?"

Late in the afternoon, all three of us walked over to the Indians' dancing circle. This evening's performance was formal at first. An announcer told us the meaning of each dance, and several beautifully-costumed dancers moved to the drums. The drummers are Indian, with a white woman who knows the high-pitched chants. A slender young girl did a high-speed, whirling dance around the circle, no matter what the beat. Older and married women took tiny steps at the center, slowly and with beautiful dignity.

Firelight flashed on faces in mysterious patterns as it must have done two hundred years ago. In the shadows, other figures stood muffled in their hooded capotes.

Finally, the announcer demonstrated the basic step and asked watchers to join the Indians in a friendship dance. Many rushed in, and the evening began to disintegrate. Noisy white children, paying no attention to the rhythms, leaped and whooped in TV-inspired imitation of wild Indians — nothing they have seen tonight — disrupting the dignity and joy of the dance. Mike looked at us questioningly, and we were pleased to see him moving in the proper rhythm.

"Oh, it's so — so ethnic!" sighed a woman with painted fingernails, dressed in snowy white buckskin.

George snorted, took my arm and drew me away.

July 19

We took a short side trip out of camp today to a fishing stream George wanted to try. He left Mike fishing a shallow area, and me happily stuffing myself with wild strawberries, while he disappeared into the willows upstream.

About an hour later, he trotted out of the willows looking over his shoulder. George is not a man who normally trots anywhere, so I was suspicious at once.

"Hurry up — get your stuff and let's get back to camp." We were halfway back to the van on a trot before I persuaded him to tell us.

Pushing through the willows along the creek, he had seen a huge mountain lion track — six inches across — just beginning to fill with water. That lion was only seconds away.

As we pulled out of the parking spot, George pointed to the cliff above — a tawny blur flashed across an open patch of rock. The glimpse was momentary, but the long tail was unmistakable. Now I've really seen a mountain lion in the wild, my greatest wish, though I'd like to have had a bit more time to focus.

July 20

A continuing problem in rendezvous camps is tourists. Rendezvous must be publicized, but rules clearly state persons in modern dress will not be admitted. Today, a line of cars appeared at the gate, filled with furious people who thought they could stroll through camp taking pictures. All dog soldiers have been called to the gate or put on guard around camp to keep people from slipping in through the woods. The folks in halter tops and shorts are greatly offended when told to go away, but we are not here to serve as a display for the curious.

Some rendezvous allow the public in on specific days. We generally avoid these gatherings, since the time a family of tourists marched into our lodge while we ate dinner. They spoke of us as if we were deaf or animals in a zoo, until George stood up, and they realized how large he is. Politely, he explained how they had offended us by entering the lodge without invitation. They still didn't seem to grasp the point until I asked where they lived, and told them we'd be by for supper sometime.

July 21

I passed word among our friends in camp that I'd have a surprise birthday party for George tonight, with dessert served at our lodge right after supper. I'd made six chocolate pound cakes at home and kept them hidden in my clothing chest.

About twenty-five friends drifted to our fire after supper for cake and coffee. George kept eyeing me, not sure what was happening. Finally I stood and announced this gathering was in honor of George's birthday, a month early so our camp friends could celebrate with us. I gave a little speech about how often I'd argued with buckskinning men about the benefits of women's liberation. I heard nervous chuckles — many of the men take this issue rather seriously.

I said the question of a man buying another rifle always causes dissension; women could think of things to do with that money. My husband had, I continued, put a deposit down on a rifle without consulting me, a situation I knew they were all familiar with.

"Therefore," I said, "I know the women will understand what I'm going to do about it."

I pulled George's check out of my belt pouch — and tore it up.

The silence was complete. George looked furious. Everyone was thinking this had gone too far.

George took a step toward me, and I dived behind Jim and shrieked, "If I live through the next thirty seconds, I'll tell you the rest of the story!"

Jim put his hand gently on George's chest, and everyone froze.

"You see," I gasped, "when George wrote out a check for a copy of this rifle, I'd already bought the original for him."

At the perfect moment, Mavis stepped out of her lodge carrying the rifle, and handed it to George.

The circle exploded with laughter. The tension evaporated. People whooped, rolled on the ground, pounded me on the back, and declared it was the best joke they'd ever seen. The men fully appreciated that they'd been teased, too, tweaked in their tender chauvinistic parts.

George's rifle was admired, everyone ate more cake and passed the jugs, and one by one most of the men took me aside to remark that I wasn't such a bad broad after all.

As the fire burned down, some people drifted away, while others pulled up chunks of firewood and sat quietly staring at the flames or visiting.

July 22

Camp is getting quieter. Most people have pulled out, and we dog soldiers have been busy hauling away trash the few slobs among them left behind. We spent most of the day cleaning up, with ample time for visiting with the friends who are left, and drinking up the beer. The booshway has decreed it would be wasteful and inauthentic to haul any beer *out* of camp.

George and Mike entered another fathers and sons shoot, and came back with a prize. George also bought Mike his own fire-starting set: tinder, flint and steel in a brass box. Late in the afternoon, as George and I leaned against the lodge, we could hear "scritch, scritch" as Mike tried to get a spark into the tinder. Suddenly we heard a new sound: "Whoosh."

We leaped for the lodge door in time to see Mike hastily set the flaming tinder into the firepit and blow on his singed hand. George helped Mike gently set larger twigs over the flame, and congratulated him on his first fire.

I cooked a last stew for supper, and we sat around the fire during the evening rainstorm, talking. George said the mountain men were the CIA of the 18th century. They learned the Indians' languages, studied the tribes, made maps, and then reported to St. Louis or to the traders at rendezvous. Lewis and Clark were legitimate explorers, but the later purpose of U.S.

policy was opening up the land to white settlement, and the mountain men were the tools of their own destruction.

July 23

A wind and rain storm struck in the night. The canvas popped, roared and hummed; the whole structure seemed to sing like a huge drum. A little rain ran down the poles, and we sleepily spread plastic tarps over our beds. We slept late this morning, then decided to pull out. Though camp is almost empty, we made it a matter of pride to adhere to the rules. Everything was neatly packed and piled before we took down the lodge, and only then did George bring the van. Within thirty minutes, we were loaded and waving goodbye to our friends, calling the traditional farewell, "Watch yer topknot!"

We put on our jeans outside of camp, and raced to Manila for huge hamburgers, french fries and cold drinks. We stayed in Rock Springs tonight, where we probably drained the motel's hot water tank.

July 24

The trains that seemed to run through the middle of the motel room woke us early, and we drove hard all day. No one talked much, remembering.

As we drove down the road at the ranch we noticed that the grass around the house looked battered, but we didn't realize how badly until we got to the house. I called my mother and she confirmed it — on my birthday we had a devastating hailstorm. My garden is completely gone, even the huge tomato vines chopped off at ground level.

Worse, most of our pasture was cut short, along with the new alfalfa we planted this spring. Father said the damage was less over east. But we've lost a good part of our summer pasture, and will probably have to sell more cattle this fall to keep from running out of feed this winter.

The temperature has been above a hundred degrees the entire time we've been gone, and Father's worn out from going over east every day. He said, "It was the first rain we've had in a month though. That's always the way in a dry year — if you get rain, you get a nasty hail."

July 25   Low 88, high 103.

Simple things were wonderful this morning, like hot water from a faucet! A chair! But we moved through our work reluctantly, mountains in our eyes and minds. The blankets are hung over the van to dry; our rendezvous clothes are in the hamper.

We went over east at 6 a.m. to avoid some of the heat. The hail was bad; some of the ground almost looks ploughed. The cows and calves look good, but water holes are drying up.

As we sat in the truck by the dam, drinking lukewarm water, we noticed a coyote trotting through the cattle. The cows began bawling and pawing the ground, and then I honked, just to liven things up. When he looked over his shoulder, he tripped and rolled over three times, gave us a look of disgust, and broke into a run.

Later, an antelope trotted along beside the pickup awhile, and we had to explain to Mike again that we don't shoot every animal we see. Antelope are such silly creatures — they'll be well to one side of the pickup, and could easily be out of sight in seconds if they ran that way. Instead they'll make a wide circle, dashing frantically across in front of the truck. Sometimes I think they just like the excitement, and we often oblige by chasing them for awhile.

I love to see them take fences. Deer sail gracefully over; antelope drop to the ground, hit the bottom wire with their back-curved horns and snap it up while their bodies pass under, all in fragments of seconds.

At sunset we took water across the highway to the steers. Mike stripped to his shorts and paddled around, ducking under the jet of water from the hose. The steers were offended, and danced around the tank, snorting and pawing, until we finally got him out so they could drink.

July 27   Low 90, high 101.

Mike and I saddled our horses and hazed the cattle out of the government lease pasture today, a month ahead of schedule. The dam is so muddy we're worried about calves getting stuck in it, and the dust is ankle deep.

Just as we topped the last hill before leaving the pasture, I looked back and saw a cow motionless on a hill behind us. I couldn't understand why she hadn't come down to water until I looked through the binoculars and realized she was lying on her side, legs in the air. George was a half mile ahead with the pickup, so I left Mike with the cows while I rode back to check on her.

She'd been struck by lightning. Her calf had his head between her back legs, trying to nurse the heat-bloated bag, and it took me a hot half-hour to get him away from her and headed up the trail with the others.

July 28   Low 85, high 102.

George spent the day fencing along the railroad tracks with Mike's help. When I took them lunch, I walked up on the tracks to catch a breeze. I was bending to pull myself up by a clump of grass when it occurred to me a rattlesnake might be coiled in the shade.

I had the thought, jerked my hand back, took a step, and saw a rattler, as if I'd created him by thinking of him. I jumped back and squeaked something at George, who came running with the shovel. The snake was very small, buzzing with brave vigor, so we tossed him to the other slope of the tracks and let him go, much to Mike's disgust.

In the evening Mike picked up a book on Jed Smith, and we all spent a quiet evening reading, and listening to the killdeer around the dam below the house. After we'd gone to bed a thunderstorm blew up; no rain, but a lot of lightning. I sat by the windows in the dark for a long time, watching for fires. In the dark house below me, I knew my father was doing the same.

July 29   Low 90, high 109.

Over east at 7 a.m. to be sure we hadn't missed any cows. We chased the orphan calf into the trailer and brought him home for oats and creep feed.

In the afternoon we went to town for groceries and treated ourselves to cold drinks, haircuts for Mike and George, and some idle window-shopping in the mall. I can hardly bear that place under normal circumstances, but going there so soon after rendezvous makes me extra conscious of the hustle, the gaudy fragile clothes, the noise and haste, after the simplicity of camp.

We ate lunch at a new Mexican place; George said the salsa was "so hot it made my tongue roll up like a window shade with the spring gone."

July 30   Low 82, high 99.

Father had a couple of neighbor kids bale hay while we were gone, but after they took their share, our pile is pitifully small. Fortunately, most of it was already cut when the hail hit, as it's unlikely we'll get another crop this year. Today George introduced Mike to the fine old sport of stacking bales when it's a hundred degrees. "Maybe it'll help impress on him the importance of a college education," George muttered, wiping sweat off his face.

I worked on my mail, and tried to clear out the garden a little. Some of the corn may survive, although even the main stalks were broken by the hail. The tomatoes are gone, but I cleared the leaves away from the parsnips and watered them well. I tilled under the lettuce and most of the salad crops. Even the onions are so broken I doubt they'll grow any more. Just as I was ready to quit I pulled a few carrots, and discovered wire worms are eating them, so I harvested all of those. We all sliced carrots tonight and spread them on the dryer to salvage what we can.

July 31   Low 86, high 100; over east again.

The cattle have settled down in the new pasture, and seem to think the dry grass there is better than the dry grass in their old pasture.

As we drove through the battered hay fields, I noticed a lot of dead birds, and few grasshoppers. Father said he'd had to spray, to save what was left of the alfalfa. The hail came a few days later and destroyed it. It's a vicious cycle — when he sprays for hoppers, the birds die, and then we have no birds to eat the hoppers. The hail was extra.

Harold says that in 1939 the water level in the field below our house was so high he could plow a furrow and water would seep into it to water the cattle; he bogged down a team of horses. Now the dam he built with that team and a fresno is almost always dry, unless we get unusually heavy snow and runoff, because the water level everywhere has dropped.

We heard distant thunder this afternoon, and saw long blue panels like drapes of rain on the horizon. A little wind swept through and kicked up a baby dust tornado in the corral, but the clouds marched past too far away to even cool us.

When My Father Waters His Trees

he puts the hose
in the fifty-gallon drum, stands in the shade till
it's full. Doorless, the green '49 Chevy truck
grates, starts, lumbers out of the yard. The running boards,
still black, snap; the jack rattles; the windshield wiper
on the floor bounces left and right. One fender is
beginning to sag but the boards in the box are
new oak. The glove box is wired shut and contains one
pair of wire clippers and a cigarette pack
put there in 1956 when Dad stopped smoking.

My father says
the green truck starts when it's too cold
for the new one. He pulls up to the tree row, dips
a bucket out, pours it on the first tree, slowly
walks back for another, arms swinging. It's evening,
he's been haying all day; he fills and then empties
the drum several times, waits for a late supper.

Sometimes
I hear the old truck start just before dawn,
while it's cool. On last year's birthday I heard him say,
'Well, I'm 69. Shall I quit, or should I plant
more trees?'

He got twenty cedar from the Forest Service,
took his long-handled spade out northeast of the house.
Most of the shoots are a foot high now, growing green.

August

August 1   Low 61, high 95; heat and drought continue; we've had no rain since the hail wiped out the garden.

August is always the month I dread most. Our house seems to be a ship caught in the doldrums, sitting motionless, while we hope for a breeze through the sails and stare around us at the heat-glare on the waves.

We started over east at 6 a.m., with a little dew on the grass. By the time we started back, the cattle were moving toward the water holes in our pasture and the 5000- acre pasture south of us. Dust rose in clouds from the trails they made.

The countryside already looked barren from the hail; now grasshoppers are crawling and hopping everywhere and eating the last fragments of green. When we drive through the pastures, clouds of them click against the windshields like heavy, winged rain. They bounce into the truck windows by the voracious hundreds, thump against our shoulders and our knees, dig their sharp claws into our bare skin until we stop flinching. The dog leaps after the first few, then gives up and lies on our laps, panting.

Pasture trails ripple with heat on the horizon. The sky seems bleached by the sun, boiled to a pale uniform blue. The grass is brown, shattering as we walk on it. In the neighbors' pastures the land looks ploughed from overgrazing. Every wrinkle in the land is exposed, seared as though the sun had dropped closer to the earth.

Cattle and antelope wander along, heads down, dust puffing under their hoofs, eating soapweed and other weeds they normally don't like. When we drive to town, we notice cattle have been turned into hayfields and into lanes leading to houses to get any grass that might be left. Usually, most people leave wide borders on hayfields for nesting birds, but everything the mowers could reach has been cut this year. And it won't be enough.

During the day, we simply endure, waiting for night and cooler air. We gasp and sweat through our jobs, and don't talk to each other much.

At night deer come into the yard and garden; I'm glad we have no way to keep them out, as they have so little to eat anywhere else.

August 4   Low 72, high 101.

This morning we crouched by the bathroom window for a half hour watching eight young grouse catch grasshoppers among the weeds. They approached slowly — fifteen minutes to cover twenty feet — with beaks open, panting. They talked and chirped to each other like domestic hens, but without the raucous assurance of, say, Rhode Island Reds. These chirps were hesitant, liquid, more in keeping with the rolling prairie grass and the constant wind.

Then they went to the puddle we fill daily. While one kept watch from a coil of hose, the others drank, tipping their heads back. One bold one chirrupped his way to the very bottom step of the porch and looked as if he might march up the steps, but one of us moved inside and he scurried away. Then he stood on the mound above the cars and seemed to deliver a lecture, calling loudly for several minutes. A moment later the dog woke up, heard him and barked. The grouse squawked and the whole flock flew awkwardly off.

August 5   Low 61, high 90. The "cooler" temperatures are the result of snow in the Big Horns to the west.

Each day is the same now. I get up early and go to the basement to write while it's cool. When George and Mike get up, we eat breakfast — George cooks — and then go over east to check water, fix fences and chase the neighbors' cattle and buffalo out. I usually pack sandwiches, sun tea, and canned fruit in the cooler, and we eat in the shade of a tree.

When we come home we rest awhile: George naps, sweating; Mike reads and listens to his tape recordings; I wash dishes, read, write a little.

About 4:00, while the plains still vibrate with heat, we take the tank of water across the highway to the steers. Mike cheers himself up by playing in it with Cuchulain, while George and I sit in the shade and visit or walk around looking at the grass. When we come back we do chores: feed the orphan calf, turn the water on the trees and what's left of the garden, or burn trash — standing by the barrel with a hose.

Constantly, whether we're inside or out, we scan the horizon for smoke, or for rain clouds.

August 6   Low 65, high 92; lots of dew this morning. Going over east we saw hints of green from a brief overnight rain.

We've enjoyed evenings on the porch this summer because it was too dry for mosquitoes, but suddenly they are everywhere, whining in our ears and flying up our noses.

George spent the day fencing and checking the cattle in the pastures close to home. Mike and I went to town for groceries. When I opened the hood of my car to check the oil I found a mouse had established a home with grass and fur on top of the battery. When Mike opened the vent on the way to town, he found the mouse's pantry: a whole winter's food supply blew out in our faces. I feel guilty that he'll have all that work to do over.

I visited my pathetic garden late in the afternoon to water the corn; the few ears are small and misshapen. A few squash may survive, and the root crops, onions and herbs seem to be recovering.

August 7   Low 57, high 90. Lots of dew this morning, but it burned off before 10 a.m. George and Mike went over east.

We talked again about George's horse, Sage. He's a beautiful horse, part Tennessee Walker with a rocking-chair gait, and he's big enough to carry George's weight without strain — my horse isn't. But Sage's other traits aren't so smooth. We bought him from a friend after he whirled and kicked her, breaking her jaw and several ribs. She'd walked up behind him on a windy day without making any noise. It might have happened with any startled horse, so we had no fear of buying him.

She never had any trouble catching him, but we do. The first time we turned him out in the pasture we had to run him down with the pickup to catch him. After that, we kept him in the corral and worked with him daily. Each day was a struggle — it took an hour to work up to him, get a halter on him, and tie him to a stout post. Then we'd work to get the bridle over his head, and he'd strain, holding his head as high as possible. When we got his head pulled down, and started to slip it over his ears, he'd rear and lash out at us with his forefeet.

All this is a ridiculous lot of trouble to go to for a working ranch horse. We don't have three hours to spend getting a horse under a saddle. Part of the problem is no doubt that we don't ride often enough; in the old days ranch horses worked every single day and were too worn out to think up new tricks.

Once he's bridled, he behaves well, except for a few minor details, like shying at everything that moves. He's never bucked, but he fell with George once, rolled clear over him, and crushed one of George's vertebra. He's too fiery to be really safe, especially since George isn't a confident rider, and we're both a little old to take unnecessary risks. So we finally, and reluctantly, have decided to sell Sage. Mike objects, but he isn't experienced enough to ride him.

August 8   Low 55, high 90.

George found a mile of poor fence yesterday, so he and Mike spent the morning putting in new posts and wire. This afternoon we spent the requisite three hours haltering and loading Sage, and hauled him to the sale ring in Sturgis for a special horse sale tomorrow. We asked them to announce that he's well broken but definitely not a horse for children or inexperienced riders.

It's so much cooler at night we're sleeping better, and realizing how worn out we were from the heat. A little rain fell in the night, and I tried to stay awake to enjoy the sound of it gurgling down the drain pipes, but I fell asleep and dreamed of high mountain streams.

August 9   Low 51, high 85.

We went over east. Mike rode Ginger and and I rode Oliver to retrieve a couple of our bulls who fell in love with the neighbors' cows. One of them came along like a gentleman, but the other broke off and galloped over the horizon. We took the first one back to the corrals and loaded him in the trailer, and then went back.

Ginger's so old she really prefers not to do heavy work in this kind of heat, so Oliver and I chased the bull down. He kept ducking away until he wore himself — and us — out.

I told Mike about my grandfather homesteading on this piece of land, and pointed out the remains of the native stone foundation that supported his house, and a little dam he dug. During the week, he rode his horse to Deadwood, eighty miles away, and worked in the mine or logging.

We left the horses over east, and drove home against a blazing sun. Cuchulain was panting in the heat, but he hates to be left at home. He's happier, and so are we, now that he has his own water jug, and drinks directly from the spout.

August 10   Low 82, high 100; the cool spell is over.

In the morning, Mike came with us to rake and stack little bits of hay Father had mowed in places we don't normally bother with.

In the afternoon we took the mower to Lindsays, to the rough, prairie-dog infested bottom we never mow. On the way, the lift bar snapped and dropped the sickle, breaking another part. By the time we'd gotten that fixed, we'd shot another hour.

Father mowed while I lay in the shade beside the truck, napped, and ate alfalfa seeds. I always used to go along when Father walked through the alfalfa fields in August to decide whether to leave it for seed or mow it for hay. He'd roll the tiny spiral seed pods between his palms to break the husks, then blow the chaff away and show me the tiny seeds, the size of pin heads. Yellow seed isn't quite ready; deep brown seed is. He'd taste the kernels, though he never told me what the flavor indicated. I licked them off my own palm then just to imitate him; now I like the flavor, a little like raw sunflower seeds.

A faint whiff of sage came on the hot wind, and nearby the earth smelled clean and dry. A tumble bug rolled his treasure of a ball of manure among the grass stems.

George brought the rake with Mike nervously driving the pickup. I mowed while they practiced shooting prairie dogs with the new rifle. The bottom is a jungle of alfalfa despite the drought because the roots have gone down until they reached water.

Rabbits have moved in now that we've cut down on the prairie dog population, and it's hard not to hit them. Several baby ones took refuge in a small clump of grass, and I got off the mower to chase them out again and again. One was so confused by the tractor noise it ran in circles and finally stopped, quivering. I picked it up gently and put it down a hole. Its poor little heart was beating frantically against my palm.

Finally I hit one, cut off his back legs, and had to get off and kill him with a wrench. I hope at least a vulture finds him so his death isn't a complete waste.

August 11   Low 58, high 102.

All three of us went over east again today to collect the missing cows from the neighbors' pasture. The thermometer read 100 degrees at 8 a.m. when we started, so we left Cuchulain at home so he wouldn't have to spend the day in the truck.

It's a good thing we took a lunch, because even though we knew the cows would be close to water, it took us all day to find them and convince them to come along with us. They were in a tiny green valley with a spring and good feed, and planned to retire there. Mike got more cowboying than he really wanted.

One cow had a calf on her, and the other should have, but there was no sign of it. The cow had dried up, so the calf's been gone awhile. We turned them back in the pasture and loaded the horses to bring them home.

As soon as we headed back, we noticed a little thundershower near the hills, and saw a shaft of lightning strike down out of a low cloud. As we got closer we began to see smoke rising so we drove faster and faster. We dropped the horse trailer in the yard, grabbed some water and sacks, and raced a mile down the highway.

Our neighbors had built a beautiful new set of corrals there last year, and moved in six big stacks for winter feed. Apparently the lightning struck one of the stacks — they were all burning — and they set the corrals on fire. Their hired man (the one with the beautiful blue eyes and white mustache) was in the center of the conflagration, frantically trying to beat out the flames. He'd swat at a post with a wet sack a few times, then begin coughing and stagger out. As we watched, another man raced in and dragged him away. Even the fire trucks couldn't put out burning pitch posts. They just kept spraying around the stacks and corrals, and waited. When everything burned down to coals, they soaked the remnants.

That's a terrible loss: the expense and work of building the corrals, besides around 120 tons of feed. To replace the feed at current prices would cost them $12,000. Probably instead they'll have to sell cattle.

When we got home, Cuchulain was missing. My folks said they'd heard him barking for a long time soon after we left this morning. It's very unusual for him to bark unless something is really wrong, but they didn't realize that. We started calling, and when we got no answering bark we separated and began to look in the buildings, in the covered well in the back yard, in the tanks. George finally found him.

Our tanks are filled from hydrants connected to the pump at the well. Each hydrant is set in a hollow concrete square, to allow us to get down inside and make repairs. One hydrant had been leaking, so the pit around it was filled with water. We keep it covered with loose boards, but Cuchulain had apparently scratched those aside and fallen in. His barking was a cry for help. His claws had dug long scratches on the inside of the pit. He struggled for a long time, but he finally sank.

We carried him up to the house, all crying, and buried him where he always watched for us to come home, right on the crest of the hill. While George and I used a pick and shovel to hack a grave out of the dry ground, Mike found several large white quartz rocks to put above him. We always saw that spot of white waiting on the hillside for us, and it will still be there.

Tonight we talked with Mike about how healthy it is to cry, and all of us cried until we were exhausted. The house seems very quiet without those busily clicking toenails. When we went to bed, we both waited for him to jump up and put his head on the pillow.

August 12   Low 60, high 90.

We had to get away from the ranch today, so took a long drive out to visit our friend Jerry at the summer cabin he's building near Hulett, Wyoming.

Once we left the interstate, heading northwest from our place, we were on a narrow paved road with no towns and few ranches, an area we've seldom been in. The ranches seem older, smaller, with log buildings and machinery even older than ours. Ranchers in our neighborhood make flat-topped stacks of hay bales, but here bales are stacked to a point — which sheds water better — under tin roofs. Eventually we got into rolling hills covered with stubby pines, then out onto the drier Wyoming plains, with Devil's Tower rising south of us.

It was a relief to work hard all day on Jerry's cabin, with little time to think. Jerry isn't able to live in the cabin yet since it has no roof, so he's set up a tent camp nearby. We cooked a stew over the campfire in the evening, and drove home after midnight.

Just before we went to bed, we stood on the hillside by Cuchulain's grave with our arms around each other, and watched the Perseid meteor shower. The sky was densely black, and the falling meteors almost seemed to sear us with their light.

August 13   Low 72, high 98. George and Mike went over east.

I spent the morning mowing below the house, a horrible job — the hay and grass are very tough, and the mower kept breaking back. George and Mike found some fence to fix, and maybe spent some time shooting at prairie dogs — they weren't back until 3:00. I just kept mowing, waiting for them.

After lunch, we cleaned out a bin in the barn and unloaded a truckload of creep feed Father bought yesterday. We have no auger, so the job was done with buckets. Mike stood in the truck and filled them, and George and I carried and dumped them. The dust and heat were terrific, but we all kept at it as if we were working off a punishment.

August 14   Low 70, high 97.

This is my "adoption birthday," the day John Hasselstrom adopted me when I was nine. I remember most clearly the old judge making Mother and John wait outside while he asked me kindly if I wanted my name to be changed. When I assured him that I did, he made me promise that if ever I was unhappy, or needed help, I was to call on him. We celebrated that day by a drive through the hills — the first one I remember — and Father bought me a Black Hills gold ring I still wear.

Several people have given us bushels of apples, so I spent the day canning apples, making apple sauce and apple butter and apple-raisin butter, slicing apples to put on the dryer, and putting them in the blender to make apple leather. Everyone feels sorry for me for losing my garden.

While I worked inside, and George stacked hay, Mike used the hand scythe to cut the tall weeds around the house; the fire danger is terrific. Father is plowing fireguards everywhere he can.

August 15   Low 76, high 98.

Haying again, though it's dirty, depressing business. We should be getting several tons of hay off this field below the house, but there's only enough for a small stack. The hail didn't leave much, but we may need every stem of it this winter. Mike helped by raking, and running to the house for jugs of water.

Late in the afternoon we drove into the cool hills, sat beside a little lake and ate sandwiches. While we were watching for deer, I noticed a bush drooping with ripe wild plums. We picked a couple of bags full — leaving some for the birds — and I made plum butter leather and put it on the dryer.

Since Cuchulain drowned, my mind has been showing me pictures of all my animal and human friends who have died, until I'm exhausted by it. Logically, I accept their deaths, but I miss them.

George dreamed last night that Cuchulain came to visit. George couldn't touch him, but Cuchulain wagged his tail, and George said he felt forgiven for not taking him with us over east that day.

Who's to say that isn't exactly what happened? Cuchulain never held grudges. I keep thinking how desperately he must have struggled to keep afloat, and how he expected us to come when he barked. But I also think of how much joy we gave him after we found him in the pet shop where he spent the first six months of his life, and how he slowly came to recognize and give love.

I think I miss him most in the bathroom, where he'd lie down waiting for me to finish, or stare up at me with his brown eyes as if eager to protect me from the monster that flushed.

August 16   Low 65, high 90. George and Mike went over east.

I woke at false dawn while it was still a little cool, walked to the garden, and dug some new potatoes to put in with a roast for lunch. It's too hot to be using the oven, but we've been eating too many sandwiches. Usually at this time of year we'd have healthy salads from the garden to go with them. I hate having to buy lettuce this early in the year.

I finished mowing the field we're working on around noon, then raked in the afternoon while George continued stacking. Mike cut weeds around the house, listened to his tapes, and read. He's missing Cuchulain; the two of them could always entertain each other.

Harold told me he re-used a cedar fence post his father put into a windmill the year he was born — eighty-two years ago. Andrew Hanson, an old neighbor, told Harold about the post years ago, and Harold kept it in the garage until today, when he put it in a gate "so I'd know where it is."

August 17   Low 72, high 98.
George found buffaloberries ripe over east, so while he checked the cattle, Mike and I picked. The bushes have thorns two to four inches long arranged around clumps of ripe berries; we wore gloves and still our hands were bleeding when we finished. I've never seen so many ripe berries. They grow in two tiny valleys in the prairie, mixed with plum bushes. We watch the valleys each summer. Both have a secret feeling, with springs seeping from the bottom and tiny cliffs of limestone jutting out — a haven for deer, antelope, grouse, porcupines, skunks, coyotes. Normally only a few berries appear and the grouse get them all; today we filled a bucket that holds thirty pounds of feed, and didn't come close to stripping the bushes. When we got home, I made jelly — the best we ever have. The berries are a rich orange in color, and too tart to eat from the bush. With just a little sugar they become tangy with a kind of wild flavor, like tasting the air of a high mountain where grizzlies live.

The cracks in the earth widen daily. The dugouts are getting dangerous for calves, turning to soupy, sucking mud, surrounded by a desert of dust. Late this afternoon I stepped off the porch and saw a coiled rattlesnake under the bottom step — attracted to the yard because we're watering. I sympathized with him, but killed him anyway because Mike is always racing outside barefoot.

August 18
We were up early this morning, and headed for Denver for the tests and a possible operation on George's throat, to correct his breathing problems.

We checked into the guest house on the base, a clean room in a remodeled barracks building, with a foldout couch for Mike. I like it, since I can walk to the hospital to see George instead of having to drive in Denver. He slept uneasily, thrashing and moaning, and I was cold — the single army blanket wasn't enough.

August 19
George's doctor peered down his throat and said the blockage is not asthma, but cartilage growth caused by the radiation he had for Hodgkin's disease. When George goes into surgery tomorrow, he'll first do a biopsy to see if the mass is malignant. If not, he'll burn out a section of it with the laser.

He warned us about the possibility of damage to George's vocal cords, and then hesitantly said a laser could also explode — which would be fatal to everyone in the room. "But," he said, seeing my face, "we've never had that happen in this hospital, or anywhere else I've been."

The anesthesiologist warned us of some additional risks: death from the anesthetic; pneumonia if stomach material gets into the lungs; air getting in around his lungs. I make this list with care, as if knowing the words and recording the risks will prevent any of this from happening, as if I were reciting a spell against danger.

Mike and I spent the rest of the day wandering through the corridors while George was examined from all angles. George got meal passes for Mike and me, and we all had supper in the hospital chow hall before George reluctantly put on the regulation baggy pajamas and perched on the edge of his bed. We stayed with him, reading, until the nurse asked us to leave about 7:00.

Just as we were leaving the hospital, "Taps" sounded, and I looked everywhere for a man with a bugle until I realized it was coming from a speaker over my head. Another illusion shattered! I have so few left.

Mike and I watched TV until 10 p.m. when I made him go to bed; I shut the door and read until midnight. I don't sleep well when George is in the hospital.

George refused to discuss the risks of the surgery with me, even when Mike was out of the room. He only said he was sick of not being able to breathe, or even walk without wheezing and gasping, and wanted to go ahead with the operation. I told him I'd hardly notice vocal cord damage, since he doesn't say much anyway.

August 20

I was up before the fake bugle sounded at 6 a.m. and got Mike going with some difficulty. We slipped into the ward while the nurses were busy. George was already sedated, smiling benignly. He told Mike not to worry, then asked him to leave for a minute.

"I hate for you to see me scared and nervous," he said.

I tried to explain to him that when we're scared together, it makes me feel closer to him. He doesn't think it odd to see me scared, but he doesn't think it should work both ways. Damn macho attitudes.

Mike and I held George's hands and walked beside the gurney down the hall, into the elevator, and to the door of the surgery. Then we joined the other refugees in the waiting room. We'd both brought stacks of books, and I read four murder mysteries before I saw George's doctor talking to another woman. He said George was next, and it was already noon!

Mike was hungry, so we went to the chow hall. He loves the food and is already talking about enlisting in the Air Force, but the minute I sat down I thought about problems, complications, laser explosions. I ate a little, and then left Mike getting a second helping and went back upstairs.

Since I hurried, naturally we had a long wait. Mike came back, but he was bored with reading, and kept asking me for quarters so he could wander around to the pop machines. I refused to give him more than two, so he did a lot of flopping on the chair and sighing before George came out of surgery. He was in the recovery room until 5 p.m. when we finally saw his unmistakable feet protruding from a passing gurney.

He was groggy, with blood around his mouth and bloody scratches on his throat. Before we got to his bed he began to throw up. I put my arms around his shoulders to raise him so he wouldn't choke, while at the same time I shrieked somewhat hysterically for a nurse. Mike suddenly disappeared.

A nurse helped me clean up the bloody vomit and get a clean shirt on him, then went away — and didn't come back for two hours! I didn't take my eyes off George. I watched the IV, listened to him breathe, held his hand. Mike sat on the other side of the bed, eyes very large.

The doctor came about 7 p.m. and told me the operation had gone well, except by the time they began, most of the anesthetic had worn off. They gave him more, but it wasn't enough, and he tried to get off the table during the operation.

"He's pretty strong, isn't he? It took three of us to hold him down until we got another shot into him."

"I suppose that accounts for the scratches on his throat."

"Scratches? Oh, er, yes, I suppose so. Anyway, that's why it took longer for him to come around."

I stayed with him until a nurse finally discovered me at midnight. By then his breathing was natural, so I felt it was safe to leave him. Mike had fallen asleep on a couch in the waiting room. I got him up and staggering, and we walked back to the guest house without saying much.

I was starving so I let Mike buy a lot of junk food and cold drinks from the machines in the guest house basement, and we snacked, but he didn't seem to want to talk. I talked a little about the operation anyway, trying to reassure him.

August 21

When we got to the hospital at 7:30 a.m. George was sitting up, face white. The man in the bed next to him had gotten up, collapsed and died between their beds. The medics worked on him for an hour, with no time to move George anywhere else; the smell of urine was overpowering. George was shaky, and his throat is sore, so it hurts him to talk.

The doctor said he was doing well, and gave him permission to leave the hospital until this afternoon. We drove to a mall and bought books, then wandered up and down the crowded aisles, looking at people and eating ice cream until noon. Mike even played a few rounds on the video machines, which we normally don't allow; both of us were too tired to argue.

While we walked, we talked about how Americans cover their feelings. I'd been telling him how cold people seemed in the waiting room as they recited the ailments of their relatives in surgery, as if it meant nothing to them.

When I started to cry after the doctor told me George would be all right, the others looked at me as if to say, "That just isn't done here." Perhaps it's the need to cover our secret places before strangers, or perhaps it's a fear of closeness, fear of loss. The only honest reaction was from a tiny girl, who came to me and laid her head on my shoulder while I was crying. Her mother looked at me as if I might molest her.

George said when he was in the terminal ward for Hodgkin's — two five-month periods in 1969 and 1970 — the atmosphere was much the same, as if giving in to fear allowed death to enter the ward. He said he noticed that the men whose wives sobbed and worried generally got worse, while those whose wives were cheerful and positive got better. He seldom talks of that period of his life, and I sometimes forget that much of his silence must be from learning to be tough in the face of almost certain death. He spent ten years believing that he was going to die, and now that the doctors have cautiously said the Hodgkins "isn't evident" (they never use the term "cured"), he must practice expecting to live.

We went back to the hospital for lunch, and then George felt tired so we went back to the ward and he slept. I read beside him until time to leave. I felt guilty leaving him, but he said he was tired of having to talk anyway.

The nightmares I expected last night came tonight. I'm awake at 2 a.m., reading and writing until I can sleep again. The scenes were mostly long white corridors where I searched for George, following a trail of blood on the white floor. But women were busy scrubbing it away, and I kept shouting to them to leave it or I'd never find him.

In the dream I passed people I actually saw today: a legless man strapped to a bed with wheels, rolling himself through the halls; a slender ten-year-old girl with only one arm; a man whose entire face was covered in bandages, with only small slits for his nose and mouth; a baby, screaming and wiggling while a nurse tried to keep it from rolling out of the stretcher.

August 22

We went to the hospital at 7:15 a.m. and were able to say hello to George before a new nurse ordered us out until visiting hours at 9. We went to the gift shop and bought him a box of chocolates and a new pack of playing cards, then had breakfast. When we wandered back upstairs, he was sitting out in the public area waiting for us — and refused to go back to the ward until visiting hours when we could come in. The nurses had to take his temperature in the waiting room.

We started talking about getting old, and he said that he wouldn't mind the aging of my body, but he'd hate it if I turned into a blue-haired lady. So I signed a statement promising never to dye my hair blue. When I handed it to him, I also slipped his wedding ring back on his finger. I'd been wearing it since they made him take it off, a constant weight reminding me of his living presence.

The doctor came at noon, checked the charts and examined George, and told us we could go. Two more laser operations will be required to completely remove the ring of cartilage. George was dressed before the doctor finished talking, and we reached Cheyenne in time for Chinese food with Jerry. George wanted to drive on home, but he looked haggard so we stayed, watching Jerry's cable TV until late.

August 23

This is George's birthday. We were up early, stiff from sleeping on the mattress on the floor. Breakfast with Jerry, and then north across the blue-grey Wyoming plains.

Eagles were everywhere today. We saw four golden eagles and three mature bald eagles between Cheyenne and the South Dakota line, all close to the road, hunting. In one pasture we saw nine gray Arabian horses trotting in a rough circle under the storm clouds, as if performing a ritual.

August 24   *Low 78, high 98; thunderclouds marched past on the north in the morning.*

George and Mike went over east, and I went to the Custer County Fair to be political. Despite all our efforts last year, the legislature passed a compact for the disposal of nuclear waste that could result in our having a huge national radioactive waste dump here. Perhaps they were aware of the mistake they made — because they did at least set up a special election at which the people will vote on whether the compact should pass.

So I spent the day running a booth at the county fair to give out information about why we must defeat the compact. The fair is held in my home-town of Hermosa, population normally four hundred; the fair swells the ranks somewhat, since everyone in the county comes.

As always when I go to the fair, I'm struck with love and a kind of nostalgia that almost overwhelm me. I grew up here; I went to grade school here; I joined a 4-H club and participated in every activity open to me at the fair — dress-making, cooking, garden exhibits. At that time, girls in the 4-H club I belonged to couldn't participate in the horse or beef cattle projects, and while I complained, it never occurred to me to campaign very hard to get the situation changed.

Now the building housing the sewing and cooking exhibits is much quieter than the horse stalls. All the subteen and teenage girls are in the 4-H horse project, and they ride wildly around the fairgrounds, chasing boys on horseback. I see myself in many of them and when one nearly runs me down, I even growl nostalgically.

When I was fourteen, a friend and I organized a horse club drill team of 4-H members, boys and girls. We devised intricate, dangerous drill patterns performed on horseback, sometimes at a gallop, and were invited to perform at fairs all over the area for several years.

Eventually, she and I — flag-carriers — crossed flags at a gallop one day, and I received a knee injury that still plagues me. We carried our flags in front of our knees, braced on the saddle, and her horse was bigger, so when we collided my horse and I were spun half around and my left knee took the impact. I was able to stay on my horse — a matter of pride to any horse person. Unfortunately, it was my left leg, the same one Oliver damaged so badly in January. Any exertion still causes a gnawing pain, like termites at the bone.

I missed the fairs for ten or fifteen years, when I was living elsewhere. Even when we visited here at the right time, my first husband scorned them, and I was a stranger walking among people who looked familiar but whose names I had forgotten.

When I moved back to the community, the conviction began to grow in me that I *should* participate in the fair in some way. It had been such a struggle of my youth to move it to our little town, and the town had gone so far to support it — building an arena, a grandstand, a women's building, stalls for the horses — expenses the town couldn't afford, all provided through the cash, sweat, labor and donated materials of the town's men. Somehow I felt I, too, should do my part, even if only exhibiting things so there would be something for visitors to look at.

Because that's what there is to do at a fair: you walk slowly through the aisles, looking at every plate of green beans, every mayonnaise jar filled with marigolds, every calf, every child's drawing, every potholder, no matter how crudely made. You pick up the articles, if you can, and examine the stitching or the finish or the size. You discuss who is showing the item and how their children are. You pause along the way to visit with others who are doing the same thing. Everyone feels an obligation to look at everything. It's a ritual, a way of appreciating other people in the community, though you may not agree with, or like them, at other times.

At first, George nearly had fits as I fell into this routine. Gradually he began to see the people with new eyes — not exactly like my view, of course, but with some knowledge of their history and habits. The universality of the experience began to register with him, and of course as he became better known — as "that Hasselstrom girl's husband," naturally — he began to relax and enjoy himself more. Slowly he is making his own friends and acquaintances in the community.

Since yesterday was George's birthday, I invited Jim and Mavis for supper and a belated party tonight. They brought noisemakers and paper hats, and I brought out the cake I'd hidden in the freezer. He's thirty-eight, and Jim, who's already forty, regaled him with promises of how weird he can get when he reaches the magic age.

August 25 Low 83, high 102. George and Mike went over east in the morning.

My folks had their traditional picnic under the tall cottonwoods in the creek pasture where the cows winter. I should have gone down and had lunch with them, but too many people crowded around my booth at the fair about noon. I missed sitting under the trees, eating cold fried chicken and listening to the cottonwood leaves whisper.

Today I saw many of my old friends, girls I grew up with. They are mothers many times over, while my experience has been as a stepmother. Meanwhile, my friends' children have children of their own, but I am not entirely left out of the conversations since my stepdaughter Heather has made me a step-grandmother. These are the topics of our conversations, topics that would have made me shriek with disgust and boredom ten years ago, and that might on a normal day still. Yet, at fairtime, I am overcome with this nostalgia, this love, and I see these people in all their ordinariness as the strength of the country I love.

They look a bit askance at me, standing in my booth selling tickets to raise money to keep a nuclear waste dump out of the area. How do I have the time? Where do I find the courage? "Of course, she has no children . . ."

But perhaps they admire me a bit, too; some of them say they do. I, in turn, admire their faith in the world evidenced by their having children; by their quiet smiles as their kids roll and tumble in the mud pool made for the tug of war in front of the grandstand; as their children mount horses much too large for them and gallop through the patterns of the pole-bending contest, with the horses barely under control.

They smile quietly as they soothe the scrapes and bumps that result, and I know their smiles are identical to the one I wear when I have finished a poem I can respect, even though it may not be perfect. They might not understand what I mean — perhaps they would — but I love them.

Mike was bored and restless this afternoon, so I hounded him until he found a partner and participated in the kids' games — the three-legged race and the sack race. He was scornful at first, believing this stuff couldn't be nearly as much fun as video games. But when it was over and he'd won a ribbon, he was excited and wanted to enter the greased pig race.

There George called a halt. I think he was afraid Mike would catch one.

August 26   Low 78, high 92; no wind, but no relief in the heat.

My uncle Harold said he's got a lot of jobs planned today for his hired man, who came home late and drunk last night.

"The best hangover cure I know is digging post holes," he said with an evil chuckle, chilling even over the telephone. "When he gets that done, he's going to shovel the horse manure out of the barn, but he don't know it yet. And if he finishes that in the daylight and ain't cured yet, I'll think of something else."

Over east with the horses in the trailer to collect six dry cows Father had enticed into the corral. They're fat now, and tomorrow is a sale day. Two of them were mine, good young cows, but I never argue with Father's judgment about when it's time to sell. Another year would pass before they might calve, and we're going to have another winter of short feed.

It does seem a little unfair that the cows have to be sold because the bulls didn't do their job; George says only I could make a feminist statement out of selling dry cows.

Since we couldn't haul them with the cows, we left the horses in the pasture, snorting and rolling in the dust. Mike said goodbye to Ginger, and I think he surreptitiously kissed her nose.

In the afternoon, we went to town for groceries, and to make our annual contribution to Mike's school clothes. We let him do the choosing, and he picked some pretty zippy stuff — a white shirt with red and black stripes, a tie with a piano keyboard on it, and red and white tennis shoes.

When we got home, just before dark, we took pictures of Mike in his new finery. He's at last taller than I am, and mighty proud of it. Much as I have always disliked teenagers as a group, he seems to be turning out fairly well.

August 27   Low 78, high 97; cloudy in the morning, but a south wind blew the promise of rain away.

After we'd helped load the cattle, we spent the rest of the morning retrieving Mike's things from every corner of the house, and trying to stuff them back into the suitcase. Around noon his mother came, and with tears all around we watched him drive away. He said he'd be back at Christmas. The airfare is a financial burden, but I don't know how we'd get through the winter without him.

The house seemed restful for about fifteen minutes after he left; after that, it seemed too quiet. We both found it hard to settle down to work, and showed a tendency to wander aimlessly to the door of his room, to look at his cowboy hat perched on the bookshelves, and his boots on the floor.

August 28   Low 55, high 93, with a mean, hot northwest wind.

George went over east alone. I wanted to go, but I think he preferred to be alone. He's always silent for several days after Mike goes, and I know he's thinking about the next two operations as well.

I tried to write in the basement, but every few minutes I was compelled to go upstairs and scan the horizon for possible fires. A cigarette tossed out on the highway would start a fire that could burn this house in five minutes, with the wind so strong. I would be lucky to save the animals and myself, and I tell myself this over and over. But I know I would be out there with a hose, trying to save the house — not, I assure myself, for the material possessions I would lose, but for the writing, the precious photographs, the little fragments of our lives that make the house ours, as well as the hours of our own labor we put into it.

George got home just after noon, with thunderclouds building up in the west. After lunch I was in the bathroom scrubbing the shower stall when I heard a terrific crack of lightning; the glare lit the bathroom, so I knew it was close. I scrambled out of the tub and ran to the kitchen window in time to see a puff of smoke rising from a little hill about a mile north of us. I screamed "Fire!" but George was already on his feet. We piled into the pickup and headed for the highway. The fire was racing straight for both houses.

When we got there, we could hear the sirens of the fire trucks in the distance. We started down the missile base road, the closest point to the fire, and a cloud of black smoke blew over us. We parked in the ditch close to the fire, wet our sacks and got busy.

When the wind changed direction, we stopped to rest. We could see pickups turning off the highway, and soon at least ten people were beating at the fire around us. The wind changed again, and the fire moved west, toward the tracks and the highway beyond. Eighteen-wheelers screeched brakes as they tried to slow down — the smoke was too thick to see through. Two fire trucks were parked on the railroad tracks spraying frantically trying to keep it from jumping to the pasture on the other side.

Suddenly two men, one wearing shorts, wandered up to us. They said they'd seen the lightning strike, and had sent their wives in the car to phone for help. One man held up the remains of a wool-lined jean jacket, and laughed. "I've been needing a new jacket!"

The one wearing shorts looked down at his legs and grimaced; they were red, and blisters were already starting to form. He held up a rag that looked vaguely like a sheepskin and said, "My wife's gonna kill me, but this was all I could find to fight with. These seat covers cost $85."

I offered to get our first aid kit and put some ointment on his legs, but they said they might as well go, since the fire trucks had arrived.

"Is this your land?" the blistered one asked.

"No, we live down there a mile or so."

"But you came to fight the fire anyway?"

"They'd do the same for us; after all, you stopped."

"We're farmers from Nebraska, on vacation." They shook hands with us, and then, dragging the remains of the sheepskin and the jacket, they tiptoed across the burned out area to a waiting car.

Just then we heard a yell and a roar, and looked back. The fire had jumped the tracks and was headed west toward the highway. We stayed where we were, to shovel or kick smoldering cow chips back into the burned-over grass, and watch for new fires. We could see traffic on the highway creeping through the smoke, and fire trucks racing to spray the tall grass in the ditches.

Once the fire had been stopped at the highway, things calmed down a little. We stayed on the south side, walking back and forth along the fire line working on sparks and cow chips. I noticed my boots were smoking, and went to the truck tank to wet them down. Several neighbors had come to wet their sacks at our hose, so we visited a little. That's one of the bizarre things I always enjoy about fires — we visit with people we haven't seen in years.

After a few minutes, two of the fire trucks raced away, and someone said they had another fire east of Hermosa and one south of us, both lightning-caused. The smoke was still intense from burning ties under the railroad tracks, and from piles of discarded ties and fence posts. The telephone line runs along the tracks, and several poles were burning. One fire truck was spraying there, but all the wood is creosote-soaked, and the water wasn't doing much good.

We spent about two hours on the fire before going home to refill the tank. While we ate supper and read, I kept looking out the windows. About 10 p.m. a little wind came up and I could see sparks blowing from the glowing railroad ties into grass, so we drove the truck into the railroad right-of-way and squirted water on any ties we saw with sparks in them. Two other ranch trucks were patrolling the edges of the burn. We talked for awhile, and they told us the fire trucks were still out on three other fires.

When we got back to the house, I called railroad employees until one agreed to send out a tank truck to watch the burning ties. I was afraid the fires could start again in the middle of the night.

August 29   Low 68, high 87; cloudy part of the morning, then bright sun and hot.

Late this afternoon I was reading the want ads, and on impulse looked at the "pets" section — and found an ad for West Highland White Terrier puppies. I called, and the woman said they had three left — so I jerked George out of his post-lunch nap and we drove to town.

They had two males and a female, and both of the males went to sleep on our laps while we were talking to the owners. We bought one. Perhaps it's too soon after losing Cuchulain, but during the years I looked for a Westy, I never found any in this area.

Perhaps this little fellow will be more trusting and cheerful than poor Cuchulain ever could be after his experiences in the pet store. We haven't found a name for him yet; we have resolved that it has to be simpler. None of our friends could pronounce, much less spell, Cuchulain. George, thinking of the laughter a Westy always caused in a rendezvous camp full of half-wolf crosses and malemutes, suggests "Soup" in honor of a rendezvous threat that unleashed dogs will become part of supper.

I'm still watering the garden, trying to keep the parsnips alive. This evening, with the soil wet, I pulled many of the old cornstalks and piled them by the garden. When the earth dries around the roots, I'll haul them to the corral to feed the calves we weaned a couple of weeks ago. We sold their mothers because all three of them had cancer in their eyes, and we'll try to feed the calves enough so that they'll catch up, eventually, with the ones we'll wean later in the year. Walking from the house to the garden, my feet create puffs of fine dust which rise into the wind to sting my eyes.

Meanwhile, I see by towering columns of dust marching on the wind that some of our neighbors are doing their fall plowing, right on schedule.

August 30   Low 85, high 100, with a hot wind blowing from the west, so we watched that direction — toward the highway — all day for fire; we've got a good fireguard to the north now. The black scar of the fire catches my eye each time I look north; if the wind hadn't switched, we'd probably have lost everything.

Sunrise: Finches are eating the sunflower seeds outside the west windows of the house; clinging to the stems, they sway gently, gobbling seed.

George and I went over east together this morning, moved the cows into the school section where the dugout supplies good water, and left Ginger in the Lester pasture where she'll spend the winter. When we move the cattle home in November or later, we'll bring her closer to home. Mike was afraid she'd be lonely, but she's probably sick of being ridden and will welcome a long winter by herself.

About 7 p.m. my father got his pickup and I tied Oliver behind, and we drove over west of the highway to find the steers we plan to sell tomorrow. They were as far away as they could get, and when I rode up they got playful, gamboling off in all directions, dodging around the few trees, snorting and shying away from me. By the time I got them collected and headed for the highway, the sun had set, and Oliver had decided he was nervous, and shied at any shadow.

Once we got them up out of the valley, they were all thirsty, so they deliberately paced over to the dam, plunged in, and drank. When they'd finished, it was dark down in the hollow, and as I tried to get them moving again the horse kept stumbling over rocks and falling to his knees. The steers waited patiently. Finally they began to work their way up a little valley to the top of the plateau where Father was waiting with the pickup.

By that time, the Charolais steers, the color of moonlit grass, were nearly invisible in the afterglow, but they quietly followed the pickup to the highway and the underpass. We herded them into the fenced-in lot before the underpass, but they refused to enter its darkness.

Father took the truck around to the other side and shone the headlights through so they could see clearly, and this spooked them even more. They broke and rushed back toward me, and I was sure they'd either knock the gate down or turn and jump the fence onto the highway. They didn't, but they refused to enter the underpass, and stood blowing and snorting, watching me. Big trucks and cars were rushing past almost over our heads, and the headlights blinded me so I couldn't see what the steers were really doing.

Finally Father came back with a whip, and we crowded them until they began drifting into the underpass. I led the horse through, since if he shied inside the tunnel he'd knock me out against the roof.

Then, in total darkness, I began driving them toward the lights of the house. By this time I could only see the white steers, but I followed the sounds of their breathing and the soft drum of their hoofs.

I could see only darkness and hear only the quiet sound of the cattle moving through the grass. The horse picked his way with some instinct, no longer tripping over rocks, and it was entirely pleasant to be driving the cattle along in the dark.

Suddenly Father's headlights struck me from behind, casting the long shadow of the horse ahead of us, and the cattle spooked and ran.

Father said later, "How'd you like to be quietly driving off about seventy-five head of someone else's cows and have those headlights hit you like that?" We agreed that neither of us are cut out for rustling.

He drove the truck ahead of me then, and the cattle followed it sedately into the corral, or we had to assume they did, since it was so dark I couldn't tell if we had them all or not.

August 31   Low 75, high 98. The wind is blowing hard again today, this time from the north, and the whole northwest horizon is smoky from huge prairie fires in Montana. We can even smell smoke here. Last night the news said 80,000 acres had burned; the last report I heard, at noon today, said 150,000 acres, and that nothing will stop it but a good rain. The crews can do nothing much but try to turn it around the many small towns in its path.

We were up early, and using the binoculars I counted nineteen steers in the corral — we got them all last night. About 11:00 the truck came, we loaded them in, and Father headed for the sale with Mother. We decided to stay home and keep a fire watch.

We said the traditional thing: "Hope you get a good price."

"Any price will be good."

He never complains about cattle prices when he's selling. He insists that a good rancher knows the markets, and sells his cattle "when they're ready." We always joke about how some ranchers send all their cattle to the sale, so buyers and other sellers are forced to sit through endless little bunches of skinny cattle that should have been kept until they were fat.

This evening I worked on the "Hands" poem I started in June, and believe I have a final draft.

Hands

The words won't come right from my hands
in spring. The fields are full
of baby calves, tufts of hay, bawling cows.
My brain is full — but words won't come.
Sometimes when I'm in the truck,
leading heifers to spring grass, I find a stub
of pencil, tear a piece from a cake sack,
and make notes, listening to the curlews'
wolf whistle. A barb tore that knuckle,
shutting a gate without my gloves. The blood
blister came when someone slammed a gate
on the branding table; I tore the fingernail
fixing a flat. The poems are in the scars,
and in what I will recall of all this, when
my hands are too broken to do it anymore.

Instead of a pencil my hands,
knotted like old wood, grip a pitchfork,
pitching hay to cows; blister
on the handles of a tiller. Slick
with milk and slobber, they hold a calf,
push the cow's teat into his mouth,
feel his sharp teeth cut my fingers —
another scar. From my hands pours cake
for the yearlings, seed for garden
that will feed my family.

My hands become my husband's, weathering
into this job he chose by choosing me; my father's
broken and aged, still strong as when
he held me on my first horse.
At night, while my body sleeps, my hands
keep weaving some pattern I do not recognize:
waving to blackbirds and meadowlarks,
skinning a dead calf, picking hay seeds from my hair
and underwear, building fires. Deftly, they butcher
a chicken with skill my brain does not recall.

Maybe they are no longer mine but Grandmother's,
back from the grave with knowledge in their bones
and sinews, hands scarred as the earth they came from
and to which they have returned.

When my grandmother was dying, when
the body and brain were nearly still for the first time in eighty years, she snatched
the tubes from her arms. At the end,
her hands wove the air, setting the table,
feeding farmhands, sewing patches. Her hands kept
weaving the strands
she took with her
into the dark.

GLOSSARY

ACREAGE: of ranch, see ranch.

AFTERBIRTH: placenta and fetal membranes expelled after a calf is born.

ALFALFA CUBES: a form of cake consisting of green alfalfa pressed into small blocks, used as a supplementary feed when cattle are not getting fresh grass.

ALKALI PANS: shallow depressions which fill with water during rain, leaving a surface accumulation of white alkali crystals with evaporation. Near the Badlands alkali makes soil nearly barren and water bitter.

AUGER: in this usage, a conveyor belt for moving loose grain or other feed from a pickup to a storage bin.

BABYSITTING: one cow remains behind with several calves while others go to feed or water.

BACK CUT: in mowing hay, after a few rounds you reverse the direction of the tractor and mow one round closer to the fence.

BACKWARD CALF: a calf that is emerging from the womb back feet first. If both back legs are extended the calf can be pulled. If only one leg or neither is in the birth canal, the calf must be moved inside the womb until two front legs or two back legs emerge. Once you start pulling you have to get the calf out before the cow's vaginal muscles strangle him. See also calving.

BADLANDS: large, barren, eroded region in southwestern South Dakota with intriguing rock formations and fossil deposits.

BAG: cow's udder, where milk is produced. If a cow has little or no bag as calving season approaches, she may be dry — not pregnant. As her bag fills with milk, we can calculate when her calf may be born. Later, if we see a cow with a full or swollen bag it may indicate her calf is sick or dead.

BALACLAVA: an extended stocking cap reaching from the top of the head down over the neck with a hole left for eyes and nose. They look wonderful in the catalogs; in practice, moisture from your nose and mouth quickly freezes on the wool.

BALED HAY, BALES: hay bundled mechanically and fastened with string or wire. "Little" oblong bales, such as we get when the neighbors bale hay for us, weigh an average of seventy to ninety pounds each. The large round or square bales weigh several hundred pounds each and require special machinery to move.

BALES, FEEDING: To feed a load of bales, one person drives and the other stands precariously on the tailgate peeling small sections of hay from each bale. I try to divide each bale into about twenty pieces, so each cow has a chance of getting her share. The wire or string that ties each bale can't simply be thrown away because it could wrap around cows' ankles.

BARBED WIRE: twisted strands of wire with sharp-pointed barbs at regular intervals; used in fencing.

BEEF PRICES: see cattle prices, sale ring.

BLACKLEG: a disease characterized by fever and swelling of the muscles; symptoms include gaseous swellings under the skin which crackle when pressed. Blackleg affects cattle six to eighteen months old, is acutely infectious and often fatal within thirty-six hours.

BLACK HILLS ENERGY COALITION (BHEC): South Dakota environmental group. See initiative.

BLACK POWDER: the original gunpowder, made of charcoal, sulphur and salt peter; still used in muzzle-loading weapons.

BLOAT: swelling of the intestinal tract of a cow caused by the gases from fermentation of green forage in the digestive process. See trocar.

BLOOD STOP POWDER: a coagulant sprinkled on wounds, especially when cattle are dehorned. The powder also helps prevent infection and forms a seal that keeps flies from getting into the wound.

BONE, CHEWING: cattle chew on bones, probably for trace minerals missing in their diet. Sometimes a cow will eat an entire bone. If it gets caught in her throat she can die of thirst or starvation, and sharp-pointed bones lodged in the flesh can cause infection.

BONEYARD: our cattle graveyard, where we haul the bodies of animals that die, a low hillside about a mile from the house chosen as an easy location to reach. Cattle that die in the pasture are left where they fall to decay naturally, with the aid of buzzards and coyotes.

BOOSHWAY: from French "bourgeois"; camp boss at a rendezvous.

BOWIE KNIFE: a single-edged steel hunting knife about fifteen inches in length, with a hilt and crosspiece, popularized by Col. James Bowie, one of the heroes of the Alamo.

BOWLINE KNOT: a kind of knot that forms non-slip loop, and took me twenty years to learn.

BRAND: an identifying mark burned into the hide of cattle or horses to prove owner-ship. Brands are registered with a state brand board, and mature cattle may not be sold without brands and papers proving brand registration. Cattle are branded as the only practical, permanent way of establishing ownership. Because the hot iron burns into the hide, a brand can establish ownership even after the cow is butchered, until the hide is separated from the meat. If a branded hide is found, it at least provides evidence of a crime. See May 12.

BREAKING BACK: when the sickle on a tractor mower encounters an obstacle it will snap backward out of line. If the tractor is then stopped until the obstacle can be removed, breakage of a sickle section may be prevented.

BREEDING: Older cows may be bred to virtually any kind of bull, but care is taken to prevent the bull from breeding his own offspring. Two-year-old heifers are often bred to Black Angus bulls, since the calves produced will be small-boned for easier calving. See also crossbreeding.

BUCKSKINNERS: persons interested in black powder weapons and the fur trade era. Buckskinners may be anyone in "real" life, but enjoy setting up their tipis in a remote spot and spending a week replicating the rendezvous of the original fur trappers of the 1840's. See rendezvous.

BULLING: when a heifer or cow is in heat, she expresses interest in sex by putting her front legs on the hindquarters of the bull or another cow.

BUTCHERING: when we can, we kill and cut up our own meat rather than having it professionally done. We never butcher steers because they bring more money at the sale ring, and generally choose a heifer to butcher because she's wild or because we believe she won't be a good cow for some other reason.

CAESAREAN: delivery of a calf through an incision in the walls of the abdomen; some ranchers do this operation themselves.

CAKE: cattle cake is a supplementary feed, compressed into bite-sized blocks of grain and sometimes mixed with molasses. Cake comes in varying sizes and with varying levels of protein. Variations of it include creep feed, which is pill-size and generally fed to calves too young to eat the larger blocks, and similar protein feeds for pigs, chickens and other farm livestock. Cake comes in fifty-pound paper sacks for ease of handling, though some ranchers buy it loose and feed it by shovelsfull.

CALF PULLER: device based on a pulley, used to help pull calves when the cow is unable to bear the calf naturally. Smooth chains are fastened around the calf's ankles and then hooked to the calf puller. A metal cradle cups the cow's flanks. A crank on a long metal pole gives extra leverage in pulling the calf out of the birth channel. When pulling a calf, one must crank slowly to avoid tearing the cow's tissues or injuring the calf. The danger of the calf puller to humans is that when a rambunctious cow swings her hindquarters, she can wave a human like a flag or mow obstacles down with the pole.

CALF TABLE: a catch device to facilitate working on cattle. It's placed at the end of a narrow chute, and features a movable opening where an alert assistant clamps a bar around the calf's neck and others around his belly. Then the table is opened so that the calf lies flat for easier access. When the job is finished, the calf is returned to his feet and turned loose. The invention of the calf table made roping and tying calves obsolete — if you could afford the calf table — and is easier on the cattle than the old method. It might also be easier on the cowboys.

CALFY: pregnant, looking as if she will calve.

CALVING: producing calves. Calves are normally born front feet first, with the head lying neatly on and between the feet. In that position they come naturally from the birth canal or, if the calf's head is too large to pass naturally, the calf puller is attached to the front feet to provide extra power. Any variation of the normal position causes trouble. Sometimes one front leg is pushed down and back — a breech birth — and the cow can't push the calf out. Someone has to reach in and pull the other leg into position before the calf can be born. Often this requires pushing the head and one front foot back inside first. Then you must grope inside for the other foot while the cow strains to push your arm out. The pressure a cow exerts can temporarily paralyze an arm.

During calving season, we watch as cows' bags slowly fill with milk, and the vulva swells, another indicator of coming birth. Some ranchers seem to be able to always predict when a cow will calve, but almost no one claims to be right all the time. George insists he can only tell if a cow is calving if he sees feet sticking out. Most ranchers calve in early spring, between February and May, but some risk December weather for calving in order to have larger calves to sell the next fall. See backward calf.

CAPOTE: the traditional long hooded coat of fur traders, made from a blanket; from French *cape* for cape or cloak. See also rendezvous.

CASTRATING: turning a bull calf into a steer calf so he'll put his energy into growth instead of sex. Normally we steer calves when they're a month old or less, using rubber rings that fit around the sac above the testicles and shut off the blood supply so the sac slowly dries up and drops off. If calves are several months old their testicles are too large for the rubber bands, so one of two other methods are used: cutting, or pincers.

Cutting involves using a knife to cut through the skin of the scrotum to remove the testicles. This method carries an extra risk of infection and maggots, though disinfectant is used. We prefer to use pincers on larger steers. The hardy soul using the pincers gets into the chute behind the steer, bends down, gets a firm grip, and clamps the pincers tight around each of two cords leading to the testicles, then stands back.

CATTLE PRICES: Most businesses today pass along the costs of operation to the consumer, but the price a rancher gets for his cattle at the sale ring is determined by the buyers present on a given day, and is not directly related to the actual expense of raising the animal. Historically, when the price of meat at the supermarket rises, the rancher is getting less at the sale ring, but his expenses have risen. More than five thousand ranchers have gone out of business in South Dakota alone in the last five years. If individual ranchers are eventually replaced, as some predict, by huge ranching corporations, expenses will be passed along to the consumer and the price of beef in the supermarket will no doubt rise dramatically.

CELL THEORY: a range management theory, also called "holistic resource management," in which a large pasture is divided into smaller units (cells) fenced with slender plastic posts and a single strand of electrified wire. The cattle are moved to a different cell every few days. proponents say this method encourages the cover grasses, gets rid of noxious weeds and can double the number of cattle on a pasture without overgrazing. Skeptics say one must be a trained botanist to recognize the precise time to move the cattle so good grasses aren't overused and poor forage is discouraged.

CHAROLAIS: A large white or cream-colored cattle breed that originated in France; both bulls and cows are larger than many breeds.

CHEATGRASS: technically called downy brome, but sometimes referred to simply as "cheat," this grass has needle-like seeds which can lodge in a cow's throat and deform or kill her. Cattle will eat it when it's green, but it matures early, dries, and then is worthless as forage while being almost impossible to cut with a mower. It's not a native grass, but an invader, and its spread may be encouraged by overgrazing. A standing rule on our ranch is never to feed hay containing cheatgrass in parts of the pasture where it has not invaded.

CHILL FACTOR: a method of combining speed of the wind with the temperature to determine the chilling quality of the day; we suspect it was invented by a diabolical weatherman to torture ranchers.

CHINOOK: A warm dry wind that sometimes moves east from the Rocky Mountains, resulting in a rapid rise in temperature.

CHUTE: a corral made only one cow wide, from which cattle may be loaded into a truck or trailer or put into a calf table for branding or other work.

COLIC: acute pain in the abdomen, which may be caused by an obstruction of the digestive tract or accumulation of gas. It can be fatal in horses.

COLOSTRUM: the first milk a cow gives after her calf is born, richer in nutrients; secretion of colostrum lasts only a few days. Some ranchers keep bottles of it in the freezer for orphan or weak calves.

CORRAL: an enclosure for confining livestock, generally built of planks rather than barbed wire to make handling large numbers of cattle safer for the cattle.

COUNTING: only adult cattle are counted for most purposes; when I say on December 6 that we brought back 168 cows, heifers and bulls, the assumption is each cow had a calf with her, so the actual number of cattle moved would be nearly twice that.

COUNTY ROAD GRADER: used to grade gravel roads and remove snow. Because Custer is a small rural county with a rapidly expanding population of people who want to buy a few acres in the country, the road maintenance budget is a touchy subject. When I wintered on the ranch alone, the County Commission's rule was not to open a rural road unless two families lived on it. They didn't agree with my contention that my parents counted as a family, even though they were in Texas, so I once was unable to get to the highway for two weeks. In retaliation I posted "Private Road" signs at the highway; they took my word for it and haven't maintained our road since then. Unfortunately this means we now have to ask them to plow snow from the road for us at $50 per hour.

COWBIRDS: related to blackbirds, these feed on cattle grubs and lice, often picking them off the hide.

COW-CALF OPERATION: a ranch where cows are bred, calved out, and the calves are sold while the cows remain on the ranch.

COW UNIT: one cow and her calf, for purposes of determining the quality of grazing. In our area, we figure ten to forty acres of grass per year, supplemented with hay and cake, is required to feed one cow unit.

COW'S TEETH: cows have no top front teeth, only a bony flesh-covered plate against which their bottom teeth clip off grass. An old cow may look healthy during the summer when the grass is green, but get thin or die in winter when we feed cake because her bottom teeth are worn down or falling out. Most cows are sold before they reach the age of fifteen.

COW CHIPS: dried patties of cow manure; used for fuel by early settlers.

COYDOG: a cross between a coyote and a dog, often very large, and combining the characteristics of both.

CRAVEN CANYON: a narrow canyon where Indian petroglyphs have been found; also the location of some uranium claims.

CREEK PASTURE: our term for our winter pasture, which lies next to Battle Creek near Hermosa.

CREEP FEED: a form of protein feed, compressed into pill-size blocks, usually for calves. If a rancher has tight bins and stout help, he'll order cake or creep loose, to be shoveled or augured from a twenty-ton semi-trailer into the bin, then shoveled into a pickup box for feeding.

CRESTED WHEATGRASS: Introduced in the late 1800s to hold soil, crested is tolerant of drought and was widely planted in arid areas for forage. When it is green in the spring, before some native grasses, it's good cattle forage, but it matures early and becomes less palatable. The roots form clumps; heavy rain washes out the earth between plants, and the result is a bumpy, barren area with nothing but crested growing.

CROSSBREEDING: Scientists and ranchers agree that crossbreeding improves beef production, especially with the first cross: when a purebred cow is impregnated by a purebred bull of another breed. Since most ranchers keep replacement heifers, each succeeding generation moves further from the pure strains. First generation calves would be, for example, half Hereford and half Angus; second generation calves would be three-quarters Angus, and so on. For this reason, many ranchers switch breeds of bulls every few years, or buy replacement heifers of pure stock to bring new blood into the herd.

CROWN: in reference to fire, means the fire moves to the tops of the trees and may advance faster than it does on the ground.

CUD: food regurgitated from the first stomach to the mouth of a cow and chewed again.

CUT OUT: separating a cow from her calf.

CURED GRASS: grass that has dried naturally in the pasture, without being mowed. In drier climates, this grass holds nutritional value and provides a major source of feed for cattle in winter when not covered by snow.

DAM: earth bank built across a gully or draw to catch runoff from rain and snow, providing cattle water. Originally these dams were built by individual labor, using a team of horses and a fresno. During the drought of the 1930s, many ranchers and farmers received money from the federal government to hire earth-moving machinery to build earth dams. Many of these dams still exist. See also dugout, well, water, rainfall, fresno.

DEHORN: removing the horns from a calf, which increases its value since horned cattle are more difficult to handlers and each other. In newborn calves the operation can be performed with a chemical paste which burns out the horn base. Once the horn gets a half inch long it must be cut out with a scoop, a sharpened circular tool that can cut through hide and bone. Horns more than an inch long are sawed off close to the skull. Dehorning leaves the calf vulnerable to maggots, flies and infection unless the wound is protected by the application of blood stop powder, antiseptic, and fly repellent.

DIRTY THIRTIES: see Thirties.

DOG SOLDIER: a form of camp police at rendezvous that originated with Indian tribes. At rendezvous, they provide information and assistance to camp members, collect fees and distribute information, keep curious spectators out, and arrange fire patrols. See also rendezvous.

DRIFTING: Cattle normally turn their backs to a wind; in a severe storm they move with the wind. If they reach a fence, they may simply stand, heads down, as snow piles up around them. Their breath can freeze a solid column of ice from each nostril to the ground, eventually smothering them. Hundreds of cattle have died this way in plains snowstorms. In winter we use pastures where they will reach shelter before reaching a fence.

DROUTHY: see drought.

DROUGHT: usually pronounced and spelled "drouth," this refers to a prolonged period without usual rain or snowfall; calves stressed by these conditions are referred to as "drouthy."

DRY COW: a cow that didn't have a calf in the current year. Because they haven't been devoting part of their energy to growing a calf, these cows gain weight more quickly, becoming slick and rambunctious. They tend to cause trouble if left with the main herd because they're more energetic. If a cow fails to calve one year she may be held over; if she fails to calve two years in a row, she may find herself at the sale ring.

DUGOUT: where water is near the surface, a shallow hole is often dug to the water level, with gently sloping sides so the cattle can walk down to drink; see also dam, well, rainfall, water.

EAR MARK: most ranchers, besides their official registered brand, have a characteristic way of slitting a calf's ear to aid in identification. We make a narrow slit called a swallow tail in the left ear; it heals quickly but shows up well when we're looking at the calves later in the summer. An ear mark is often easier to see than a brand after the calf's hair gets thick.

EAR TAG: a plastic tag, inserted through a hole punched in a calf's ear, often numbered to help identify the calf's dam and/or sire. An ear tag provides additional identification of ownership.

FALSE DAWN: about an hour before dawn when the sky lightens briefly, then grows darker again before the sun actually rises, which probably accounts for the saying "It's always darkest before the dawn."

FARM: generally devoted to raising grain crops, whereas a ranch primarily raises beef cattle.

FEED BUNKS: troughs, often built of heavy lumber, where cattle may be fed to prevent waste.

FEEDING: cattle prefer to be fed on clean ground, though they may be eating and defecating at the same time. If we feed cake in snow more than a couple of inches deep, they'll scuff snow over most of it and lose it. To prevent this, we lead them with the pickup until they've trampled down a path, then shoulder a sack of cake and feed back along the track. This is risky business when they're hungry, since they run with no regard for the rancher in their way. But feed can't simply be dumped in a pile, since the stronger, more aggressive cows would get it all.

FENCE: Our fences consist of three to five strands of barbed wire fastened to posts. Today most ranchers use steel posts, which can be driven into the ground, for at least half the fence, and wooden posts for corners and intermittently in the fence to strengthen it.

FENCING: repairing or rebuilding fences. In the west, fence-fixing conforms to unwritten rules: when facing a stretch of fence shared with another ranch, the right half is yours to fix. This works if the neighbors fix their fences. But the rancher who turns his cattle into his pasture first is responsible for checking all the fence around his pasture, and if it's down, it must be fixed, no matter whose job it is. A lazy man can escape fixing fence for a long time, but he can't complain if his neighbors' cattle eat his grass. Fencing is expensive and time-consuming, so tempers fray when not everyone does his part.

Fences are damaged in many ways: wind may pile tumbleweeds so deeply that their weight breaks wires and posts, or the weight of snow piling up on the tumbleweeds may accomplish the same thing. Cattle scratch themselves on wire and posts and force their heads between the wires to get the naturally greener grass on the other side. Hunters sometimes cut fence or remove staples and push the wires down to drive over them. For this reason, many ranchers try to make gates easy to shut, with adjustable closings, to encourage strangers to close them.

FENCING TOOLS: the most useful, and what we mean by "hand me the fencing tool," is a combination cutter, hammer and pliers. George calls it "a pair of pliers designed by a committee."

FIGHTING FIRE: Though the community fire departments have pumper trucks, much fire-fighting in our area is still done by individuals with wet gunny sacks, as described in the entry for September 1. Though most landowners contribute money to the fire departments, we still aren't able to buy the best equipment nor to hire a full-time staff. When someone spots a fire, we call a fire alarm number, and volunteers race to the fire house and take the trucks to the fire site. If all the trained volunteers happen to be out of the community, we're in trouble.

FIRE: prairie fire can be caused by lightning, by a cigarette thrown from a passing car, or by sparks shot from the smoke stacks or overheated wheels of the elderly engines that haul trains through our pastures.

FIREGUARD: a plowed strip several feet wide. Since fire won't burn earth, a fireguard may stop the fire, unless a strong wind is blowing.

FLIES: Biting flies can make a cow's life miserable, and anything that makes a cow miserable costs money in lost beef. One species of heel fly is picked up from manure, travels through the cow's system until it reaches the skin, forms a larval stage called a grub, and hatches there in the heat of early summer. As the grubs hatch, cattle run off pounds and even gallop through fences. Whole herds will run until they're exhausted unless we spray or otherwise treat the flies.

FOOD DRYER: a closed box with screen shelves above four lightbulbs, used for drying foods indoors.

FRESNO: a device that looks like a wheelbarrow without wheels or support, used with a team of horses to move earth in building a dam. The horses pulled the fresno as it scraped up earth and human muscles provided the dumping power.

GARBAGE DUMP: country people are responsible for their own garbage, which leads to elaborate disposal methods. Vegetable waste is fed to chickens or composted; meat scraps feed barn cats. Anything combustible is burned when the fire danger is low enough. Cans and bottles that can't be recycled are hauled to a natural or specially dug hole in the prairie — ours is an old homestead foundation — and dumped so the wind won't blow them around, which would be hazardous for the cattle.

GATE: in pastures, usually made of barbed wire and require strength to shut properly. Some ranchers add loops of chain to pasture gates so strangers can close them easily. One of our strongest unwritten rules is that one must always close a gate. People who leave a gate open "just for a few minutes" often find cattle out when they get back.

GRAPPLE FORK: an attachment for a tractor that operates like a human hand to grasp loose hay from a stack and load it for feeding.

GRASS FAT: a cow fattened only on grass, as opposed to one fed supplements of cake, corn, or other feed.

GROUSE: plump bird with brown and gray feathers; they feed hidden in the tall grass, and if startled fly awkwardly off with a chuckling sound. They're good eating, but if you're a hunter, we don't have any on our land.

GUMBO: a fine soil that is particularly sticky when wet.

GUNNY SACK: a cloth feed sack, usually burlap. Years ago, they were used to sack feed, but have been largely replaced by paper, which isn't much help fighting fire.

HAULING WATER: When a pasture still has good grass cover but the water sources have dried up, we set a metal water tank at a central location near salt, and haul water from homw to the cattle in a 300-gallon tank carried on the back of a pickup. See also water, dam, dugout, well, rainfall.

HAWK, THROWING HAWK: in buckskinning, the term for a tomahawk or small axe used for wood cutting and in contests of throwing skill.

HAY: dried alfalfa and other grasses used for winter supplementary feed. Loose hay is simply stacked in large loaf-like piles and may retain nutrients for fifteen years or more. See baled hay, grapple fork.

HAYING: the process of cutting, raking, drying and storing alfalfa and other hay grasses for winter supplementary feed. See also mowing, raking, stacking.

HAY HOOKS: a hook about eight inches long with a handle attached, used for moving bales of hay.

HAZE: used as a verb, to chase, as hazing a cow out of a corral.

HEAT: recurrent periods of ovulation and sexual excitement, estrus, the only time when the cow can be impregnated.

HEAVY COW: a cow carrying a calf.

HEEL FLIES: see flies.

HEIFER: female calf, from birth until she has her first calf, usually at the age of two; after that she's referred to as a cow.

HYDRANT: a pipe with an outlet for drawing water from the main pipe without the use of a pump.

INDIAN RESERVATION: a tract of land set aside by the federal government for the use of an Indian tribe; South Dakota has nine such reservations.

INITIATIVE: South Dakota was the first state to legalize initated measures. The impetus behind the initiative referred to in this journal began in 1979. I joined Black Hills Energy Coalition when a mining company staked uranium claims in Craven Canyon, near my grandmother's ranch. The initiative we sponsored at that time would have banned uranium mines, mills, waste dumps or nuclear power plants without a statewide vote. We lost, but this campaign inspired a later initiative to give voters the right to decide if the state should host a major national nuclear waste dump.

KILLDEER: a bird that nests along streams or ponds, and whose cry sounds like "killdeer, killdeer."

LAND: the first cut around a hayfield, as in "mowing out a land." After a few rounds, you must back cut. We make the first land and back cut far enough from the fence to leave cover for birds and other animals.

LARIAT: a long rope with a moving noose for roping cattle; also called a lasso.

LEE SIDE: the side sheltered from the wind.

LICE: plural of louse, a flat, wingless, sucking external parasite.

LIFT BAR: bar which can be used to raise the extended sickle bar on a mower, which is usually more than seven feet long, so the tractor with mower attached is narrow enough to pass through gates.

LINDSAY PASTURE: it's customary for pieces of land to be known by the names of the original homesteader or a prominent owner long after those people have sold the land or died. In this case, John and Anna Lindsay sold their land at retirement to the Hasselstroms, and have since died. This practice can be hard on people new to the country; sometimes directions are given this way: "Turn left by the old Peterson place and drive south until you come to the Jones place . . ."

LONGHORN: a breed of cattle with exeptionally long horns, up to six feet from tip to tip.

LONG JOHNS: long underwear; ours are bright red, a blend of wool and cotton.

MAGGOT: legless soft-bodied larva of various flies, usually found in rotten matter.

MARMOT: called woodchucks in some areas; their smaller cousins, pikas, live among the jumbled chaos of peaks above timberline.

MAUL: tool used for pounding steel posts into the ground. Looks like a piece of pipe welded shut and weighted at one end, and usually with handles on the outside. By grasping the handles, minimal force is needed to bring the maul down and drive the post into the ground. Using a sledge hammer is less satisfactory because when it strikes the post it can bounce back.

MEADOWLARK: bird about the size of a blackbird, with a bright yellow breast and throat outlined with a V of black; unique and lovely song.

MINERAL: a supplement needed when cattle are not getting green feed; comes in various forms, including blocks which the cattle can lick and powder which can be mixed with loose salt.

MISSILE BASE ROAD: a paved highway north of our ranch which leads to a former Titan missile site. The site was never armed but because the road is paved — a rarity — it makes a useful reference point when giving directions. Like many such references, it's totally useless if the directee wasn't around twenty years ago when the missile base was there.

MOWING: Using a tractor-drawn mower, we start at one corner of a field and cut the hay in concentric squares until we reach the middle. Though time-consuming, mowing is seldom boring. Many natural elements conspire to add excitement: wasp nests, sweat bees, badger holes that can tip a tractor over, wire that can tangle in sickle blades. See also haying, windrow, raking, stacking, power takeoff.

MUZZLE-LOADING: guns from the black powder era are loaded by pushing black powder, a patch and ball down the muzzle in the correct order. See rendezvous.

NUCLEAR WASTE VOTE COALITION: a statewide environmental group which was active in passage of an Initiative requiring a statewide vote before a national nuclear waste dump could be sited in South Dakota.

ON THE GROUND: Our main job in spring is getting calves on the ground, i.e., born and on their feet in good health.

OPEN WINTER: a winter with little snow, so the grass remains open, or uncovered, and cattle may graze throughout the winter.

PAIRS: each cow and her calf is a pair.

PAIR UP: getting each cow together with her own calf.

PETROGLYPH: a prehistoric carving or line drawing on rock; some of those in Craven Canyon consist of lines of dots chipped into the rock.

PITCHFORK: an oversized fork with a long handle used to throw or pitch loose hay.

PITCH POST: a wooden fence post cut with the sap still in it, which increases its ability to withstand weather. When we remove such posts from a fence after the bottom eventually weakens we often save them for use in starting branding or heating fires, since a few slivers of the hardened pitchy wood catch fire easily and burn very hot.

PLOWING: A few years ago, state news stories spoke of the plowing of thousands of acres in South Dakota that had *never before been plowed,* mostly by new owners who thought they'd make a profit on wheat. We had a dry summer, they sold out, and the new owners have the job of trying to return the land to grazing use. In some parts of the state large corporations are still buying acreages like this and plowing them up, and the result will be disaster. This land is so fragile that even grazing has to be done with care.

POSSIBLE POUCH: a leather bag used to carry the various pieces of gear a fur trapper needed — every thing he could "possibly" need, hence, possible or possibles pouch.

POWER TAKEOFF: an extension of the drive shaft of a tractor; by turning it powers other attachments such as a mower or post-hole digger. For safety the power takeoff is kept covered; if a person becomes caught, it simply keeps turning until the engine is turned off. Men have been caught by a pantleg in it and found hours later twisted into an unrecognizable mass.

PRAIRIE DOG: a burrowing rodent with tawny fur and a bark like a small dog. They tend to live in ever-growing communities, digging a new hole for each new generation of pups, and may bear pups several times a year. Because they multiply quickly, and dig grass out by the roots, a prairie dog colony can kill hundreds of acres of grass in a summer. Ranchers deplore the amount of grass they eat almost as much as the large holes they leave, which are traps for horses and cattle to break legs in. Natural predators like coyotes can get a few, but when they retreat to their deep holes in rock-hard dry earth, very few animals bother them. Some ranchers used to kill prairie dogs with poison grain, but most such poisons act in a chain; that is, they kill not only the prairie dog but anything that feeds on it later: eagles, coyotes, owls.

PRICES: for cattle, see cattle prices.

PROLAPSE: when an organ slips out of place; we use the term to refer to a cow's uterus being pushed outside. If we don't get to her quickly the uterus becomes swollen and covered with filth, making it more difficult for us to push it back in; we put antibiotics in with the uterus, and stitch the vulva closed so that she won't force it out again. By the next year, if the stitches haven't torn out they may have to be cut before she can calve, but other than that the cows usually recover well from a prolapse.

RAINFALL: Officially, the average rainfall per year in western South Dakota is 16.1 inches at lower elevations, 18.3 in the higher Black Hills. Our own actual records for the following years show these rainfall amounts: 1980: 6.45 inches of rain; 1981: 6.15

inches; 1982: 17.65 inches; 1983: 8.12 inches. We did get additional moisture in the form of snow; between Jan. 1 and April 3, 1986, for example, we got 75.7 inches of snow.

RAKING: After hay is mowed, it must be raked into windrows. A number of advances in machinery design have simplified this process, including the swather, which mows and rakes in one operation. However, we still use one of the first types of rake built, the dump rake, attached to a tractor with a long rope from a trip lever to the tractor seat. The operator pulls on the rope to dump the load of hay.

Raking is a long slow process enlivened only by the intricacy of turns — it's easy to turn too short and bend or break the rake tongue — and watching the blisters form and pop on the hand pulling the dump rope. The greatest danger in raking is wanting to get it over with too fast; it's easy to tip our rake tractor over if it hits a rock or hole.

Hay is usually raked as soon as the field is mowed, but if it's too green or damp from rain when it's stacked, the stack may catch fire spontaneously or the hay may spoil. On the other hand, if the hay is allowed to dry too long, leaves will fall off and the hay will lose much of its nutritional value. Knowing when it's dry enough but not too dry is one of those skills requiring both instinct and experience. See also haying, mowing, stacking, windrow.

RANCH, SIZE OF: The question, "How big is your ranch?" is one of the few questions to which a lie is considered an acceptable answer. The question is regarded as an invasion of privacy, just as if an acquaintance asked, "How much money do you have in the bank?" An answer is meaningless anyway without knowing how many cows the acreage will run. Between ten and forty acres of average grazing land on the plains is required to support a cow unit — one cow and one calf — for one year. In some areas the acreage needed is much less or much more.

RANKIN RIDGE: a lookout site in Wind Cave National Park considered one of the best for hearing the elk bugle during mating season in September.

REDWING BLACKBIRDS: recognizable because of red shoulder patches and a peculiarly melodic song.

REGISTERED CATTLE: cattle whose pure breeding is proven by registration with the national breeding organization and supported by papers that accompany them each time they change hands. Such cattle sell for high prices, since they are used to improve a breeding operation.

RENDEZVOUS: When beaver tophats became fashionable in England, men began trapping beaver — along with other saleable fur — in the Rocky Mountains and similar locations. From 1825 through 1840, the mountain men met fifteen times to exchange their beaver and other pelts for necessities and frivolities brought to a central location by traders from St. Louis. Each location was decided at the rendezvous of the year before, and the information passed by word of mouth. At the appointed time, usually in July or August, wagonloads of merchandise arrived at a camp established by trappers and Indians. The trappers sold their pelts, bought supplies for the coming year, and then celebrated. They bragged, fought, fornicated and caroused enough to last them through the coming year before returning to the isolation of trapping beaver alone.

Today, rendezvous is a gathering of enthusiasts of black powder shooting and the history of fur trapping. In recent years two national organizations, the National

Muzzle Loading Rifle Association (NMLRA) and the National Association of Primitive Riflemen (NAPR) have held a joint national rendezvous, often near a site of one of the original gatherings, attracting several thousand enthusiasts from all over the world. People who attend rendezvous are dedicated to the idea of making the rendezvous look as it might have before 1840, but because families are usually involved, modern rendezvous are much tamer than historical ones. A rendezvous is intended for enjoyment as well as serious trading of replicas of goods current during the fur trade, and is kept as much like a trip back in time as possible. Participants wear clothing taken from patterns current in the 1840's, carry authentically styled weapons, use black iron cookware over open fires, and light their tipis or lean-to shelters with candle lanterns. Radios, modern clothing, camping gear, guns, plastic, and similar gear are prohibited. Some modern conveniences, like plastic water containers, are allowed if they are kept covered. Ideally a rendezvous should look as if it might be happening between 1825 and 1840. In order to encourage the sport, various publications are produced and local and regional clubs hold meetings throughout the country.

REPLACEMENT: heifer kept for breeding to replace older cows sold for age, infirmity, or other reasons. In order to improve bloodines, some ranchers buy replacement cows.

RESERVATION: see Indian Reservation

RUNOFF: rain or water from snowmelt that does not soak into the ground but runs off; some is later caught in dams.

SALE RING: where cattle are sold at auction. The rancher's only choice is to sell the cattle at the price bid, or take them home. See also cattle prices.

SALT: essential to cattle; fed in fifty-pound blocks the cattle lick, or loose in wooden boxes, in which form it can be mixed with vitamins and minerals such as a vitamin A and D supplement. A good ration of salt also insures cattle will drink enough water, which helps prevent waterbelly and other diseases.

SCHOOL SECTION: sections of western land were set aside for the support and establishment of schools in the homesteading era. If unused for the location of a school, the land was leased to ranchers for grazing, and in many cases still contributes financial support to state schools.

SCOURS: diarrhea causing white excrement and an especially foul smell. The odor and color make it easy to spot, and calves sick with it just lie around with swollen bellies and don't suck. It often seems to be brought on by cold damp weather, but we've also had it in warm springs. Scours pills obtained from the vet are given with a piller, a long tube large enough to accommodate one or two pills, with a plunger to eject them. The tube is put down the calf's throat, using care not to get it in the windpipe, and the pills pushed out far enough down so the calf can't regurgitate them.

SCYTHE: Single-edged blade with a wooden handle, used for cutting weeds where an ordinary mower can't go because of rocks.

SERVICE: as used on June 26, means maintenance on the tractors and other machinery, such as checking oil, gas, radiator, tires, and greasing moving parts. We also speak of bulls "servicing" or breeding cows.

SICKLE: a movable cutting bar on a tractor mower, made of separate triangular teeth riveted to the bar. Sickle teeth can be replaced or sharpened individually.

SILO: a tall cylindrical structure in which feed is stored.

SIZE: of ranch, see ranch.

SLICK: a fat cow, often a dry one, is sometimes referred to as slick, meaning her hair is especially shiny and glossy because she is fatter and in better health than the cows that are raising calves. Also, sometimes an unbranded calf is called a "slick."

SNOW FENCE: fence constructed of vertical pieces of thin, narrow wood, put up in the fall to catch snow to keep drifts from blocking roadways.

SNOW PLOW: see county road grader.

SOAPWEED: see yucca

SPOOKED: frightened.

STACK: a pile of hay that may weigh from five to twenty tons. The haystack is not simply a haphazard pile, but a carefully built structure. The stacker gathers several windrows in one load, then delivers them to the stack from all sides, so that the hay is almost woven together, keeping the pile higher in the center. This stacking technique helps the stack resist strong winds and moisture, and keeps the hay inside fresh longer. Many novice stackers have worked all day stacking, only to have the stacks completely blown apart by winds during the night. Hay also settles; the stack that was thirty feet high in July may be only a wet mound a third that height in November. If built correctly a stack of hay resembles a loaf of bread, slowly turning golden the first year, and darker shades of gray in succeeding years. When I was thirty we used a stack my father had built when I was fifteen. The outer foot or so was gray, dusty, leafless stems; under that was hay so fresh we could smell the dry scent of alfalfa blooms.

When haying was done with horses, and in the early days of mechanical stackers when hired labor was cheap, one man always stayed on top of the stack. His job was to move the delivered loads with a pitchfork, weaving them even more tightly together. Excitement was provided when a rattlesnake was delivered with a load of hay.

STACKER: A stacking attachment like a huge fork, mounted on a tractor so that it can be raised and lowered, and equipped with a device that pushes the hay forward off the tines of the fork. In winter, the stacker head is replaced by a grapple fork for feeding. See also haying, mowing, raking, windrow, and related terms.

STAPLE: U-shaped piece of metal, pointed on each end, driven into a post to hold barbed wire in fencing.

STEER: a castrated male calf.

TABLE: as in Cuny Table, used in western South Dakota for the level top of an elevated piece of ground, with the land falling away from it on all sides; similar to a plateau, but smaller. The tables in South Dakota are all found in the western end of the White River Badlands, and usually named for individuals who settled on or near them.

TAILING UP: a cow weakened by lack of feed, injury, or birthing may need assistance to get to her feet. As she starts to get up, grab her tail and pull backwards, giving her leverage to stand. Then use the tail as a handle to help keep her upright until she can stand on her own. This is lots of fun, and is highly recommended as an outdoor sport.

TAIL-TWITCHING: in steers, a symptom of waterbelly; see waterbelly.

TALLY: counting calves branded; we record the number of steers and heifers branded with our two brands.

TANK HEATERS: used to heat water for cattle in winter, to reduce the need for chopping ice off the tanks. Ours use a small drum of gasoline regulated to drip into the bottom of a hollow metal drum in the water. Once the drip is ignited and air flow regulated, they'll burn until the gasoline runs out, and provide enough heat to minimize ice. Lighting them is risky; George often singes his mustache.

TEAT VALVE: a hollow plastic tube made for draining milk from a cow's udder. Inserted into the cow's teat, with hooks to keep it from sliding out, it can be left in place so the milk drains continuously, or capped so milk can be drained periodically. But the cow must be kept away from a calf, who could swallow the teat valve while sucking.

TEETH: see cow's teeth

THIRTIES: the 1930s were periods of great drought and suffering on the plains, when huge clouds of dust often created drifts inside houses; they're still referred to here as the "Dirty Thirties" by people who remember having to turn plates upside down to keep dirt out of them before dinner was served.

TIPI RINGS: circles of stone used to hold down the cover of a hide tipi. Since the Indians often returned to the same camping spots year after year, many of these circles of stone can still be found, half-buried in grass, on the prairies.

TRAIL: In our arid climate, if you drive across a pasture once, the tracks of the pickup can be seen for months. If you drive the same route again, you've made a trail; four times and we call it a road.

TRANSPLANT: to get a cow to accept a calf not her own by tying her own calf's skin on the new calf, and leaving them together in a confined space overnight. After a few days, when the calf's smell has become familiar to the cow, the extra hide is removed; see April 30.

TRIPLE SEVEN: The name and brand of a ranch south of us.

TROCAR: a sharp-pointed instrument used, in this case, to puncture a calf's hide to let out air created by bloating. If the air is not released, the pressure of the air can be fatal.

TUMBLEBUG: a beetle that rolls manure into round balls to protect its eggs and provide food for the hatchlings.

TUMBLEWEED: a poor forage weed that breaks off at maturity and is blown across the prairie; sometimes huge rolls of it move together, looking like brown snowdrifts and collecting against fences and in any sheltered spot.

TURKEY VULTURE: also known as buzzard, though incorrectly; see vulture.

TWO-BOTTOM PLOW: a plow with two sets of shares or cutting blades, for turning over earth in a furrow.

TWO-YEAR-OLD HEIFERS: Two-year-old heifers are often kept as replacement cows, and calve first in the spring of their second year. This is a little like an eleven-year-old girl having a baby; it can be done, but you must beware of complications.

These heifers must be watched around the clock, and frequently require help from the rancher or veterinarian to calve successfully. In succeeding years they can usually calve alone, unless the calf is unusually large. In some cases, because they are so young their calves must be pulled, and they require extra feed. See calf puller.

UDDER: see bag.

UNDERPASS: a passage under a highway for cattle or vehicles.

URANIUM: see Initiative.

VACCINE GUN: a needle used to give vaccinations to cattle.

VACCINATE: each calf is vaccinated to prevent blackleg, a bovine disease that was epidemic before vaccination was required. We also give the light-colored calves a shot to prevent louse infestations; the black cattle don't seem to get lice — or else the lice can't be seen on them.

VULTURE: a large, carrion-eating bird with dark feathers and a naked head and neck.

WALLEYED: when a cow is frightened or angry, she rolls her eyes so the whites show; this is referred to as being "walleyed."

WASTE DUMP: see Initiative.

WATER: one of our most vital resources, adequate water is essential to a ranching operation. On the western plains, few ranches have running natural streams; we have none. A cow drinks 25 to 50 gallons of water daily, so 100 cows might require 5000 gallons of water on a hot day. At the same time, evaporation of open water, such as that in a dugout or dam, amounts to thousands of gallons a day. Some pastures have only a single water source; if that goes dry in summer, we usually haul a metal water tank to the pasture and fill it daily from a 300-gallon tank carried in the back of the pickup.

In winter, if water is provided from a dam or dugout, a daily job is to chop holes in the ice for the cattle to drink. Once the ice reaches a foot thick, or the snow gets deep enough to make getting to the cattle questionable, we generally bring them to the main corrals, where water is provided from wells, and where we can operate heaters to prevent ice. See also dam, dugout, well.

WATERBELLY: occurs when a steer's urinary canal is blocked with stones and his bladder swells with urine he can't drain. Vets can operate on it because the urinary tube runs upward beside the calf's rectum. They can cut it and sew it to the hide so the bladder drains there instead of in the normal location under the belly. We call it "turning a steer into a heifer" and if it's done soon enough, it can save a calf. Often, however, the bladder has ruptured before we can get the vet, and the calf dies even if he's operated on, leaving a legacy of a $75 bill plus mileage. We try to prevent it by providing plenty of salt and water for steer calves, so any mineral deposits are washed out before they grow large enough to create a blockage. We watch steers for the symptoms of swelling under the belly and for twitching their tails.

WELL: Drilled wells provide some water in our area, with the resulting water flow piped into tanks for the cattle, but underground water supplies aren't easy to find. Some ranchers dowse to locate water. Drillers always hope for a flowing well, one in which underground water pressure is sufficient to bring water to the surface without mechanical aids. Even if a well originally flows, a few years of use may reduce the water pressure or supply so that a mechanical aid is needed to bring the water to the surface. If the well doesn't flow, we use a windmill or pump to raise water. Windmills have generally disappeared in the west since gasoline pumps became available, but that trend may be reversed in the future since wind is almost always available, and free. It is generally illegal now to allow water to flow with no shutoff method.

WINCH: a hoisting or towing machine consisting of a rotating drum around which the cable or chain winds as the load is lifted.

WINDROW: a long row of cut hay piled up by a rake or swather and left in the field to partially dry before being stacked or baled.

WINTERIZE: to check and replace anti-freeze, and check oil and fuel levels in machinery.

YEARLING: a calf, either sex, a year old.

YELLOW THUNDER CAMP: a site in the Black Hills established by traditional Indians and members of the American Indian Movement as part of an effort to regain land promised to the Lakota by the 1868 treaty. Despite the objections of Forest Service personnel and some private landowners, the camp has existed for several years.

YUCCA: tall spiky plants with sharp-edged leaves and a stalk of creamy bell-shaped flowers that may reach almost six feet in height; several species grow larger in the southwest. Indians used the roots in making soap, hence the slang name "soapweed."

ZERK: a valve placed at a convenient location on moving machinery parts, and fitted with a head that allows grease to be pumped through it from an ordinary grease gun, then closed so the grease doesn't run back out.

Linda Hasselstrom, a cattle rancher, writer,
and environmental activist, was born in Texas
and raised on the plains of southwestern
South Dakota, where she now lives with her
husband, George. She divides her days
between ranch work and writing. Her poems,
short stories, and articles have appeared in
over 70 magazines and anthologies. In 1984
Hasselstrom received a National Endowment
for the Arts grant in poetry. Her first volume
of poems, *Caught by One Wing*,
was published that same year.